impressionism
on the seine

impressionism
on the seine

edited by
MARINA FERRETTI BOCQUILLON

essays by
ANNE L. COWE
MARINA FERRETTI BOCQUILLON
VANESSA LECOMTE
DOMINIQUE LOBSTEIN

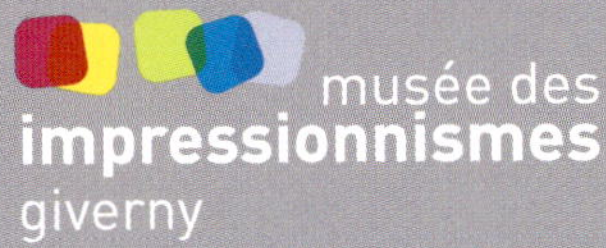

SilvanaEditoriale

PUBLISHED IN CONJUNCTION WITH THE EXHIBITION

impressionism
on the seine

ORGANISED BY THE MUSÉE DES IMPRESSIONNISMES GIVERNY
FROM 1ST APRIL TO 18 JULY 2010.

This exhibition received exceptional loans from the musée d'Orsay, Paris

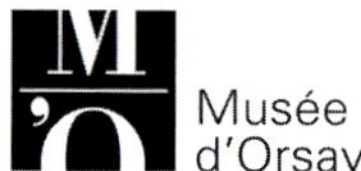

Exhibition organized on the occasion and with the support of the festival Normandie Impressionniste 2010

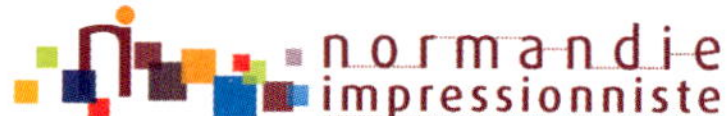

ISBN: 97888-3661620-6
Distributed by: Silvana Editoriale

Front cover
Georges Seurat, *The Seine at Courbevoie (By the Water)*, 1885, private collection (see cat. 32)

EXHIBITION

Curators
Marina Ferretti Bocquillon,
Scientific Director - Curator
with the assistance of Vanessa Lecomte,
Associate Curator,
in association with Diego Candil,
General Director

Registrar
Céline Mittelette

Conservation
Véronique Roca

Installation
Didier Dauvel
Didier Guiot
Olivier Touren

Education
Hélène Furminieux
Renata Hernandez

Public Relations
Géraldine Raulot and Élodie François,
in Giverny
Catherine Dufayet Communication,
in Paris

Tourism
Laurette Roche

Administration
Cindy Buffière
Catherine Fox
Xavier Poc

ACKNOWLEDGEMENTS

We would like to extend our heartfelt thanks to all the collectors whose generous loans have made this exhibition possible:

Belgium
Musées royaux des Beaux-Arts de Belgique, Brussels
Collection du Musée d'Art moderne et d'Art contemporain, Liège

United States
Terra Foundation for American Art, Chicago
National Gallery of Art, Washington

France
Musée des beaux-arts, Brest
Conseil général du Val d'Oise, Cergy-Pontoise
Musée d'Art, Histoire et Archéologie, Évreux
Musée Malraux, Le Havre
Centre Pompidou, musée national d'art moderne / Centre de création industrielle, Paris,
Musée de l'Orangerie, Paris
Musée d'Orsay, Paris
Musée Camille Pissarro, Pontoise
Musée des Beaux-Arts, Reims
Musée des Beaux-Arts, Rouen, long term loan from the musée d'Orsay, Paris
L'Annonciade, musée de Saint-Tropez, long term loan from the Centre Pompidou, musée national d'art moderne / Centre de création industrielle, Paris
Fondation Bemberg, Toulouse

The Netherlands
Collection Triton Foundation

United Kingdom
The National Gallery, London

Switzerland
Association des Amis du Petit Palais, Geneva

Without forgetting the many private lenders who wish to remain anonymous.

From the curator

The curator of the exhibition would like to express her warmest thanks to Diego Candil, director of the musée des impressionnismes Giverny, for his constant trust and support. She would also like to thank in particular Vanessa Lecomte, associate curator, who helped with rare efficiency in the preparation of the exhibition. Her thanks are also due to Céline Mittelette, registrar, who managed to adapt to the sustained rhythm of the museum's curatorial team.

Heartfelt thanks are due to a large number of individuals who contributed throughout the preparation of the exhibition and the catalogue:

Roland Abily, Odile Aittouarès, Naomi Aplin, Annamaria Ardizzi, Didier Arnal, Catherine Arnold, Maurice Amatteis, François Auffret, Marine Bancilhon, Laurianne Barban, Roger Barbe, Juliet Bareau, Stéphane Bayard, Benoîte Beaudenon, Véronique Beauregard, Romain Beignon, Stephanie Belt, Hadrien Bocquillon, Léonore Bocquillon, Philippe Bocquillon, Valérie Bouba, Pierre Bouho, Violette Boulet, Francine Bouré, Ivo Bouwman, Michela Bramati, Emmanuel Bréon, Françoise Cachin, Florence Carotine, Dominique Chardeau, Jacques Chardeau, Mr. and Mrs. Olivier Chardeau, Gilles Chazal, Françoise Chibret-Plaussu, Florence Chibret, Dario Cimorelli, Judy Cline, Jean Pascal Cogez, Pina Comar, Mr. and Mrs. Willem Corda, Anne L. Cowe, Jérôme Crépatte, Philippe Cros, Françoise Daniel, Guy-Patrice Dauberville, Michel Dauberville, Claire Denis, Nathalia Denninger, Michel Devarieux, Christian Devleeschauwer, Jean-Marc Dos Santos Malhado, Marina Ducrey, Catherine Dufayet, Ann Dumas, François Dupouy, Dominique Durussel, Bénédicte Duthion, Christophe Duvivier, Marion Eybert, Martino Foca, Christine Fournié, Vanina Gasly, Bruno Gaudichon, Gilles Genty, Marielle Gerritsen, Claude Ghez, Léonard Gianadda, Geraldine Glynn, Francine Guidi de la Rosa-Dawans, Femke Gutter, Valérie Haerden, Claire Hallinan, Gaël Hamayon, Amélie Hardiviller, Colin Harrison, Annette Haudiquet, Tom Heaven, Pauline Heerema, Guillaume Henry, Dorian Hill, Danielle Hodel, Waring Hopkins, Deborah D'Ippolito, David Jaffé, Kimberly A. Jones, Frédéric Juret-Rafin, Daragh Kenny, Alexandre et Irina Klein, Marie-Pierre Kopf, Frédéric Laux, Brigitte Léal, Isabelle Le Bot, Nathalie Lecerf, Laurence Le Cieux, Jean-Louis Laville, Géraldine Lefebvre, Hervé Le Guern, Margueritte Le Mière, Ghislaine Le Normand, Matthieu Leverrier, Dominique Lobstein, Emmanuelle Long, Olga Makhroff, Marie-Edmée de Malherbe, Daniel Malingue, Jackie Maman, Dominique Maréchal, Mira Mariani, Bristol Mariott, Lidia Masolini, Caroline Mathieu, Armelle Maugin, André Mayer, Dan Mayer, Deborah Mayer, Sandra Mazière, Giacomo Merli, Alain Meyst, Odile Michel, Valentina Miolo, Jean-Paul Monery, Monique Moulene, Pieter Muys, Ruth Nagel, Jean Naudin, Jurgita Navelikaite, Thierry Normand, Alessandra Olivari, Christian Olivereau, Pascal Otheguy, Alfred Pacquement, Hélène Pastianis, Élodie Pauls, Adeline Pelletier, Nicholas Penny, Matthieu Petit, Corinne Picarello, Mathilde Pigallet, Joachim Pissarro, Nicolas Portnoï, Gaëlle Pottier, François Puget, Pascale Réa, Catherine Régnault, Christopher Riopelle, Dr. Jean-Pierre De Rycke, Pilar Saez Lacave, Françoise Safin-Crahay, Laurent Salomé, Catherine Scelles, Gérard Sebaoun, Jennifer Seeds Martin, Sabrina Sémati, Olivier Simmat, Dawn Somerville, Societé des Amis de Jongkind, Paris – La Haye, Vérane Tasseau, Alicia Thomas, Mireille Triballier, Claire Vachon, Viviana Vai, Peter van Beveren, Christophe van Runckelen, Hélène Verdier, Stéphanie Videau, Willemien de Vlieger-Moll, Trish Waters, Nicolas Wierczynski, Katherine Wodehouse, Barbara C.G. Wood.

We are very grateful to the Terra Foundation for American Art for its generous loan. Our heartfelt thanks to: Elizabeth Glassman, Elizabeth Kennedy, Katherine Bourguignon, Donald H. Ratner, Cathy Ricciardelli, Francesca Rose, Amy Zinck.

Without the help of the festival Normandie Impressionniste we would not have been able to give the project the same breadth. We would particularly like to thank: Pierre Bergé, Annick Bouillot, Jérôme Clément, Laurent Fabius, Jacques-Sylvain Klein, Jade Lobato de Faria, Laurence Philippot, Nicolas Mayer-Rossignol, Anne Samson.

This exhibition would not have been possible without the generous support of the Conseil général de l'Eure and in particular of: Jean Louis Destans, Yves Bousquet, Gaëlle Cachereul, Christian Chermeux, Stéphanie Cléradin, Benoit Forcuit, Evelyne Gliozzo, Jean-Loup d'Hooren, Philippe Huthwohl, Éric Mémeteau, Claire Scotton, Laurent Sodini, Dominique Soulier, Sonia Verbist.

The members of the board of directors gave us invaluable trust and support: Jean Louis Destans, Francis Courel, Guy Cogeval, Claude Béhar, Dominique Chauvel, François Erlenbach, Laurent Fabius, Michel Jouyet, Christian Jutel, Hugues Gall, Elizabeth Glassman, Claude Landais, Alain le Vern, Anne Mansouret, Philippe Nguyen Thanh, Michel Ranger, Philippe Thiébaut, Gérard Volpatti, Amy Zinck.

The exhibition benefitted from the efforts of talented staff at the musée des impressionnismes Giverny: Khaddija Belhajjame, Emmanuel Besnard, Marie Bosson, Cindy Buffière, Cheickne Camara, Didier Dauvel, Catherine Fox, Élodie François, Hélène Furminieux, François Gouley, Didier Guiot, Cyril Hermand, Renata Hernandez, Frederic Ksiezarczyk, Hermann Le Bas, Laurent Lefrançois, Pascal Mérieau, Céline Muller, Xavier Poc, Géraldine Raulot, Véronique Roca, Laurette Roche, Olivier Touren.

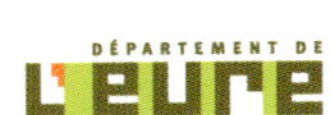

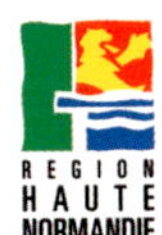

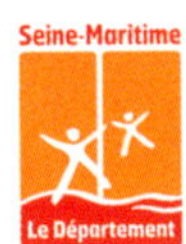

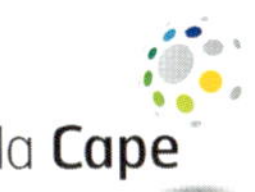

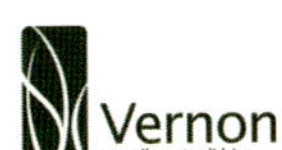

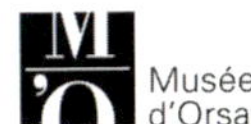

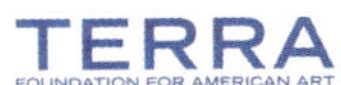

The musée des impressionnismes Giverny is still reverberating with the success of the two exhibitions held in its first season. It has won over art lovers and tourists the world over, and in a single year has conquered the hearts of the people of Normandy and Île-de-France. For the representatives of the institutions of the board of the EPCC, this is a recognition of the value of the project.

This success has led to expectations which, in this first exhibition in 2010, will not be disappointed. "Impressionism on the Seine" offers a dual reading, overlapping and complementary, of the work of artists around the central theme of the Seine valley, a territory so emblematic of the Impressionist movement.

Founded on a pedagogic approach, this exhibition casts light on the artistic evolution of Impressionism from its precursors, followed by the Impressionist group and its great masters, then the neo-Impressionists or Nabis. Illustrious names punctuate this anthology: Claude Monet, Auguste Renoir, Camille Pissarro and Georges Seurat, to cite only a few of the most celebrated. It will also be an opportunity to discover other lesser known painters, such as Stanislas Lépine and Armand Guillaumin.

The other reading offered to visitors relates to the history and the development of a territory often considered to be the cradle of Impressionism, a slant that embodies the very essence of the festival Normandie Impressionniste of which it is part. At the crossroads of the 19th and 20th centuries, in a period marked by rapid change, the industrial revolution was underway and landscapes were beginning to alter. Railway, and the development of ports and factories, led to the slow evolution of a rural world firmly rooted in its traditions.

This project would not have been possible without the unfailing support of the musée d'Orsay and its President, Guy Cogeval, as well as of the generous lenders, be they museums or private collectors, to whom I extend all my gratitude. I would also like to thank Pierre Bergé and Laurent Fabius, President and Vice President of the festival Normandie Impressionniste, for their contribution to the museum's ambitious programme. Finally, I would like to thank once again all the members of the board, as well as the museum's teams, for their unceasing hard work.

JEAN LOUIS DESTANS
President of the EPCC

It is with pleasure that the musée d'Orsay takes part in the exhibition "Impressionism on the Seine" through the loan of thirteen paintings by Claude Monet, Auguste Renoir, Alfred Sisley, Camille Pissarro, Gustave Caillebotte and their friends. The work which is forcing us temporarily to reduce our exhibition space is also an opportunity to present an important part of our collections "hors les murs." Two major itinerary exhibitions are already ensuring that our collections can be appreciated abroad, in Madrid, Canberra, Tokyo, San Francisco and Nashville.

We are happy to be able to help the young musée des impressionnismes Giverny by lending important works. We believe that a generous lending policy is a natural part of the mission of major museums. And the close collaboration between the musée d'Orsay and the musée des impressionnismes Giverny is all the more natural, reinforcing the links that have united the two institutions since the latter's conception. The public will thus have the opportunity to rediscover famous paintings, presented in the heart of the area that witnessed their birth. New possibilities for comparison and analysis will give visitors the chance to look from a fresh viewpoint at works with which they are sometimes already familiar.

GUY COGEVAL
President of the musée d'Orsay

There was a sort of readiness and anticipation in this beloved Normandy of ours, a latent desire that we wished to express in concrete terms.

The image of Normandy idealized by the beaches of Boudin, the rocks of Courbet and the gardens of Monet lives on in the hearts and minds of every one of us. This is the origin of Normandie Impressionniste, a popular festival spread out over the whole of upper and lower Normandy, aimed at everyone and open to all the arts of our time. Propagated by the vital forces active in the region, the initiative saw the blossoming of dozens of projects in the space of just a few months.

Normandie Impressionniste is a unique example of the mobilization of an entire territory for a large-scale project of culture, education and tourism involving about fifty local communities, two regions and over two hundred events.

The great exhibition "Impressionism on the Seine" at the musée des impressionnismes Giverny lies at the heart of the festival. The greatest masters of Impressionism and others of lesser renown reveal to us in a succession of works the strength and clarity of this bond between one of the most beautiful regions in France and one of the most fascinating movements in the history of art. Normandy is the cradle of Impressionism. Impressionism and Normandy are inseparable and unforgettable.

With our warmest greetings,

PIERRE BERGÉ
President of Normandie Impressionniste

LAURENT FABIUS
Vice President of Normandie Impressionniste

JÉRÔME CLÉMENT
Chair of the advisory council of Normandie Impressionniste

JACQUES-SYLVAIN KLEIN
General Curator of Normandie Impressionniste

It is the banks of the Seine that provide the setting for most of the key moments of Impressionism, starting with the origin of the term itself in a view of Le Havre, *Impression, Sunrise* (1872, musée Marmottan Monet, Paris). The new school of painting blossomed in Chatou, Bougival, Louveciennes and above all Argenteuil, whose name itself suffices to designate the enticing period of early Impressionism.

The group scattered around 1880 and its members moved away from Paris. Claude Monet moved to Vétheuil in 1878, then Poissy and finally Giverny. Alfred Sisley chose to live in isolation in the vicinity of Moret from 1880 on. Gustave Caillebotte bought a property in Petite Gennevilliers in the same period and Camille Pissarro settled at Éragny-sur-Epte in 1884. Berthe Morisot lived close to Mézy, where her old friend Auguste Renoir often visited her, as from 1890. Never too far away, the Seine remained a source of inspiration for many of them until the end.

They were not the only ones to undertake impassioned analysis of the sparkling light reflected on the surface of the river. George Seurat, Paul Signac, Pierre Bonnard and many others later chose to live and paint its banks. Then came the young Fauves, including Henri Matisse, Albert Marquet, Maurice de Vlaminck, André Derain and Othon Friesz.

From Paris to Le Havre, the whole of the Seine valley is today becoming a place of memory. The museums follow one another in close succession from the capital to the mouth of the river, like so many tributes to the one of the most brilliant pages in the history of painting. From the musée d'Orsay to the musée Malraux by way of Rouen and Vernon, they offer the art lover a broad range of Impressionist works. And many are the towns that conjure up the memory of the artists they inspired or watched over as they grew. The house of Maurice Denis in Saint-Germain-en-Laye has become the Musée du Prieuré, Mantes celebrates Maximilen Luce and Honfleur cherishes the memory of Eugène Boudin. The places that the Impressionists chose to paint have in turn become shrines of memory, such as Monet's garden at Giverny, the Musée de la Grenouillère at Croissy-sur-Seine and the Fournaise house in Chatou.

The works gathered together at the Giverny musée des impressionnismes invite you to take a walk in the very heart of the places that inspired them. They recount a history of Impressionism and offer above all the rare delight of rediscovering works in the settings in which they were born.

DIEGO CANDIL
General Director

MARINA FERRETTI BOCQUILLON
Scientific Director - Curator

Contents

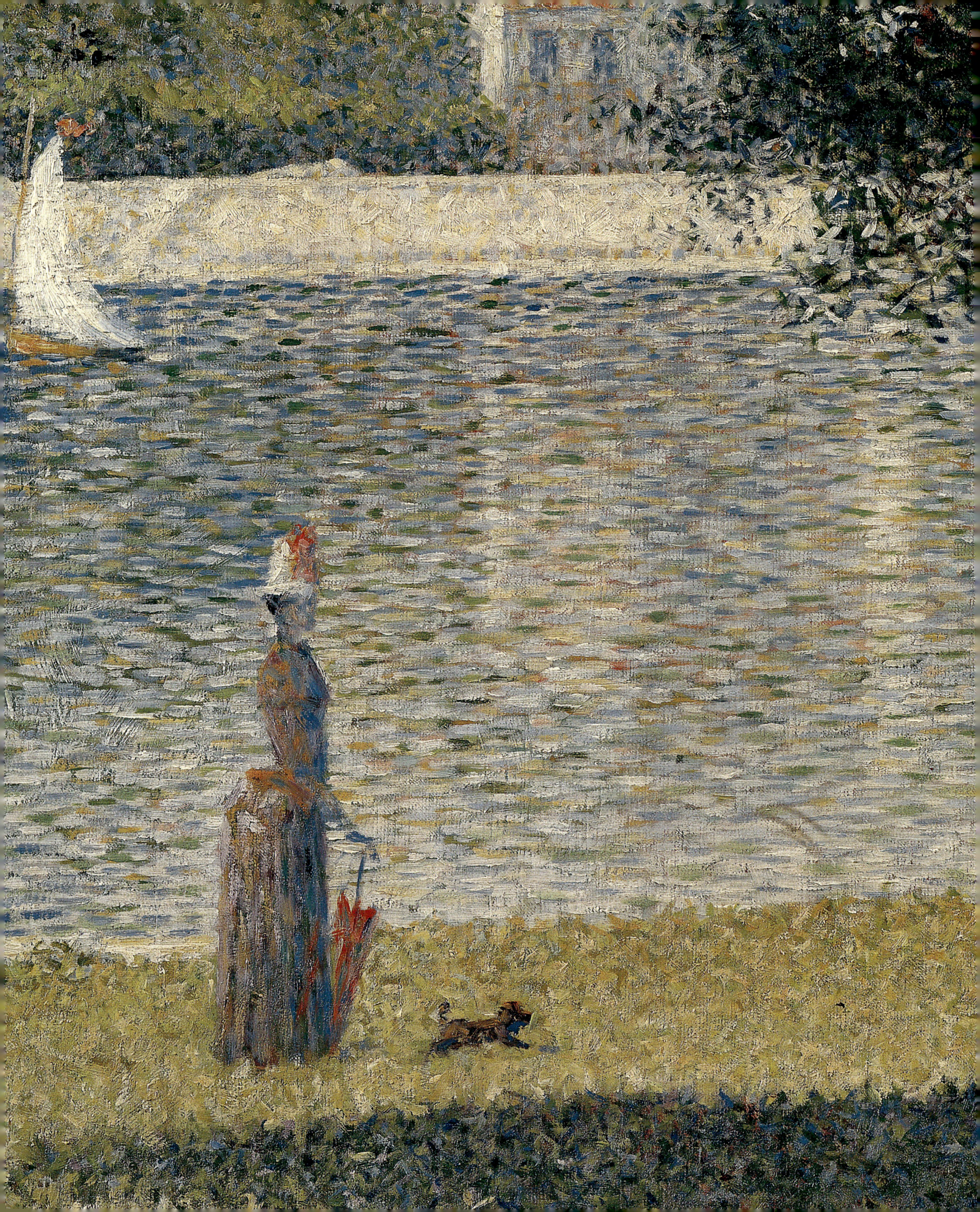

Impressionism on the Banks of the Seine

MARINA FERRETTI BOCQUILLON

Georges Seurat, *The Seine at Courbevoie (By the Water)* (detail), see cat. 32

If the Seine was the cradle of the New Painting all the way from Fontainebleau to Le Havre, this is because it was then the home of all innovations. It was on its banks that a new and hedonistic world convinced of the virtues of progress took shape. The Impressionist painters took a keen interest in this universe in the full swing of change and invented a different way of painting. They saw the Seine come to accommodate both industry and the leisure activities of city-dwellers, observing the latter closely and often sharing in their pleasures. While some were more sensitive to work, including Camille Pissarro, Alfred Sisley and Armand Guillaumin, others gave priority to the depiction of leisure, including Claude Monet, Auguste Renoir and Gustave Caillebotte. These two complementary aspects of modern times were, however, seldom separated. It was life itself that they sought to describe, and the sparkling figure of a lady out walking or the gleaming sail of a pleasure boat often stands out in their paintings against the background of factory chimneys and iron bridges.

Several of them chose to live close to the river because it offered them new subject matter. They sought isolation in order to work in peace and quiet, which did not prevent them from turning up on the riverside among the residents. From Asnières to Louveciennes by way of Argenteuil, Chatou and Bougival, from Vétheuil to Honfleur via Mantes, Giverny and Rouen, they found inspiration in fashionable resorts or instead sought out secluded spots. They gave these places a fame that they certainly never imagined.

The Seine was of no less interest to the naturalist writers who had also resolved to describe contemporary life. Guy de Maupassant in particular knew the river extremely well. "How many times have I wished to write a short book entitled *Sur la Seine* to recount the carefree life of energy, gaiety, poverty and rowdy, boisterous exuberance that I lived in my twenties. [...] How simple and good and also difficult it was to live like that, between the office in Paris and the river at Argenteuil. My one great and all-absorbing passion for ten years was the Seine. [...] I think I loved it so much because it gave me, or so I believe, the sense of life."[1] He continues a few lines further on: "as others have memories of sweet nights, I have memories of sunrises in the drifting, errant mists of early morning, as white as the dead before dawn and then, with the first rays, gliding over the meadows tinged with pink to delight the heart." Some more than familiar paintings instantaneously spring to mind, *Impression, Sunrise* or *Morning on the Seine*.[2]

It should be noted straight away that not all the painters who participate in the exhibitions of the Impressionist group displayed the same interest in the Seine. Edgar Degas paid it no attention at all and Paul Gauguin very little. Édouard Manet painted it only occasionally but the canvases it did inspire—*Argenteuil* (fig. 1) and *Boating* (1874, The Metropolitan Museum of Art, New York)—are among his most resounding masterpieces. Paul Cézanne preferred the Oise, which is essentially just one of its tributaries. On the other hand, the members of the group that can best be defined as "Impressionists" painted the Seine with great passion. It is at the heart of the work of Monet, Sisley and Guillaumin. Renoir depicted it very often, as did Gustave Caillebotte and Camille Pissarro. The artists of the post-Impressionist generation also paid frequent tribute to the river, as in the most celebrated cases of Paul Signac, with his numerous early views of the stretch from Asnières to Les Andelys, and Georges Seurat, with *Bathers at Asnières* (1884, The National Gallery, London) and *A Sunday Afternoon on the Island of La Grande Jatte*. Then we have painters like Vincent Van Gogh, Maurice Denis and Pierre Bonnard. Nor should we forget the young Fauves, who also vied with one another in celebrating the Seine, before turning to the more glaring colors of the South of France, like so many others at the turn of the century. At the dawn of the twentieth century, the modern landscape finally occupied the place of honor. This was the result of a very slow development.

Landscape and Feeling for Nature

Nature remained the domain of country folk for a long time and the activities associated with them, regarded as repetitive and utilitarian, provided very little inspiration for French artists. In the fifteenth century, when the Duke of Berry commissioned Pol de Limbourg to illustrate his *Très Riches Heures*, the primary purpose was the portrayal of his sumptuous castles, even though each miniature is accompanied by the precise depiction of a stage in the cycle of agricultural work. For centuries nature offered practically no pleasures other than those of the hunt, as attested by splendid paintings such as Carle Vanloo's *The Hunt Lunch* (1737, musée du Louvre, Paris), which shows an elegant alfresco banquet. The landscape appears only in the background, like a stage set. Few are the cases where nature is observed without being subordinated, as in Jean-Antoine Watteau's *Pilgrimage on the Isle of Cythera* (1717, musée du Louvre, Paris), to preparatory rearrangement as a setting for imaginary scenes.

Everything changed in the nineteenth century, when France underwent industrialization and urbanization. While Pierre-Henri de Valenciennes advocated the practice of painting *en plein air* and invented the concept of the landscape portrait, more and more artists took up a genre previously regarded as minor.

The marked development of landscape painting during that period was bound up with a more general taste for nature. The number of public parks and gardens increased considerably in the

1. Édouard Manet
Argenteuil, 1874
Oil on canvas,
148.5 × 114.5 cm
(58 ½ × 45 in.)
Musée des Beaux-Arts
Collection, Tournai

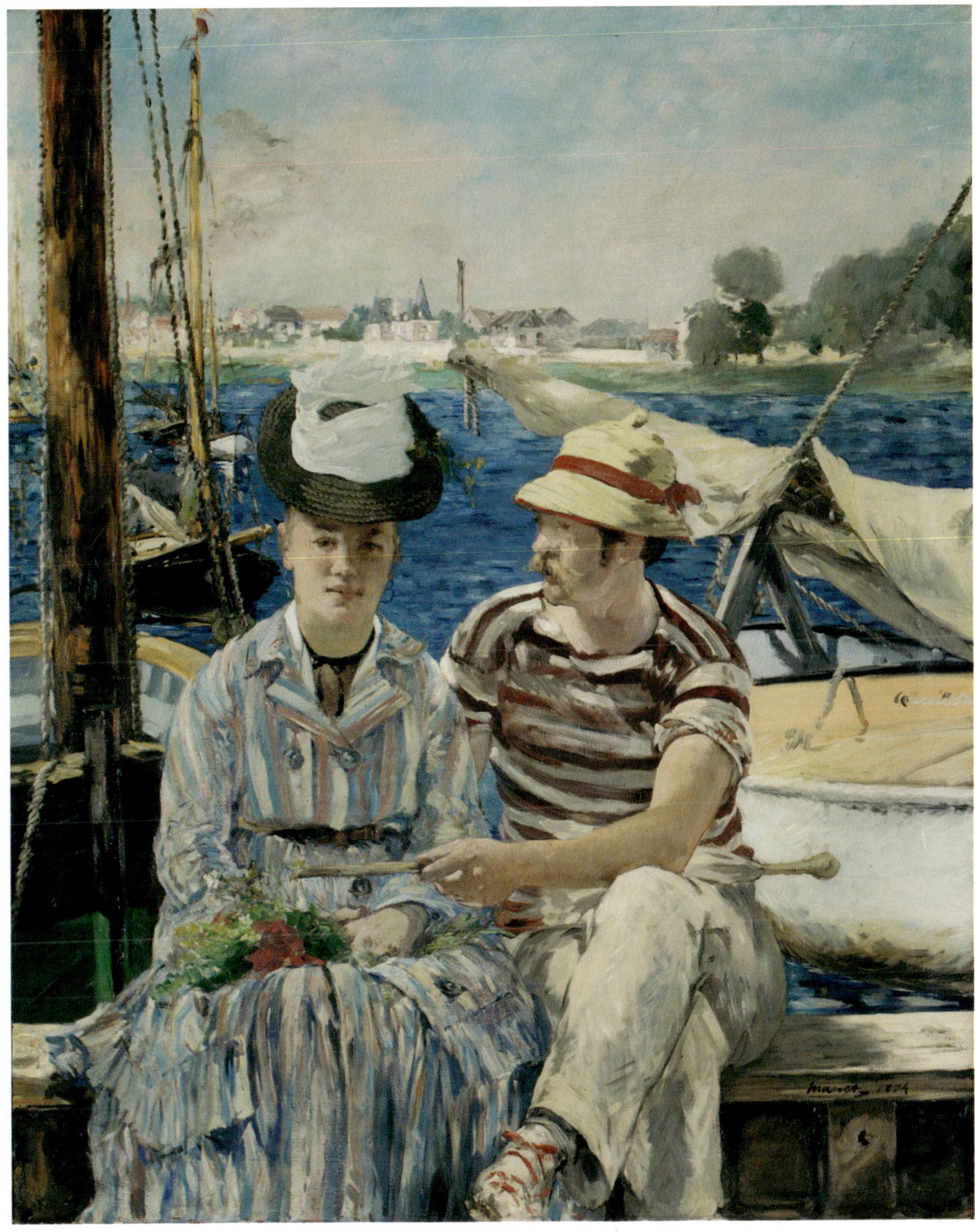

cities at the same time. Paris had nineteen hectares of green space in 1848 but no less than 1,800 in 1870. The urban remodelling planned by the prefect Haussmann and carried out by the architect Alphant led to the creation of the Bois de Boulogne, the Bois de Vincennes and the Parc des Buttes-Chaumont, to name only the most important parks.[3] The rural exodus bore fruit, as the woodland and countryside around the big cities also lost no time in becoming pleasant places of recreation. This passion was already the expression of nostalgia for a paradise lost, or in any case greatly endangered. It was forgotten that nature had been a powerful

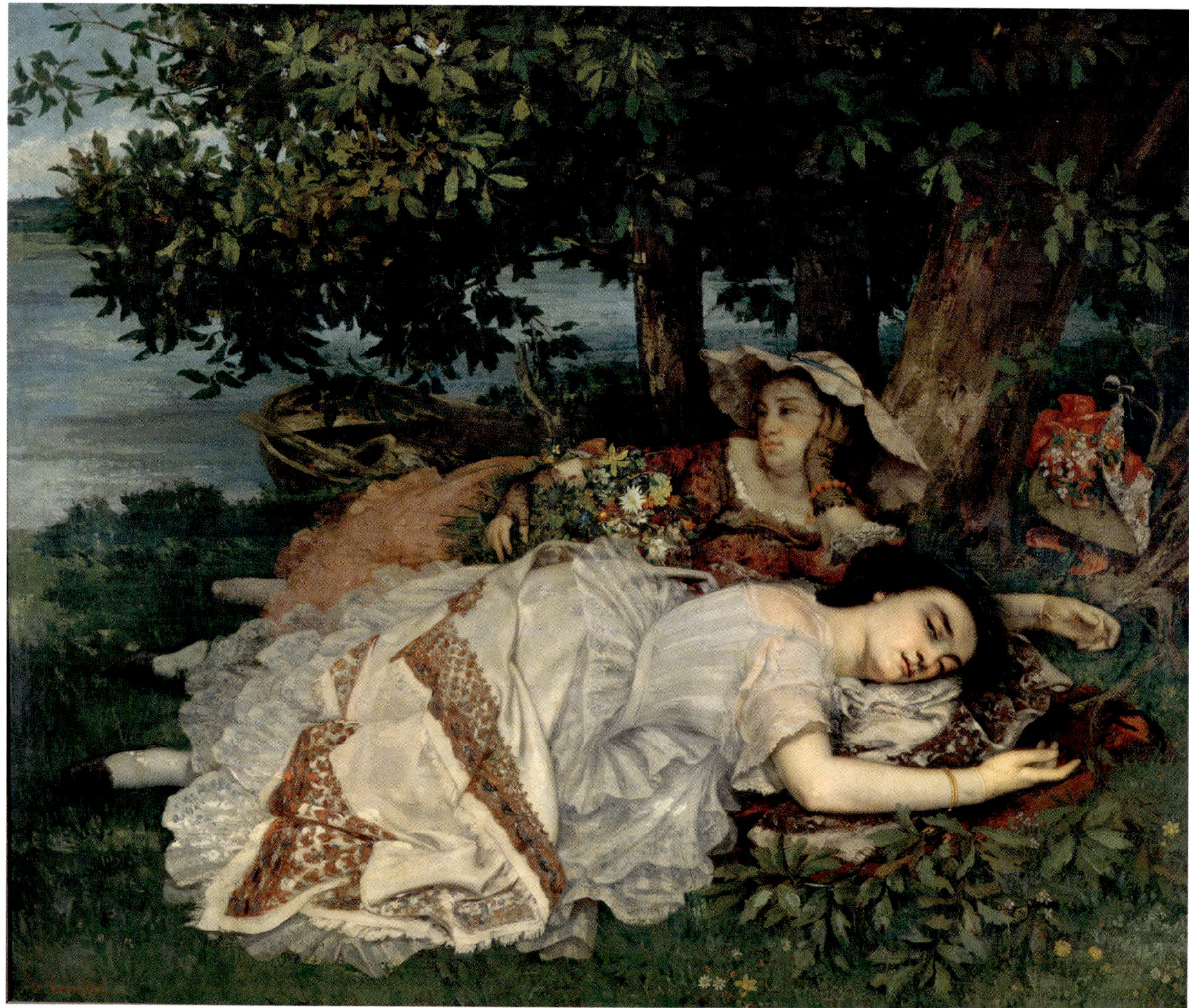

2. Gustave Courbet
Young Ladies on the Banks of the Seine, 1856–57
Oil on canvas, 174 × 206 cm (68 ½ × 81 ¼ in.)
Petit Palais–musée des Beaux-Arts de la Ville de Paris, Paris, 377

threat for centuries to country folk, whose efforts for the whole year it might suddenly destroy, and to sailors, who saw even greater risk in its caprices.

This feeling was born in France at the end of the eighteenth century, when the idea of nature was already being detached from the rural landscape. When Louis XIV decided to leave the Louvre and move the court to Versailles, this was a political choice. And if he did feel a sincere love for gardens, he intended them above all as manifestations of boundless royal power. At the end of the century, Marie-Antoinette's hamlet reflected very different aspirations: the return to a simpler and more intimate life and escape from intrigue together with the wholly Voltairean idea that wisdom consists in cultivating one's garden. This was also the period that saw the emergence of the English-style landscaped garden, whose natural appearance was soon preferred to the traditional order of Le Nôtre's works, as well as the pre-Romantic sensibility expressed in Rousseau's *Rêveries*.

With Romanticism, nature truly became the mirror of the soul. In painting as in literature, it reflected the torments and emotions of the soul. A taste for direct observation was, however, already emerging.

Camille Corot and Paul Huet began painting in the woods at Barbizon in the 1820s. While the practice of painting studies *en plein air*, in oil or watercolour, had in fact been spreading since the second half of the eighteenth century, it was not until the invention of paint in tubes by the American John Rand in 1841 and of the portable easel around 1857 that it developed on any real scale.[4] The age of realism had arrived. With the painters of the Barbizon School, Théodore Rousseau, Jean-François Millet and Gustave Courbet, the artist looked at nature through eyes seeking to be objective. Strongly symbolic messages were also conveyed, however, as the art of landscape came to express regional roots or national identity. Gustave Courbet's formidable *The Oak of Flagey* also known as *The Oak of Vercingetorix* (1864, Murauchi Art Museum, Tokyo) is an evident example.

A new clientele had appeared since the breakdown of the social structures of the *Ancien Régime*. The active and enterprising middle classes adopted different values from the aristocracy, no longer seeing history, mythology and the Bible as the touchstone of knowledge. They gave priority to concrete values, preferring to observe and seek to understand a familiar world. When they travelled, it was not necessarily to make a pilgrimage or on a *Grand Tour* designed to complete a meticulous education, but often for practical or commercial reasons. Stendhal's hero, the first "tourist" in French literature, is an iron merchant who travels around France, observes the places where he stays and finds out about their characteristics.[5] Middle-class art lovers asserted their own aesthetic values, as they had already done in the fields of politics and economics, and thus supported the emergence of a new artistic vocabulary. More direct and apparently simpler, it responded to new criteria, with heroic deeds and myths giving way to the idea of truth and straightforwardness. As Françoise Cachin notes in a study on the landscape as a place of memory, "Barbizon replaced Versailles."[6]

This was the time of picnics, of democratic hunting parties. Nature had gradually become a place to get away from it all, with the first excursion trains handling a massive outflow of population from Paris on Sundays. In 1866 it was at Asnières that the brothers Edmond and Jules de Goncourt set the boating scene of *Manette Salomon* with the hopeless would-be painter Anatole[7]: "The summer arrived and Anatole switched from painting to leisure, the joys of the water, the Parisian passion for boating [...] Enjoying the day, the fatigue, the intoxication, the free and vibrant open air, the glitter of the water, the sun beating down, the gleaming flame of everything that dazes and dazzles in these flowing promenades, the almost animal inebriation of life imparted by a great seething river, blinded by light and good weather." To convey the sensuality of a nap outdoors, the authors recalled a painting by Courbet that had caused outcry at the Salon a few years earlier (fig. 2): "The group scattered and let the worst of the heat go by in one of those unrestrained siestas, stretched out on the grass, in the shade of the branches, and showing nothing of society but a glimpse of a straw hat, a red patch of jacket, a hint of petticoat, whatever floats and survives a shipwreck in the Seine."[8] It is instead in the setting of the woods of Fontainebleau that they present the painter Coriolis, seized by quasi-mystical emotion on his arrival at Bas Bréau: "He felt that he was beholding one of the great majestic spectacles of nature and stopped for a few minutes in a kind of rapture and awed silence of the soul before this entrance to the avenue, this triumphal gate where the trees extended their vast foliage, filled with the joy of the day, as an arch over their magnificent columns. At the end of the winding avenue, he looked at those splendid and severe oaks, as old as gods and as solemn as monuments, beauteous with a splendor crowned by the centuries."[9] Tourists and artists had definitively taken the place of hunters in the forest of Fontainebleau, where nature was regarded with the respect due to a venerable monument. The Impressionist painters were to see through less deferent eyes.

Tired of the teaching in the Gleyre studio, Monet, Renoir, Bazille and Sisley went to Barbizon in 1863. Like their elders, they set themselves to learn from nature and the forest inspired their first masterpieces. Bazille's *Landscape at Chailly* (1865, The Art Institute of Chicago) and Sisley's *Avenue of Chestnut Trees near La Celle-Saint-Cloud* (c. 1866–67, Petit Palais, Paris)—which was painted, despite its title, on the edge of the forest of Fontainebleau[10]—already attest to a freer and more colorful vision than that of their predecessors. And while Manet had created his *Luncheon on the Grass* (1863, musée d'Orsay, Paris) in the studio, Monet made the effort to paint his own ambitious *Luncheon on the Grass* (fig. 3) *en plein air*.

These two canvases are not landscapes but scenes of modern life on an unusually imposing scale. They show neither woodcutters nor hunters but city-dwellers relaxing. The gleam of the light-colored dresses rivals the sumptuous still life of the picnic in Monet's painting. Above all, the solemnity manifest in the paintings of Rousseau or Courbet gives way to a new fluidity. Like a photographic plate, the painting seeks only to capture the savor of a fleeting moment. With his very particular atmosphere and light, Monet's imposing *Luncheon* retains the freshness of a snapshot. The shifting flow of the Seine with its shimmering light and reflections soon took the place of motionless ponds, immemorial rocks and age-old oak trees in the paintings of the young Impressionists. Living in a universe that was moving faster all the time, their authors adapted their technique accordingly. The world had changed and so had their mental representation of it. In order to depict a less structured society and communicate a feeling of vivacity, it was necessary to use lively brushstrokes, light colors and colored shadows. In order to preserve the effect produced, it was necessary to avoid any freezing of sensations through overly precise drawing or composition of a too evidently geometric character.

This sensibility is already to be glimpsed in the work of Charles-François Daubigny, who commissioned the boat builder Baillet in 1857 to design a boat, the *Botin*, equipped for painting on the Seine, closer to nature. It is also to be found in Corot (cat. 4), the least realistic of the Barbizon painters but also the one that Pissarro and Berthe Morisot were to acknowledge as their master. It was stronger still in the work of Eugène Boudin. Monet once said that if he had become a true painter, it was due to Boudin, whom he met in Le Havre.[11] When he painted the port of Le Havre and the beaches of Normandy, Monet was long to remember his elder's "extraordinary enchantments of air and water"[12] (cat. 9, 12). Monet also met Johan Barthold Jongkind in 1862: "He became my true master from then on. It is to him that I owe the definitive education of my eye."[13] It was in London, where Monet took refuge with Pissarro during the Franco-Prussian War of 1870, that he completed his education through elective affinities with the discovery of the works of the great Romantic painter Joseph Mallord William Turner, who explored and painted the banks of the Seine back in 1821, long before the Impressionists.

For a certain time, and in any case until the turn of the century, the Seine took the place of Barbizon in works of the modern painters.[14] From Moret to Le Havre, the river and its tributaries—the Loing, the Yerres, the Oise and the Epte—were the Impressionists' favorite subject matter together with the beaches of the Channel. They wished to be realistic and chose to paint what was familiar to them. Monet travelled a great deal in France and in Europe but after a last stay in Venice in 1908, he devoted himself exclusively to painting his garden in Giverny. On being invited by the young American artist Walter Pach to go and paint in the United States, he explained, "one must know a place thoroughly before one can paint it. That's why I stay here in the country where I was born."[15]

3. Claude Monet
Luncheon on the Grass
(Central panel), 1865–66
Oil on canvas,
248 × 217 cm
(97 ¾ × 85 ½ in.)
Musée d'Orsay, Paris,
RF1987-12

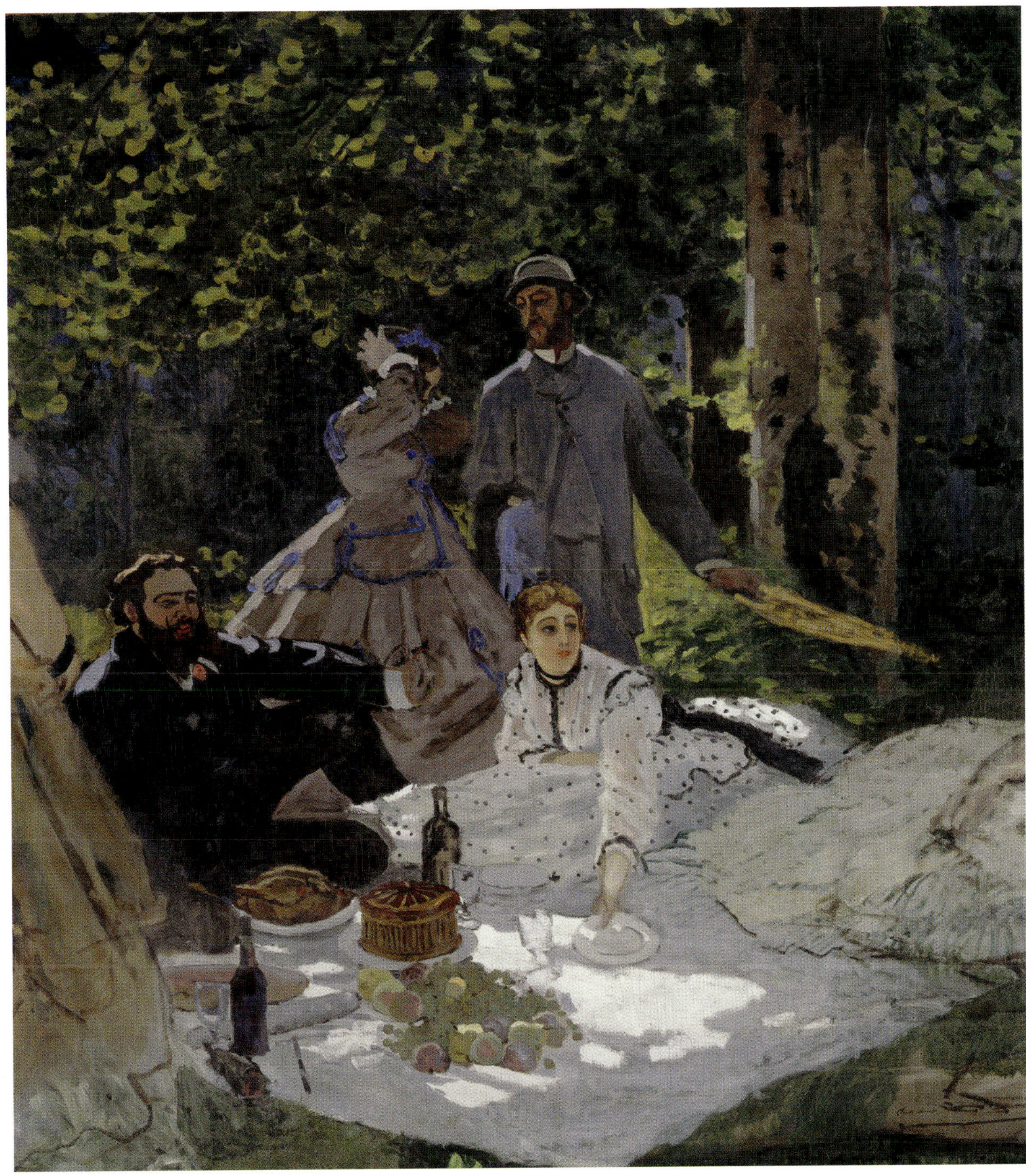

"Paris, Rouen and Le Havre are One Big Town with the Seine as its High Street"

As all the encyclopaedias tell us, the Seine stretches for 776 kilometres from its source on the Langres plateau. It is not until Montereau, however, that it swells on receiving the waters of the Yonne and then those of the Loing downstream from Moret. Apart from Moret and its surroundings, where Sisley lived from 1880 until his death in 1899, it is primarily the course of the Seine in the area of Paris and in Normandy that interests us here. The river begins to meander in this stretch, where it is joined by the Essonne, the Orge, the Yerres—where Caillebotte lived for a long time—and finally the Marne. In Paris, where it had held the attention of artists for years, it was a favorite subject of the pre-Impressionist painters. It is joined by the Oise in the Basse Seine. Its valley offers the yachtsman wonderful scope for exploration all the way to Rouen. The waters of the Epte and the Andelle increase its volume still further in Normandy

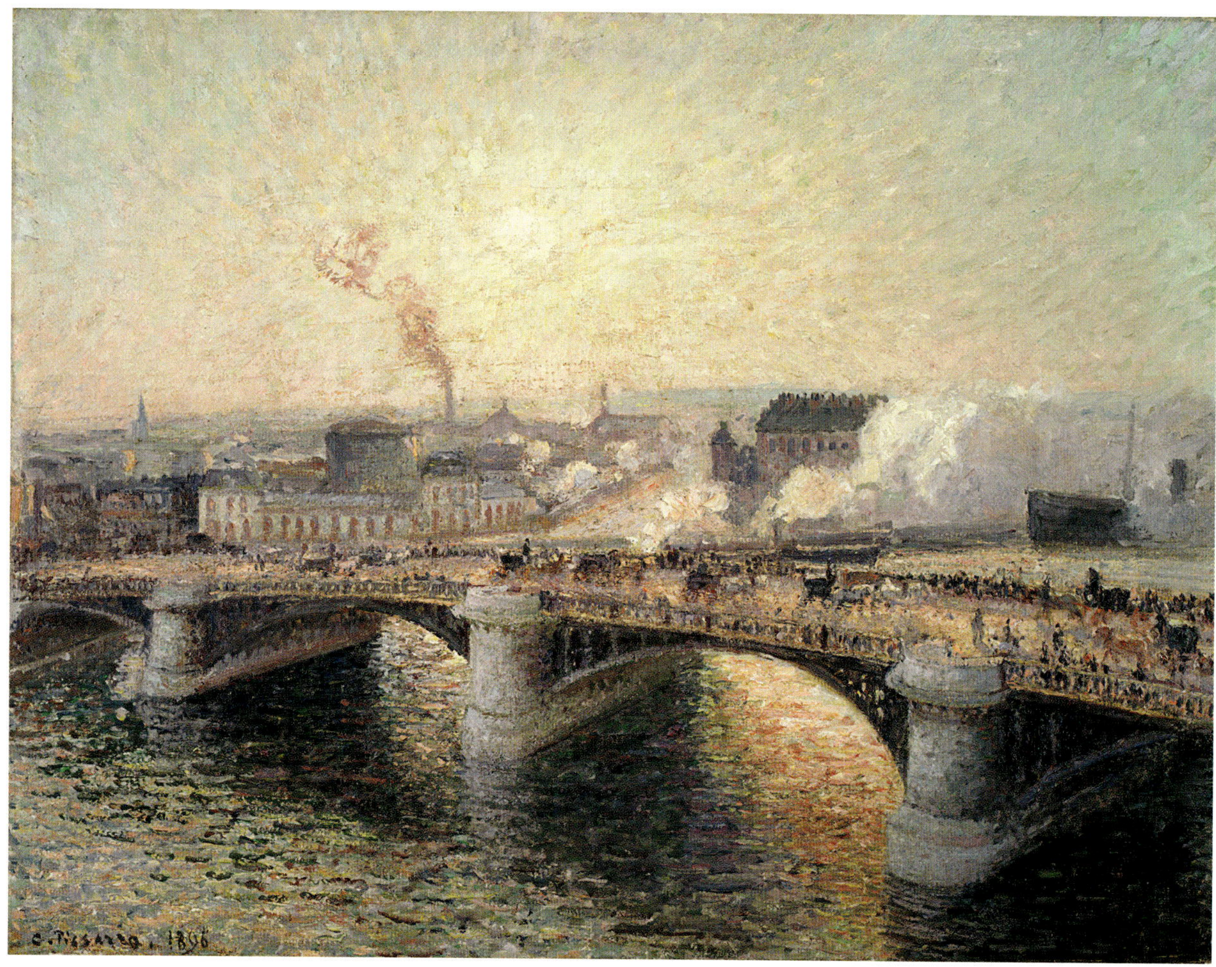

4. Camille Pissarro
The Pont Boieldieu in Rouen at Sunset, 1896
Oil on canvas,
74.2 × 92.5 cm
(29 ¼ × 36 ½ in.)
Birmingham Museum
and Art Gallery, 1950p23

and the maritime stretch downstream of Rouen bears intense traffic before flowing out into the English Channel south of Le Havre.

Without actually attaining the level of tentacular urbanization announced in 1870 by Michelet, who envisaged the three great ports of the Seine forming "one big town with the Seine as its high street,"[16] the river underwent rapid industrial development very early, not least due to its ideal location between the capital and the English Channel.

The first railway line took Parisians to Le Pecq as early as 1837. The Paris–Rouen line opened five years later and was extended to Le Havre in 1847. The Saint Lazare station handled 13,254,000 passengers in 1869 and the possibilities of movement were expanded at the end of the century by the bicycle and then the car. (Monet, Bonnard and Signac were keen motorists.) The transport of goods also increased and steam revolutionized the design of shipping. The great ports of Le Havre, Rouen and Paris underwent modernization. Pissarro never tired of painting them, and if he often returned to Rouen, "the city of a hundred bell-towers," it was not for its churches but above all because he was fascinated by its modern and industriously bustling quays[17] (fig. 4). The port of Le Havre instead held a very particular significance for Pissarro, as it reminded him of his arrival from Saint-Thomas des Antilles. He was to make it the subject of his last series of paintings right at the end of his life in 1903 (cat. 23).

The landscape of the banks of the Seine also lost its rural appearance outside the big cities. Locks had been built in the 1830s and steam tugs now towed the barges formerly hauled by men or horses. The number of warehouses, tanneries, paper mills, foundries and factories multiplied on the water's edge throughout the century. Tall chimneys and iron bridges formed part of the landscape and the painters had no hesitation in including these outward signs of the Seine's industrial dynamism in their works.

Pissarro juxtaposed the paper mill of Port-Marly and its traditional wash house in 1872 (cat. 5) but deliberately ignored the Grenouillère, which had attracted the attention of his friends Renoir and Monet two years earlier. Despite the evident tribute to Corot, who had painted this harmonious bend in the Seine before him, it was the universe of work that he depicted.[18] At the opposite extreme, Sisley's *The Seine at Bougival* (cat. 8) presents an exceptionally idyllic landscape of sky, water and trees devoid of any human presence whatsoever. The artist stopped at a precise point known as the "backwater," navigation being prohibited downstream of the Machine de Marly, upon which he turned his back. The countryside appeared unspoilt, as long as you chose your viewpoint carefully. This virgin landscape on the banks of the Seine was, however, to remain as isolated a case in the artist's oeuvre as it was in the work of his friends. The increasingly numerous factory chimneys erected in Argenteuil rose quickly above the old church tower and the abrupt lines of iron bridges, often wreathed in the plume of steam from a train engine,[19] were recurrent structural features in the canvases of Monet, Renoir and Caillebotte. It was the accentuated outlines of coal cranes and gasometers that fascinated the young Émile Bernard, Signac and Van Gogh in Clichy.
The signs of modernity attracted the attention of the Impressionists and their followers in Paris too. The construction of the underground railway near the old village of Passy altered the face of the banks of the Seine. Henri-Edmond Cross offered a depiction of this district where change was in full swing, with the metal scaffoldings of the Métro bridge rising like so many potential Eiffel Towers, that was not devoid of lyricism (cat. 22). At night, the old bridges also showed them a new face because of the unprecedented charm lent by gas lighting. Maximilien Luce often expressed their poetry, finding extraordinary scope for innovation in the pale garland of gas globes and street lights with the glittering play of reflections on the surface of the river (cat. 21).

The Seine, the Mirror of Sunday Pleasures

The advent of leisure time accompanying industrial development had no less impact on the landscape. From Paris to Rouen in particular, the Seine became the "mirror of Sunday's extravagant delights."[20] Like their contemporaries, painters often noted the striking contrasts presented by the outskirts of the capital: places of pleasure on one side and the industrial universe on the other. The contrast was particularly marked between Asnières, the paradise of boating, and the resolutely industrial waterside of Clichy, and no less striking between the factories of Port-Marly and the very residential town of Bougival. The roles were less clearly defined in the vicinity of Argenteuil and Gennevilliers, where industry and leisure coexisted indivisibly and the ballet of the immaculate sails developed alongside the plumes of smoke from tugs. The regattas organized by the Cercle de la Voile presented a glittering spectacle on Sundays against the background of factories, workshops and shipyards.
The English, manufacturers of the first trains, also exported their taste for sport to France, with the vogue for boating taking its place alongside walking and hiking in the 1830s. Maupassant took a keen interest in this pastime and made frequent references to it in its stories. *De Paris à Rouen* communicates his enthusiasm for "a delightful trip through the most wonderful countryside in the world and the best suited to description. [...] We simply went down the Seine,

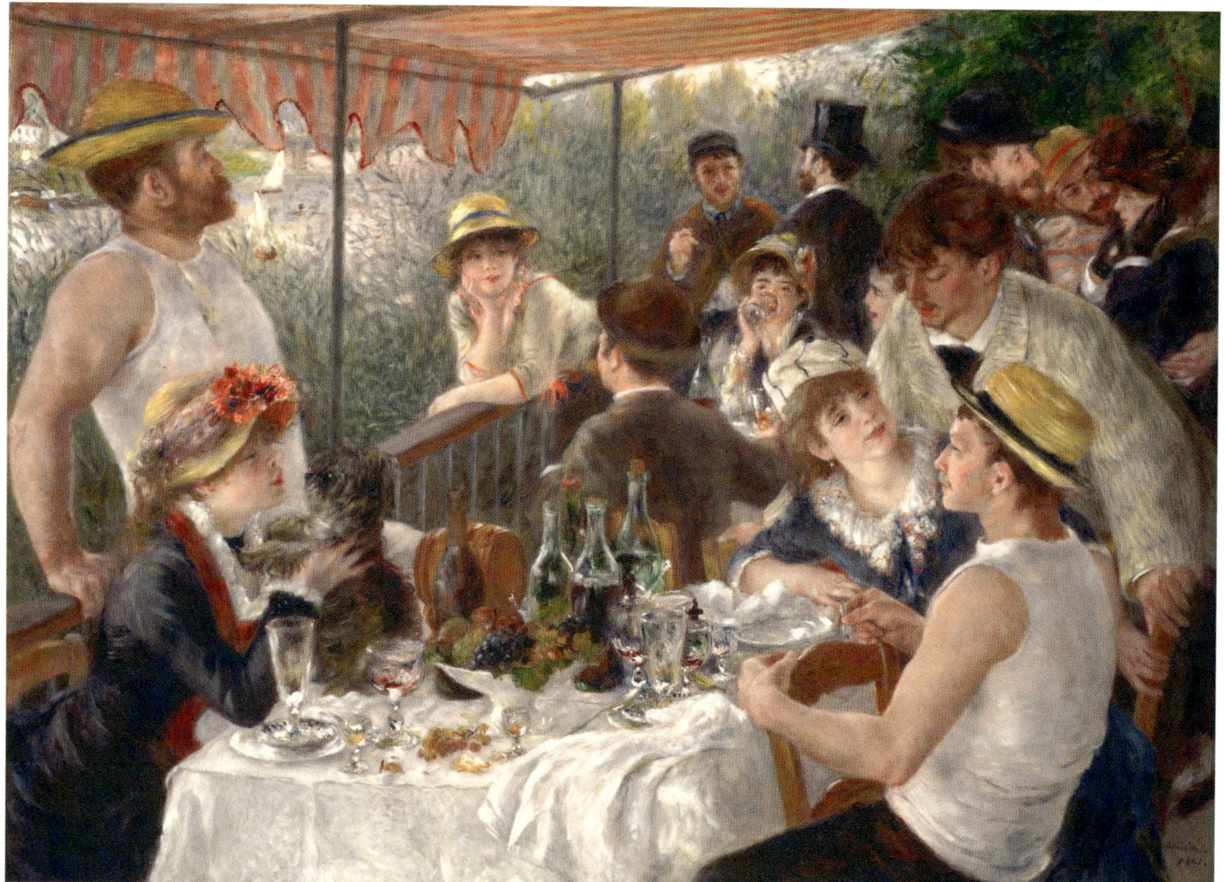

5. Auguste Renoir
Luncheon of the Boating Party, 1880–81
Oil on canvas,
130.2 × 175.6 cm
(51 ¼ × 69 ¼ in.)
The Phillips Collection, Washington

that calm and beautiful river, from Paris to Rouen in one of those small two-seater boats called skiffs. So light that one of us can carry it alone, long, slim and elegant, varnished to a mirror finish inside with mahogany fittings, sharply pointed like a needle of wood, so flat that it does not enter the water but glides over it like a skater, so fragile that a foot out of place would break it at once, so narrow that an abrupt movement would make it capsize, our craft was as dear to us as a human being."[21] Caillebotte and Signac, rowing enthusiasts like Maupassant, then became skilled yachtsmen with the new craze for sailing.

While Asnières was the main centre for rowing, the Parisian sailing clubs made their home in Argenteuil, where the Seine widens out, the Société des régates parisiennes in 1853 and the Cercle de la Voile de Paris shortly after in 1858. Argenteuil thus became a fashionable resort. It was there that Monet observed the bustling life of the Seine from his floating studio, as attested by one the most Impressionist works of his friend Manet (fig. 7). The latter's family had a property at Gennevilliers and he often went to visit Monet, who had already left the area when Caillebotte, a keen yachtsman, bought a property at Petit Gennevilliers[22] in 1881 and became the President of the Cercle de la Voile. Caillebotte sponsored the membership of the young artist Signac, who was also drawn there by his twofold passion for painting and sailing (cat. 43).

While yachting and regattas remained a sport for gentlemen, the preserve of the upper middle class, the Seine also offered other and more democratic pleasures. The riverside cafés with dance floors, where a far more mixed company relaxed on Sundays, were also often mentioned by Maupassant, who set various scenes of his short stories at the Grenouillère: "Couples strolled beneath the high foliage along the Seine, where the boats glided by. There were young people, working-girls and their sweethearts, the latter in their shirt-sleeves with coats on their arms, tall hats tipped back and a jaded look. There were tradesmen with their families, the women dressed in their best and the children flocking like little chicks about their parents."[23]

Located on the island of Croissy opposite Bougival, the Grenouillère was a bathing establish-

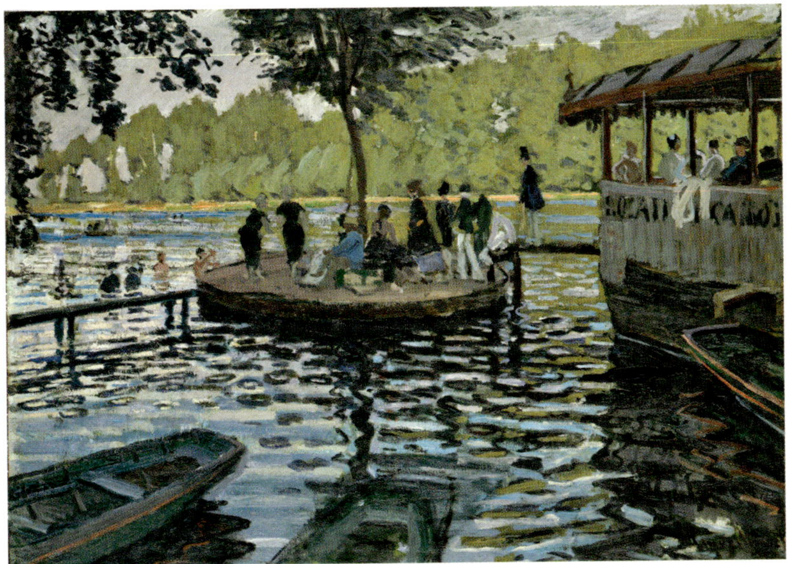

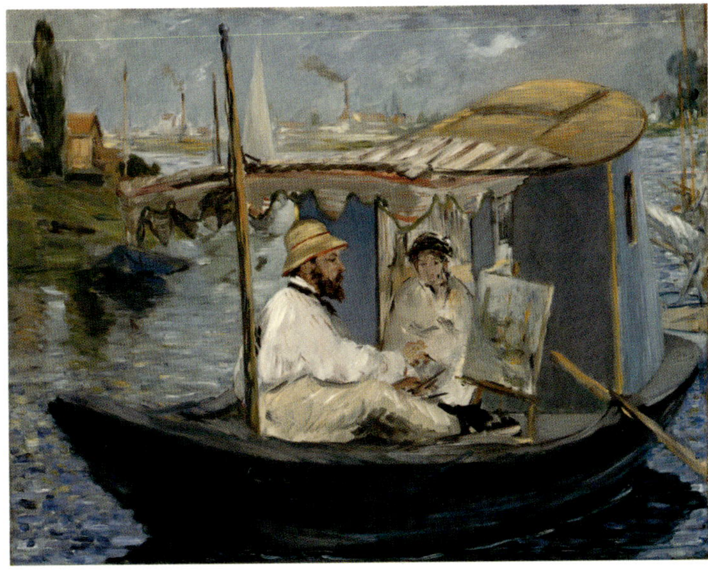

6. Claude Monet
La Grenouillère, 1869
Oil on canvas,
74.6 × 99.7 cm
(29 ½ × 39 ¼ in.)
The Metropolitan Museum, New York, H.O. Havemeyer Collection, Bequest of Mrs. H.O. Havemeyer, 1929, 29.100.112

7. Édouard Manet
The Boat, 1874
Oil on canvas,
82.7 × 73 cm
(32 ½ × 28 ¾ in.)
Bayerische Staatsgemäldesammlungen, Neue Pinakothek, Munich, 8759

ment that reached its peak of glory from 1860 to 1889. People went there to swim, row, drink, dine and dance at little expense. The accent was on gaiety and pleasure far more than sporting prowess. Renoir went there with Prince Bibesco before embarking on a large painting of the place at the same time as Monet. While these planned works were never produced, the sketches they both painted in 1869 can be seen today as the true laboratory of Impressionism (fig. 6). Renoir was also a regular patron of the nearby Maison Fournaise in Chatou, which became a museum in 1992. Maupassant discovered it in 1873 and Alphonse Fournaise, the owner and boat builder, took care of his ships. In addition to the joys of rowing, the place offered the services of a hotel and a restaurant run by Madame Fournaise. The couple's children Alphonse and Alphonsine helped their parents in this highly successful enterprise. Maupassant described the atmosphere of the place under the name of the "Grillon restaurant" in *La Femme de Paul*[24] and used it as the setting for a scene in *Dimanches d'un bourgeois à Paris*: "She had found friends, a band of almost naked, gesticulating rowers, scarlet to the tips of their ears, who arranged all the details of the competition at the tops of their voices in front of the house of the builder Fournaise."[25]

Well-known for her charms, Alphonsine Fournaise inspired Degas, who also patronized the establishment, and especially Renoir who painted her portrait (cat. 30) and depicted her leaning on the balustrade of the terrace in his *Luncheon of the Boating Party* (fig. 5). This emblematic image, including her brother Alphonse, Renoir's future wife Aline Charigot, the actress Ellen Andrée, Maupassant and perhaps Caillebotte together with other habitués of the celebrated restaurant, marks the completion of the project commenced at the Grenouillère. The pretty Aline reappears in *Oarsmen at Chatou* (cat. 31), a canvas painted by Renoir not far from the Maison Fournaise.

As on the coast of Normandy, fashionable city dwellers were henceforth to form part of the landscape on the banks of the Seine, where they brought the light touch of a straw hat, a brightly colored dress or a parasol. Manet, Monet, Renoir and Caillebotte depicted this universe painstakingly, never neglecting the effects of fashion, because each detail counted for reasons of an artistic or symbolic nature. Thus, while rowers on the Seine all wore white, red and black stripes were *de rigueur* on the Marne.[26] The design of bathing costumes also took specific shape based on the model of the Pont Neuf school of swimming.[27] Like the Parisian elegance of hats and crinoline, sporting outfits also formed part of the modern image. Seurat drew up an extraordinary and by no means humourless inventory of these things in 1886 with his *A Sunday Afternoon on the Island of La Grande Jatte*, capturing the Sunday promenade of a secularized society (fig. 8).

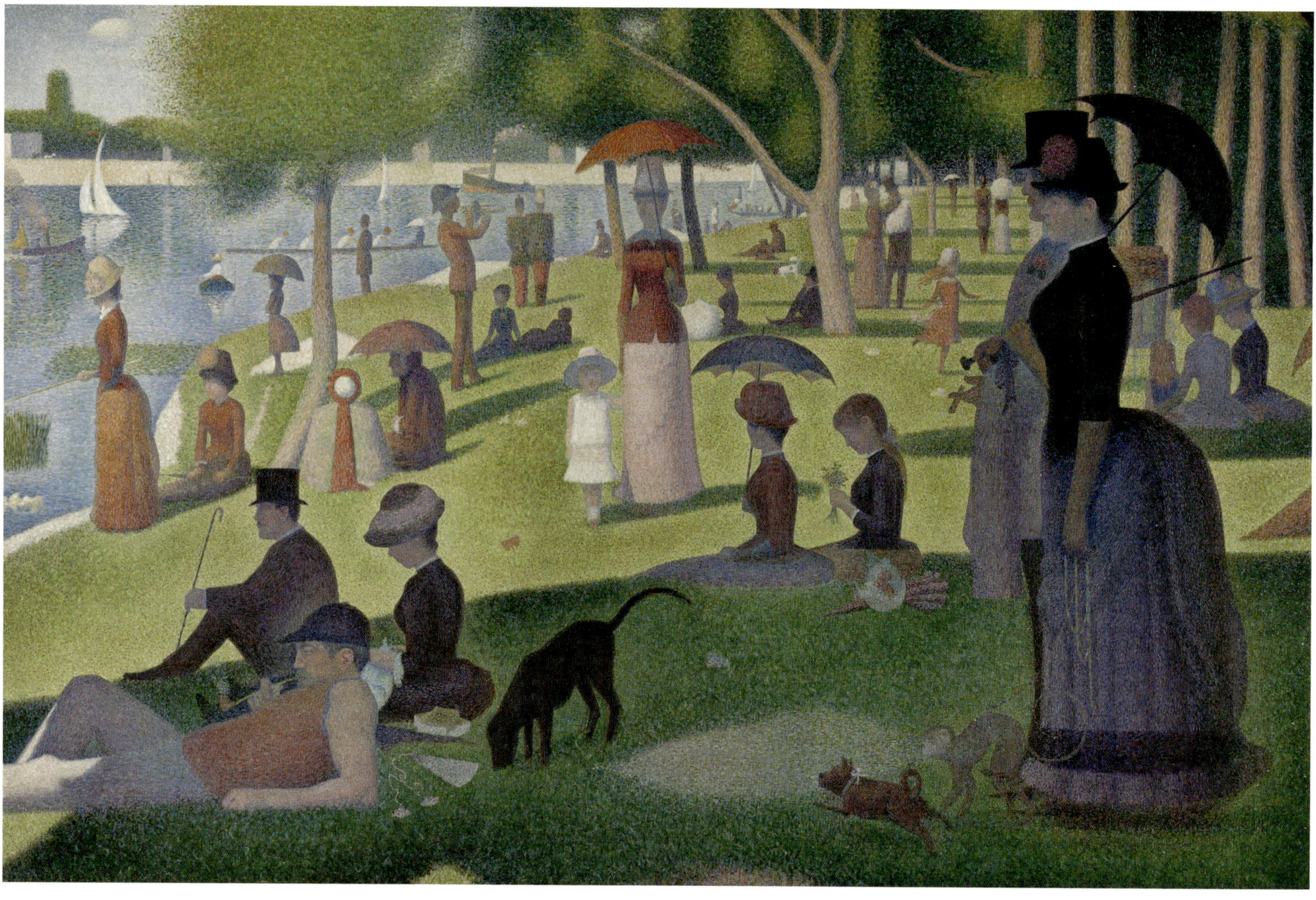

8. Georges Seurat
A Sunday Afternoon on the Island of La Grande Jatte, 1884–86
Oil on canvas,
207.5 × 308.1 cm
(81 ¾ × 121 ½ in.)
The Art Institute of Chicago, Helen Birch Bartlett Memorial Collection, 1926.224

Living and Painting by the Water's Edge

The future Impressionists developed the habit of meeting up on the outskirts of the capital from 1867 on. Numerous painters and writers were to settle more or less permanently on the banks of the Seine during the 1870s, as the progress of transport made it no longer imperative for an artist to live in Paris. Driven by the desire to get closer to nature and have their own gardens, they moved out of the city, even if visiting the Salon and exhibitions, buying supplies and meeting their friends and dealers meant a journey by train or car.

Monet had more addresses on the Seine than any of the others and spent the whole of his life along the river between Paris, where he was born, and Le Havre, where he grew up and where he painted *Impression, Sunrise* (1872, musée Marmottan Monet, Paris), the work from which Impressionism took its name.

Monet was living in Saint-Michel near Bougival in 1869. Renoir's family had been living in Louveciennes since 1868 and the two painters met up regularly. They also saw Sisley, who moved to Bougival in 1870 and whose house was destroyed shortly afterwards by Prussian soldiers together with all the canvases in it. The same fate befell Pissarro, who had settled in Louveciennes in 1869. When he returned in 1871 from London, where he had taken refuge with Monet, his house had been plundered and he found only 40 of the 1,500 canvases he had left there. A whole chunk of his work disappeared, *Barge on the Seine* (cat. 6) being one of few works to survive the catastrophe. Sisley moved to Marly-le-Roi in 1874 and then to Sèvres. Berthe Morisot, who became Mrs. Manet in 1874, when she married one of the painter's brothers, rented a house in Bougival in 1880 and spent the summers there. Caillebotte regularly visited the family property on the Yerres, a tributary of the Seine upstream of Paris, where he both enjoyed and painted the delights of boating (cat. 28, 29). Monet had chosen to live in Argenteuil, where he had his own garden for the first time. This was one of the great periods in the first stage of Impressionism. Manet himself learned from his young disciples. Apart from Degas, who remained Parisian, most of them either settled or made regular stays outside the city and preferably on the banks of the Seine, leaving the bad memories of the Commune and prohibitive rents behind them.

Many of the Impressionist painters chose in the 1880s to move still farther away and settle in the countryside, as Pissarro had done earlier. Monet moved from Argenteuil to Vétheuil in 1878, then Poissy in 1881, and finally Giverny less than two years later.

The painters were not the only ones to take this choice. Among their best-known contemporaries, Émile Zola moved far from the Parisian suburbs in 1878 to settle in Médan, where he was visited by his friends and fellow naturalist authors. It is again to Maupassant that we owe the most abiding image of the "*terrible réaliste*" in his garden: "Médan. We go down to see Zola. He appears in the midst of a through of masons and gardeners, directing the building of his farmyard. He is cheerful, happy to see his trees growing."[28]

Zola drew upon Monet a great deal in creating Claude Lantier, the hero of *L'Œuvre*, his *roman à clés* about the contemporary art scene. It is certainly Monet that he had in mind when he wrote the passage where Lantier decides to take his girl-friend very close to Giverny. "He knew a small village after Mantes called Bennecourt [...] and, without worrying about the two-hour train journey, took her there for lunch, just as he would have taken her to Asnières. She was delighted with the never-ending journey. Even better if it were at the end of the world!" Enchanted, the lovers decide at once to rent a house with garden, where they settle: "after lunch, endless wanderings, long treks over the apple orchard, along the grassy paths through the countryside, walks by the Seine, in the meadows, as far as Roche-Guyon, explorations further afield, real journeys on the other side of the water, in the corn fields of Bonnières and Jeufosse. A man obliged to leave the town sold them an old boat for thirty francs and they also had the river, for which they developed a wild passion, spending whole days there, sailing, discovering new spots, remaining hidden beneath the willows on the banks, in the small inlets dark with shadow."[29]

Sisley also went away from the capital in 1880 and cut himself off from the group by moving upstream from Paris to Veneux-Nadon near Moret-sur-Loing, where he settled in 1882.[30] Though often forced to change address by his always precarious financial position, he remained in the area until his death in 1899. Caillebotte moved in the opposite direction, selling the house at Yerres and buying a property in Petit Gennevilliers opposite Argenteuil in 1881 with his brother Martial. The Seine then became his primary subject and he abandoned the urban views of Haussmann's Paris. He sailed down the river all the way to Le Havre in 1884, stopping on the way to visit Monet.[31] He returned to Vétheuil in the autumn of the same year as well as the next three summers.

Camille Pissarro settled permanently in Éragny-sur-Epte near Gisors, just twenty-five kilometres away from Monet, in 1884. Berthe Morisot also chose the vicinity of Giverny in 1890 when the family went to stay at Blotière near Mézy (cat. 41). Having spent the summer at Roche-Guyon in 1885, Renoir did not settle in the area but visited his friends there regularly. The Manet family bought the property of Mesnil at Juziers near Mantes in 1891 and Berthe withdrew there with her daughter the year after her husband died. She still saw her old friend Monet and the faithful Renoir. Cézanne also visited Giverny but lived in Provence, where he enjoyed his splendid isolation.

Monet attracted many people to the village in Normandy where he had moved to be alone. He received many visits at first from his Impressionist friends, as we have seen, but these soon dwindled as some died and others settled far away. On the other hand, an authentic colony of painters, mainly American, settled in Giverny (cat. 38, 39, 40) and helped to establish the renown of the place and the landscapes of Normandy in the United States.

The Seine was fashionable. Many artists of the post-Impressionist generation continued to live or stay there. The young Signac often went to Asnières, where his mother lived as from 1880. It was also at Les Andelys that he painted his first series of neo-Impressionist landscapes during the spring and summer of 1886.[32] He loved sailing on the Seine with his friends and stayed for several months in Herblay with Luce in 1889 (cat. 42, 45).

Monet's friends also included Pierre Bonnard, who bought his house La Roulotte at Vernonnet in 1912 and lived there until 1938. As still attested by over a hundred works today, he never tired of painting the view of the garden stretching right down to the Seine.

At the dawn of the twentieth century, Maurice Denis had been living in Saint-Germain-en-Laye since 1893 and the Fauves Derain and Vlaminck worked in Chatou and Bougival. The Seine continued to inspire young painters and especially Matisse, whose studio in Paris was on Quai Saint-Michel, very close to Marquet's. Like many others, however, he was soon to move to the South of France. Signac discovered Saint-Tropez in 1892 and Renoir was often resident as from 1903 in Cagnes, not far from Cannet, where Bonnard moved in 1926. The Mediterranean was in turn to become the home of all innovations.

[1] Guy de Maupassant, *Mouche, Souvenirs d'un canotier* (1890), in *Contes et nouvelles 2* (Paris: Éditions Gallimard, bibliothèque de La Pléiade, 1979), 1169.
[2] Claude Monet painted *Impression, Sunrise* (1872, musée Marmottan Monet, Paris), the painting from which Impressionism took its name. He was also the author of a series of canvases entitled *Mornings on the Seine* in 1896–97.
[3] Adolphe Alphant, *Les Promenades de Paris* (Paris: Veuve A. Morel, 1863, 2 Vols.); Robert L. Herbert, *Impressionism: Art, Leisure, and Parisian Society* (New Haven & London: Yale University Press, 1988), 142; Alain Corbin, *L'avènement des loisirs* (Paris: Aubier, 1995, Éditions Flammarion, 2009), 180–83.
[4] Vincent Pomarède, "Quelques fragments pour une histoire du paysage entre 1780 et 1850," in *Reflets de la Seine impressionniste* (Rueil-Malmaison: Atelier Grognard, Éditions du Valhermeil, 2008), 10.
[5] Stendhal published *Mémoires d'un touriste* in 1838.
[6] Françoise Cachin, "Le Paysage du peintre," in Pierre Nora, *Les Lieux de mémoire*, Vol. 11, La Nation (Paris: Éditions Gallimard, 1986), 439.
[7] See also Dominique Lobstein, "Asnières-sur-Seine. Which Subjects for Which Artists?," p. 43.
[8] Edmond and Jules de Goncourt, *Manette Salomon* [1867] (Paris: Éditions Gallimard, Folio classique, 1996), 181–83.
[9] Ibid., 333.
[10] Chantal Georgel, *La Forêt de Fontainebleau : un atelier grandeur nature* (Paris: Musée d'Orsay, 2007), 99–100.
[11] Georges Jean-Aubry, *Eugène Boudin d'après ses lettres et documents inédits* (Neuchâtel: Ides et calendes, 1922, reprinted in 1968), 35.
[12] Charles Baudelaire, *Salon de 1859*, in *Œuvres complètes* (Paris: Éditions Gallimard, collection de La Pléiade, 1985–87, Vol. II), 665–66.
[13] François Thiébault-Sisson, "Claude Monet : les années d'épreuves," *Le Temps*, 26 November 1900, 3.
[14] See Dominique Lobstein, "Les Peintres de Salon à la conquête de la Normandie," in Frances Fowle, *Monet and French Lanscape: Vétheuil and Normandy* (Edinburgh: National Gallery of Scotland, 2006), 81–91.
[15] Walter Pach, "At The Studio of Claude Monet," *Scribner's Magazine*, June 1908, Vol. XLIII, n° 6, reprinted in Charles F. Stuckey, *Monet. A Retrospective* (New York: Hugh Lauter Levin Associates Inc., 1985), 252.
[16] Jules Michelet, *Histoire de France* (Paris, Éditions Flammarion, 1870, Vol. 4), 33.
[17] For Camille Pissarro's work in Rouen, see the exhibition "Une ville pour l'impressionnisme : Monet, Pissarro, Gauguin à Rouen," Rouen, musée des Beaux-Arts, June 2010.
[18] Richard Thomson, *Camille Pissarro. Impressionism, Landscape and Rural Labour*, exh. cat., Birmingham, City Museum and Art Gallery (Glasgow: the Burrell Collection, 1990), 24.
[19] See Paul H. Tucker, *Monet à Argenteuil*, Paris, Éditions du Valhermeil, 1990, 29–30 [*Monet at Argenteuil* (New Haven: Yale University Press, 1982)]
[20] Louis Morin, *Les dimanches parisiens. Notes d'un décadent*, 1898, 213 and 40, quoted in Corbin, op. cit., 219.
[21] Guy de Maupassant, *De Paris à Rouen*, in *Chroniques 2* [1883] (Paris: Union Générale d'Editions, coll. 10-18, 1980), 219–27.
[22] Annick Coulfy and Olivier Millot, "Monet, Sisley, Caillebotte, régates impressionnistes à Argenteuil," in *Reflets de la Seine impressionniste*, op. cit., 54.
[23] Guy de Maupassant, *Yvette*, written in 1884 and included in *Contes et nouvelles 2* (Paris: Éditions Gallimard, bibliothèque de La Pléiade, 1979), 264.
[24] Guy de Maupassant, *La Femme de Paul*, published in *La Maison Tellier* in 1881 and then in *Contes et nouvelles 1* (Paris: Éditions Gallimard, bibliothèque de La Pléiade, 1974), 191–308.
[25] Guy de Maupassant, *Dimanches d'un bourgeois à Paris (Essai d'amour)*, in *Contes et nouvelles 1* (Paris: Éditions Gallimard, bibliothèque de La Pléiade, 1974), 160.
[26] Benoît Noël and Jean Hournon, *La Seine au temps des canotiers* (Garches: AROM, 1997), 106.
[27] Corbin, op. cit., 116.
[28] de Maupassant, *De Paris à Rouen*, op. cit., 222–23.
[29] Émile Zola, *L'Œuvre* [1886] (Paris: Éditions Gallimard, Folio, 1983), 173–74.
[30] See Anne L. Cowe, "Sisley and the Seine: a River of Change," p. 29.
[31] Christopher Loyd, "An Unknown Sketchbook by Gustave Caillebotte," *Master Drawings*, Vol. XXVI, 1988, 107–18.
[32] See Vanessa Lecomte, "Paul Signac and Félix Vallotton in Les Andelys," p. 55.

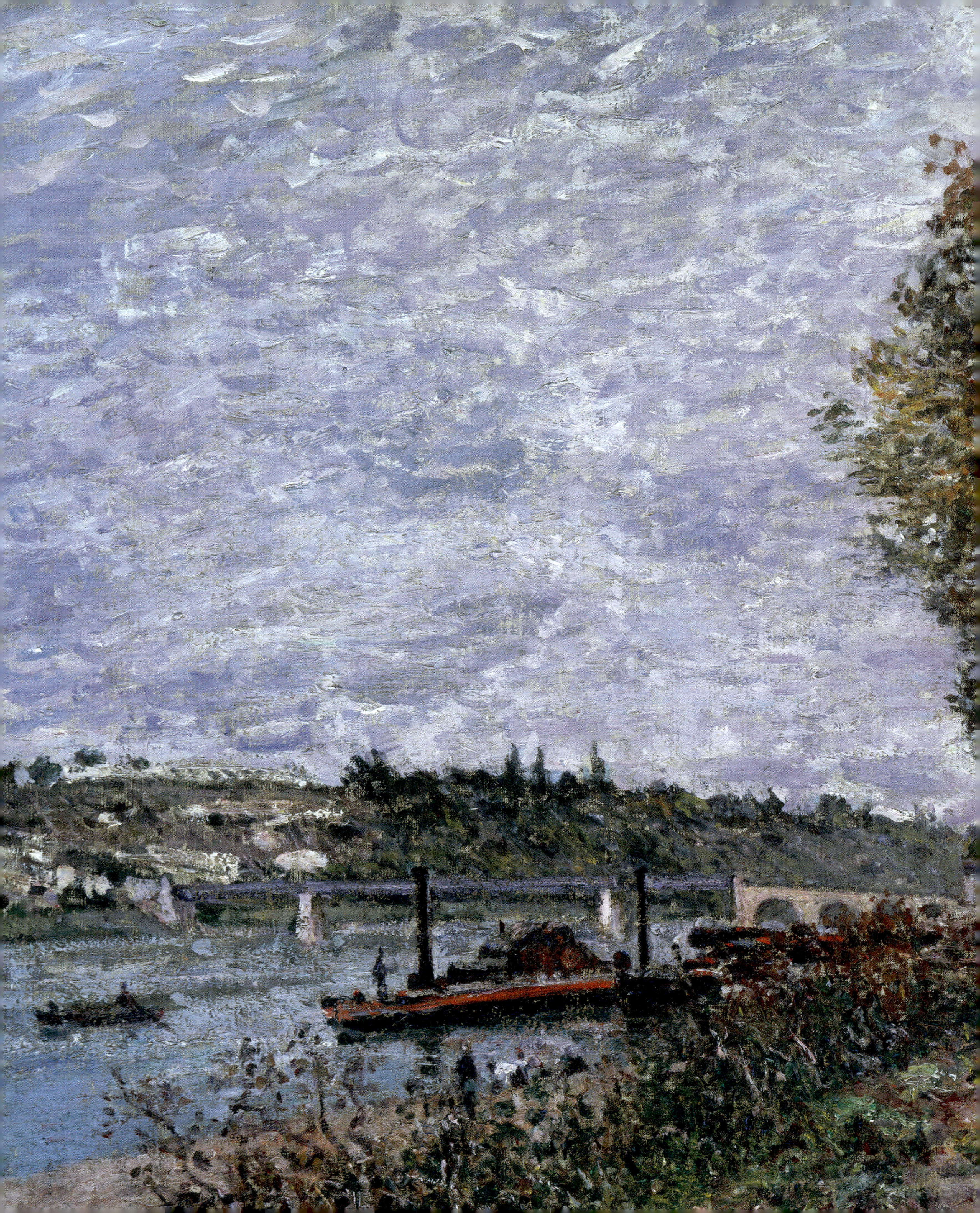

Sisley and the Seine: a River of Change

ANNE L.COWE

The Seine of the Impressionists was both rural and urban, a place of leisure and industry, of tradition and modernity. While the artists painted it in various roles, however, its overriding significance had long been established. The Seine was the artery connecting the regions of France to the heart of the nation—Paris. From its earliest foundations on the Île de la Cité, Paris had functioned as a port, surviving and thriving from the cargos delivered to its quays. The Seine fed, cleaned, watered, built and fuelled the city. By the nineteenth century France had developed the most coherent network of waterways in Europe—through the Seine, its tributaries and canals, boats could reach the Loire, Rhine and Rhone basins, not to mention the sea. The wealth of the nation was transported on the river to sustain the life of the city.[1]

Historically a consumer rather than supplier,[2] Paris's main export was its sphere of influence. The expansion of the nineteenth century, however, saw the city limits spill into residential and industrial suburbs with their own demands on the river. But it was the development of the railways which affected its function most. As well as transporting freight, the trains carried city-dwellers to the countryside and tourism dawned on the banks of the national river.[3] The reflections shifting on the rippling waters, which carried with them a wave of social change, encapsulated the essence of the Impressionist landscape.

The presence of the Seine was a key feature in portraying modern day France, and a constant allusion to the capital through which it flowed. Archetypal images of suburban leisure, Monet and Renoir's paintings of *La Grenouillère* (fig. 6 p. 23) depict some of the thousands of pleasure-seekers who flocked to the suburban stretches of the river by train during the summer months. Bathers bob in the water as if washed there downstream from the city. Likewise, these artists' paintings of pleasure boats at Argenteuil connote quite specifically the recreational culture of the Parisian bourgeoisie, for example in *The Port at Argenteuil* (cat. 25), in this case

Alfred Sisley
Overcast Day
at Saint-Mammès
(detail), see fig. 6 p. 37

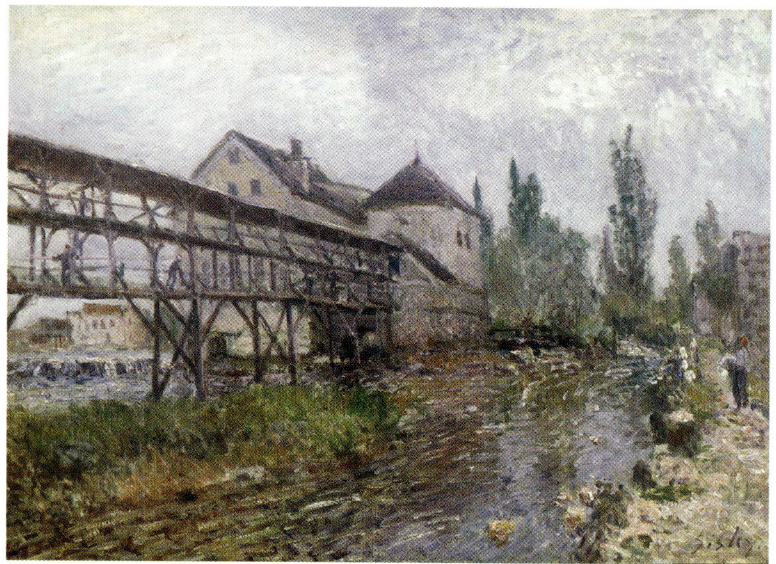

1. Alfred Sisley
Watermill near Moret, 1883
Oil on canvas, 54 x73 cm (21 ¼ x 28 ¾ in.)
Museum Boijmans Van Beuningen, Rotterdam, 3023 (MK)

to the deliberate exclusion of any commercial or industrial river activity, which might have detracted from the hedonistic sense of urban escapism.[4]

The contrasting roles of the "recreational river" and the "working river" are often discussed with regard to Impressionist depictions of the Seine.[5] In most cases it is Pissarro's works which are used to represent the latter. Quite different to those views of La Grenouillère, paintings such as *The Seine at Port-Marly, the Wash House* (cat. 5) and *Barge on the Seine* (cat. 6) consciously focus on the river's functional purpose—the trailing plumes of smoke serving as reminders of modern industry. The Seine in this context connotes not escapism, but acts as an indelible reminder of the capital's influence. Such a comparison between works by Pissarro and Monet may be rather simplistic, however, these were two artists with forthright personalities who showed great confidence in the ideas they expressed. More subtle and diverse, however, are the paintings of the Seine by Alfred Sisley—arguably the most emphatic and certainly the most prolific in developing the role of the river within his paintings.

Sisley's rivers and watercourses are more than a simple vehicle of or allusion to human activity. They assume an active and independent function in the composition. Works from throughout his career reveal a preoccupation with the movement of water. His flood scenes from Port-Marly, for example; the historic pumping house and aqueduct at Marly-le-Roi; the regattas from his sojourn by the Thames; locks, weirs, canals and bridges abound. Sisley's paintings expound a complex and dynamic relationship between the water and those who exploit it; a dialogue between the forces of nature and the ingenuity of man. The focus of this study will be his most extensive analysis of the "working river," at the village Saint-Mammès.

An Artist in the Country

The end of the 1870s and the beginning of the '80s is a period often referred to as the "Crisis of Impressionism," when sales were low and the group seemed to lose coherence in both its artistic vision and social network.[6] As Monet had done already and Pissarro would do in 1883, Sisley decided to move his family to live in the countryside beyond the suburbs, where the cost of living was cheaper. Leaving Sèvres, Sisley rented a house in the village of Veneux-Nadon, situated on the edge of the Forest of Fontainebleau where the river Loing joins the Seine. He continued to live in the area for the rest of his life, finally settling a few kilometres away in the historic town of Moret-sur-Loing in 1889. The water activity which surrounded the rivers and the adjoining Loing Canal were a rich source of inspiration for the artist.

Only two hours from Paris by train, Moret was a popular destination for artists and other visi-

2. *Saint-Mammès. Quai de la Bosse,* postcard, published in Auguste Clément, *The Village and the Ancient Priory in Saint-Mammès,* Dammarie-les-Lys, Éditions Amatteis, 1985 [1900]

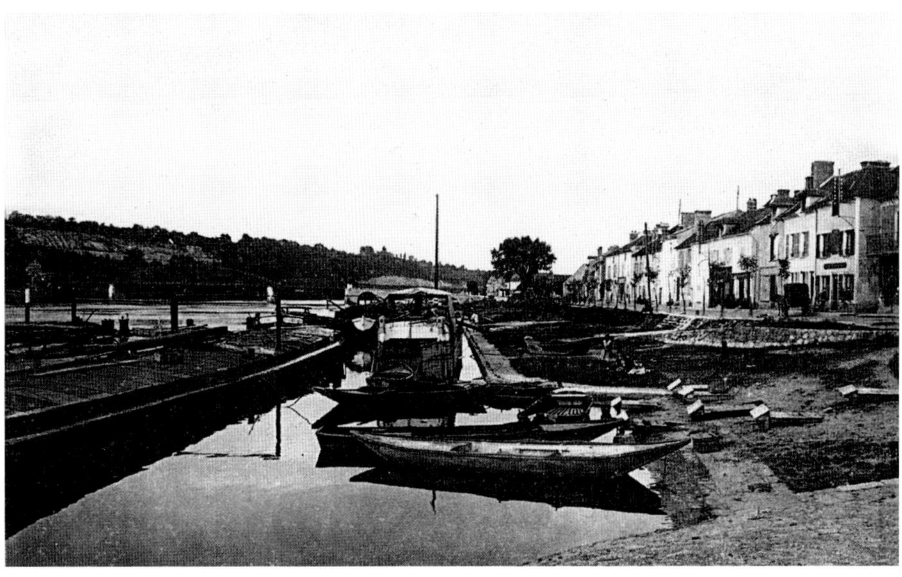

tors. A report by a Moret school mistress, Miss Collin, for the Universal Exposition in 1889, described "High season brings a large number of tourists, attracted not only by the charm of its surroundings, but above all by its historic monuments."[7] Artists such as Théodore Rousseau, Léon Fleury and Edmond Petitjean, for example, all painted the mediaeval gatehouse and bridge, which served as the grand entrance to the town.[8] For artists exhibiting regularly at the Paris Salon exhibitions, such conventionally picturesque details were recognisable as a sample of provincial France—a form of visual escapism for the Parisian viewer.[9]

In 1882, however, Sisley wrote to Monet saying he thought Moret was "rather a chocolate-box landscape."[10] While the historic motifs of Moret did become a more common feature of his paintings in later years, his earlier impressions of the area quite literally turned their back on that popular form of artistic tourism. *Watermill near Moret* (fig. 1), for example, is located directly adjacent to the historic bridge and gatehouse, which are conspicuous by their absence. He depicts a vibrant interaction of man and water. White brushstrokes in the background mimic the water rushing over the weir in the background, harnessing the power of the river to work the mill. In the foreground the rapid movement of the river flowing and the plunging perspective accentuate the to-ing and fro-ing of the workers on the gangway. And, as if no facet of the river is wasted, Sisley also includes some laundrywomen on the bank to the right.

Nonetheless, it was the village of Saint-Mammès which was one of the first themes to dominate his work (fig. 2). Situated on the angle of the confluence of the Seine and the Loing, most of the houses and buildings at Saint-Mammès stretched along the banks of the two rivers. The village served as a river port, not for cargo but a stopping place for barges as they arrived at the end of the Loing Canal. There they would take on a pilot who would guide the barge through the more erratic waters of the Seine, usually to Paris. The Abbé Clément explained in his history of the village in 1900, "The village lives from river haulage. From Saint-Mammès to Paris and beyond, most of the men pilot the boats that arrive via the canal, this 'chemin qui marche,' from Montargis, Orléans and central France."[11]

Saint-Mammès: Morning (fig. 3) depicts a view looking south across the Seine which flows from left to right. On the far side a number of barges are clustered around the mouth of the Loing, poised either to set off downriver to the city, or waiting their turn at the lock which would allow them access to the Loing Canal and further into France. For those who had travelled from elsewhere, Saint-Mammès was a place to take on provisions, the hire of animals for haulage, as well as for boat building and repairs.[12] The life and work of the community revolved around the water. As one might expect the life of a countryside village to live through the fields surround-

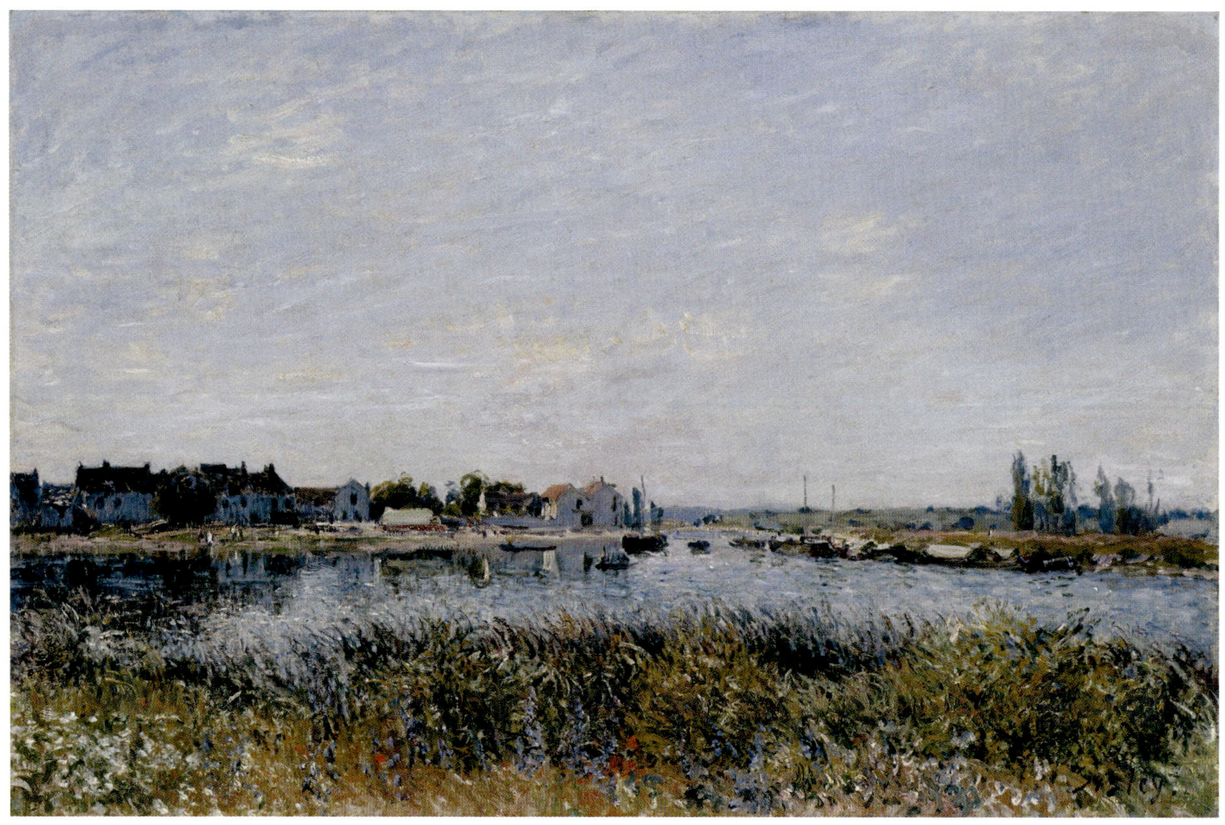

3. Alfred Sisley
Saint-Mammès: Morning, 1881
Oil on canvas, 50.2 × 73.7 cm (19 ¾ × 29 in.)
Museum of Fine Arts, Boston, Bequest of William A. Coolidge, 1993, 1993.45

ing it, so the *Mammèsiens* found a livelihood and identity in the rivers flowing past their doorsteps. When Sisley painted there, however active and industrious Saint-Mammès was, a tourist beauty spot it was not.

Socially and artistically the artist seems to have more or less detached himself from the "recreational."[13] There is a recognisable element of personal distancing in Sisley's works. With the exception of his paintings of the regattas at Hampton Court, from his trip to London in 1874, there is little sense of Sisley's integration into leisurely society. This is in contrast with Monet, Renoir and Manet's paintings of Argenteuil, for example, where their mutual enjoyment in the recreational context is quite apparent. Even where Sisley's works depicted pleasure boats at Argenteuil and Villeneuve-la-Garenne, they were consciously accompanied by images of working folk.[14] He may not have felt at ease among the decadent Parisian bourgeoisie, and the likes of the wealthy Gustave Caillebotte who was an avid yachtsman.[15]

From early on Sisley appears to have been distinguished as an outsider. Despite being born in Paris into a wealthy family, his parents were English (and probably Protestant). The artist therefore had a British passport and was consistently characterized as English.[16] The family business had failed in the Franco-Prussian War of 1870, leaving Sisley without financial support in times of hardship. The critic Arsène Alexandre, who wrote about Sisley in the catalogue for the artist's posthumous studio sale, described the change in his character after 1870: "His work continued fresh and radiant, while his character split; he became gloomy and unsociable: the artist continued to be charming to passers-by while his temperament became increasingly black. His painting was as lacking in suspicions as ever, while his own mind was full of them."[17]

His bleak financial situation when he moved to the Moret area may have been one reason he seems to have identified more with the "working" river than the pursuits of the bourgeois tourist. Neither was he a working class labourer, however; and his paintings of the people in Saint-Mammès never breach the boundary of individuality. Their identity is instead defined by their activity.

The Bargemen of the Seine

Views of barge-workers by other artists cast them in a specific class role—one generally lower than that of the Parisian artist or his bourgeois audience. Stanislas Lépine's *The Seine at Bercy* (cat. 3), for example, depicts men in the process of unloading cargo while the businessman patron looks on. At his side the pilot of the barge answers to him. The hierarchical structure is clearly indicated by their body language and dress, just as the raised perspective elevates the viewer from the industrial dockyard environment. Monet's *The Coal-Dockers* (cat. 13) places the dark faceless workers in a similar rather pejorative role as they move back and forward like part of a machine. Where Monet included scenes of work in his paintings, the effect was often to emphasize the class distinction.[18] His paintings of barges in front of bourgeois villas in Asnières do just that, showing little empathy for the common working man.[19] In complete contrast, however, Pissarro's imagery consistently flaunts his social conscience and ideals. Particularly in his later works, figures are singled out to characterize the virtues of labour.[20] Sisley, however, painted a community, not individuals.

The reputation of those working on the barges in Saint-Mammès may not have been one to aspire to, however. Clément wrote in 1900, "The local people are, in general, better then their reputation… They say of themselves: 'We're *rowdy*' (I soften the expression) 'but we're not wicked!'"[21]

The life of these bargemen, the "*mariniers*," was in some respects gypsy-like. Those who did not have houses on land frequently set up makeshift homes on the riverbanks. Men who were not working on the boats were often at one of Saint-Mammès' many bars, which were notorious for their rowdy behavior. These establishments acted both as business forum and social meeting place. One Mammèsien reminisced, "At six o'clock in the morning the women went to run errands, the men to the café…"[22] A local history written by the former mayor of Veneux-Nadon, described their villagers' bad reputation saying, "The difficulty of their work made them tough."[23]

Barge-life and irregular schooling also led to low levels of literacy, a fact lamented by the school teacher Mr. Rausoir in his 1889 report on the Saint-Mammès commune. Commenting on the low grades in his table of school results, he noted the indifference of many toward schooling, with "education completely lacking in the family."[24] For those *mariniers* whose skills had been handed down through the generations, it may have been difficult to see the merits of any other form of learning.

From the Parisian outsider's viewpoint, it was a profession which defined a lifestyle, forming a proud but rough-hewn character, with an intuitive knowledge of the river. Like the peasant farming the French soil, the *marinier* working the French waterways evoked a sense of tradition and closeness to nature which inspired both artist and writer. The critic Arthur Baignères was especially struck by the new "type" discovered by Roger Jourdain in his painting *The Barge* at the Paris Salon of 1879.

"M. Jourdain has certainly shown his best painting; to the rear of a boat, which is cut by the frame, a family is gathered… This barge is inspired; and in these days, when everything has been seen and interpreted. M. Jourdain is an innovator: he has discovered the art of river haulage."[25]

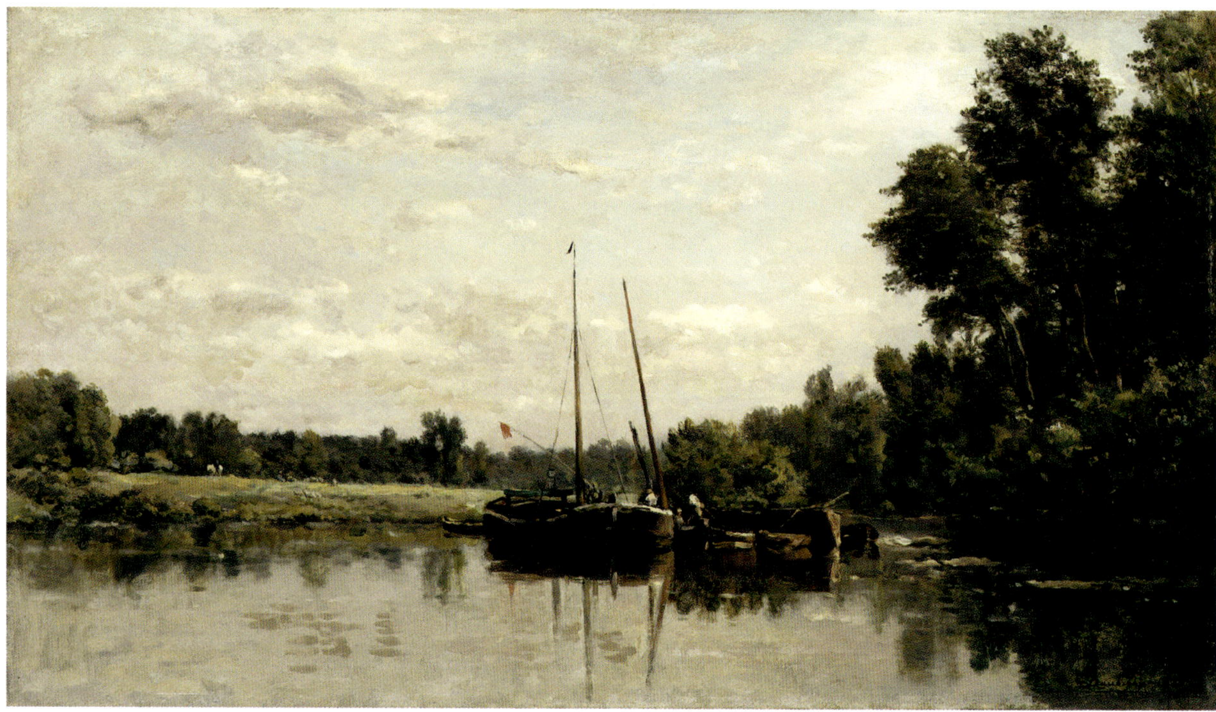

4. Charles-François Daubigny
The Barges, 1865
Oil on panel,
38 × 67 cm
(15 × 26 ½ in.)
Musée du Louvre, Paris,
RF 1362

A character in Jules de Glouvet's novel titled *Le Marinier : Au bord de la Loire* from 1881 is bargeman of the Seine, who states:

"– I'm a man of the water, like my father and my ancestors long ago. I must have boards below me and a gaff in my hands, otherwise I get bored."[26]

Inhabitants of Saint-Mammès were not considered Mammèsiens unless they were a *marinier*; and you were not a *marinier* unless your family had been *mariniers* before you.[27] The history of the Loing Canal went back generations to the 1720s and the Seine had been used to transport cargo for centuries before. This sense of engrained skill and tradition, combined with the slow heavy movement of the barges, could evoke a living sense of reassuring constancy—the ever-flowing river personified.

Charles-François Daubigny's paintings of barges from the 1860s (fig. 4), themselves painted from a boat, rely on their implied timelessness in creating an escapist rural calm. Whereas the stretches of river he painted would often have been busy with noisy tugs and other river traffic.[28] Daubigny's depictions of barges could almost appear contemporaneous with those in John Constable's paintings of the river Stour in England from fifty years before. Similar works by Pissarro, for example *Barge on the Seine* (cat. 6), do not shun modern subject matter in the same manner but display an equivalent steadfastness—described by Scott Schaefer as "slow and torpid."[29] Pissarro's iconography alludes to an old and traditional way of living. Indeed, we can start to question the status of the barges within the modern context. The Seine's symbolic relationship to life and death has a rich foundation in art and literature, a tradition explored in depth by Richard Brettell.[30] If the notion is applied to the paintings of barges, however, perhaps we can consider their slow movement as the passing of life—with an inevitable end.

A Vision of Modernity

Timing was a crucial element in capturing the impression of an ephemeral moment. It implicitly referred to the contemporary and modern, but also indicated that further change was inescapable. Sisley himself wrote to his friend the journalist, Adolphe Tavernier, saying, "… the water of the Loing here, so beautiful, so tranluscent, so changeable…"[31] The brief and cursory brushstrokes with which Sisley depicts the transient waters are exemplary of the Impressionist effect. And in his paintings of Saint-Mammès he uses the same technique to convey the itinerant lifestyle of the *mariniers* and the constant activity of the barges, at one with the shifting waters. The critic Gustave Geffroy described Sisley's paintings as, "the painter's response to the life of people along the riverside, the boatmen, and all who passed in their heavy vessels pursuing a nomadic and Bohemian existence on the water."[32]

In paintings such as *Saint-Mammès: Morning*, the emphasis is very much on the single instant. The early sunlight connotes a very specific time of day as it glistens on the water, casting long shadows through the flickering reeds. The scattered reflections of the houses appear almost to emerge from the water and the boats break free from the bank as if propelled by the artist's brushwork. For Sisley movement was a fundamental and emotional element of his art. Tavernier quoted him saying, "After the subject itself, one of the most interesting aspects of the landscape is movement, life... It is the painter's emotion which brings it to life and it is that same feeling which awakens the emotion of the spectator."[33]

In this respect, the overall effect appears one of optimism. Alexandre wrote, "He watched each pleasure leave him in turn, except for the joy of painting, which never departed."[34] In comparison to Pissarro's barges, it is hard to consider any of Sisley's boats as "slow and torpid." Instead, the allusions are to beginnings and departures. His detailed fascination in the community activity denotes productivity and prosperity and, while recognizing the engrained tradition of these *mariniers*, his outlook appears forward-thinking and progressive.

Although France was at that time in the grips of economic recession, and the vineyards were being ravaged by phylloxera and mildew, for Saint-Mammès the early 1880s would have been a time of optimism. After the election of Jules Grévy's "Opportunist" Republic in 1879, a grand plan of investment in the national communications network was implemented, headed by Charles de Freycinet. Focussing on roads, rail and waterways, the purpose of the plan was both economic and strategic.[35] Internationally, the plan was an expression of renewed logistical strength and advanced economic prowess. Speaking in 1880, the American civil engineer Moncure Robinson, was particularly impressed, "There is no country in the world where so small a proportion of the capital invested within the last forty years in canals and railroads has been wasted or where travelling is safer, or in which travel and trade are accommodated at more reasonable rates than in France."[36] Nationally, the scheme was intended to create employment and stave off recession.

The effects of the Freycinet plan would have made a significant impact on the village. In addition to removing tolls from public waterways,[37] a key feature of the Freycinet plan had been to standardize the width of 4,000 km of canals (costing two billion francs).[38] Sisley mentioned some of the works on the canal to Monet in 1881, albeit disapprovingly, "On my side, when I arrived there were plenty of nice things to do, but they've been working on the canal, they've cut down trees, built quays, straightened the banks."[39] Yet despite these earthworks, he was apparently entranced by the effect of the Freycinet plan on the village's productivity. It may even be said that Sisley's attention and enthusiasm in depicting the active barge community was indicative of political sympathies toward the policies of the new Republic.[40]

With the standardization of canals came the standardization of barges, creating work for the boatyards. Vanessa Manceron's study of the barge industry at Saint-Mammès explains that the traditional *Berrichon* barge (27.5 × 2.62 m; 55-60 tonnes) could now be replaced by the new *Freycinet* (32.5 × 5.10 m) with the much larger capacity of 350 tonnes.[41] Sisley's *Boatyard at Saint-Mammès* (fig. 5), for example, shows one of the new *Freycinets* in construction. The small figures, rallying around the hull, accentuate its impressive size as the Seine flows past behind, ready to carry its bountiful loads. It is just one of many paintings of the Leveau boatyard, situated in front of the buildings on the spur of the confluence. This particular boatyard opened in 1880, when Sisley had just arrived in the area.[42] His paintings view the site from many different angles, depicting different stages of the boats' construction and the activity of the villagers around it.

The artist wrote to Tavernier in 1892, "The subject, or theme, should always be represented in a simple and comprehensible form, which grips the spectator. The latter should be drawn [...] along the road the painter shows him and should see first whatever caught the artist's eye."[43] The viewer is not only led through a spatial progression but also a temporal one. *Overcast Day at Saint-Mammès* (fig. 6) takes the process another step further. The steam tug—*toueur* or *remorqueur*—shows another form of modernisation, this time on the river. Whereas the meandering Seine was more erratic than the canal, requiring careful navigation around the invisible undulations below its surface, modern engineering had found a solution. As well as extensive dredging on many sections, large chains had also been laid along the navigable course of the riverbed. The *toueur* would mechanically pull itself and a convoy of barges. Obviously struck by the spectacle, Monet and Renoir painted such a convoy together in 1869[44] (fig. 7).

Significantly, it was at Saint-Mammès that the style of transport changed from canal to river. As explained by Jules-Michel Regnault, former mayor of Veneux-Nadon: "This modernism brought a new sort of life to Saint-Mammès among the *mariniers*. It is in Saint-Mammès, in fact, that the traction changed, animal on the canal, steam on the Seine."[45] From Sisley's perspective Saint-Mammès was not only a place of aquatic movement and a fusion of man and water, it signified a juncture between old and new. In comparison to Renoir's distanced painting of the convoy, the implications of modernity in Sisley's works appear far more profound. *Overcast Day at Saint-Mammès* appears to express an emotional involvement in the scene. Although the light and atmosphere may pertain to a specific moment, the subject suggests the progression of time. As the rowing boat, barge and steam tug show stages in a technological evolution, the juxtaposition of the green poplars on the bank and the dead ones being felled suggests a natural cycle of renewal.

But the ephemeral light in which Sisley bathes his Saint-Mammès subjects is not without its fragility. His modern-day barges were not as steadfast as Pissarro's. With steam tugs there was less need for the skilled Mammèsien *pilote*, and public investment did not make lasting success a certainty. Perhaps for these reasons, the initial sense of community cohesion displayed in Sisley's early works from Saint-Mammès wavers in later paintings.

The Freycinet plan had been a controversial issue when it was first instigated and its critics were not without reason. Freycinet had taken a considerable risk in investing so heavily in the waterways and the railways at the same time. Countries like Britain had decided to develop the railways only, being faster, more reliable and more versatile than water transport could ever be.

5. Alfred Sisley
Boatyard at Saint-Mammès, 1885
Oil on canvas,
55 × 73 cm
(21 ½ × 28 ¾ in.)
Columbus Museum of Art, Ohio, gift of Howard D. and Babette L. Sirak, the Donors to the Campaign for Enduring Excellence, and the Derby Fund, 1991.001.068 8

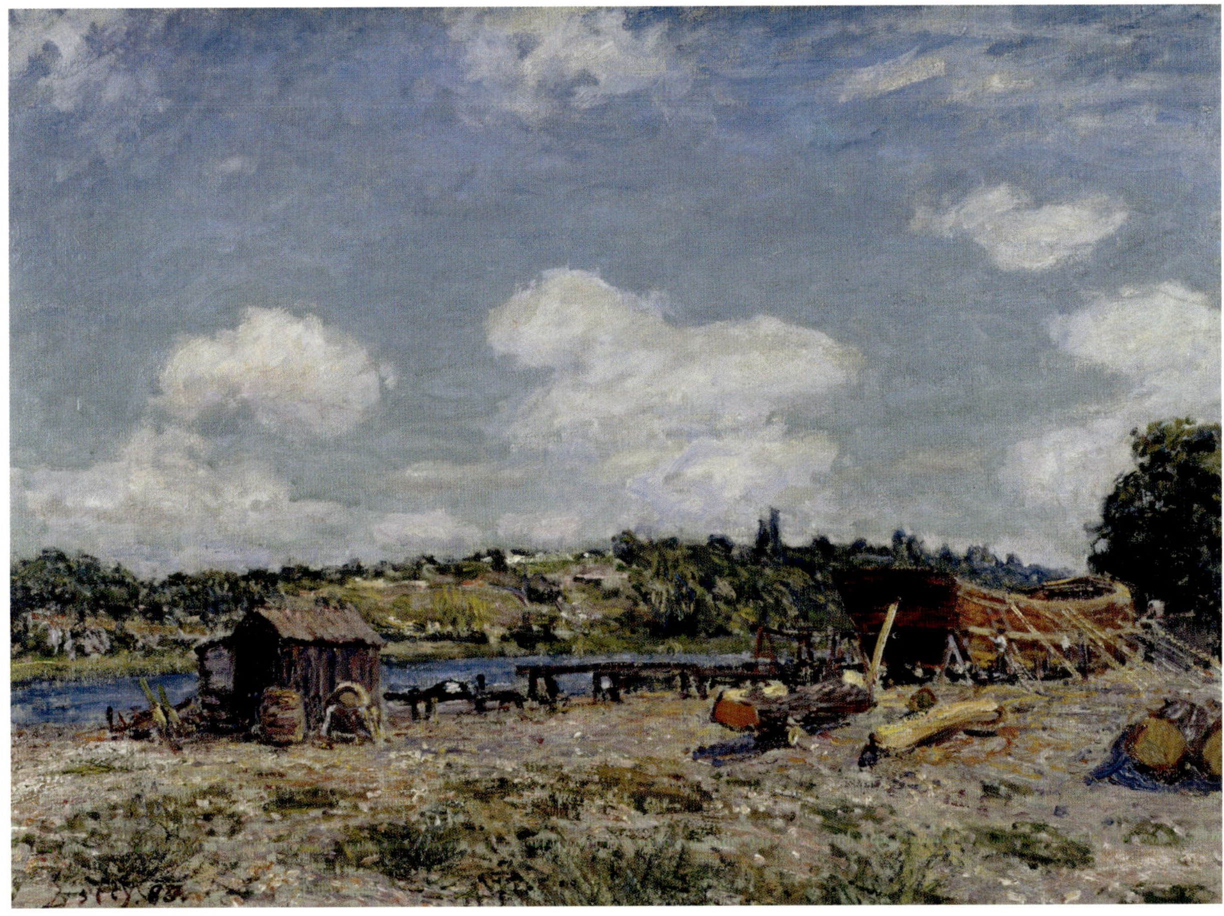

6. Alfred Sisley
Overcast Day at Saint-Mammès, 1880
Oil on canvas,
54.9 × 74 cm
(21 ¾ × 29 ¼ in.)
Museum of Fine Arts, Boston, Juliana Cheney Edwards Collection, 1939, 39.679

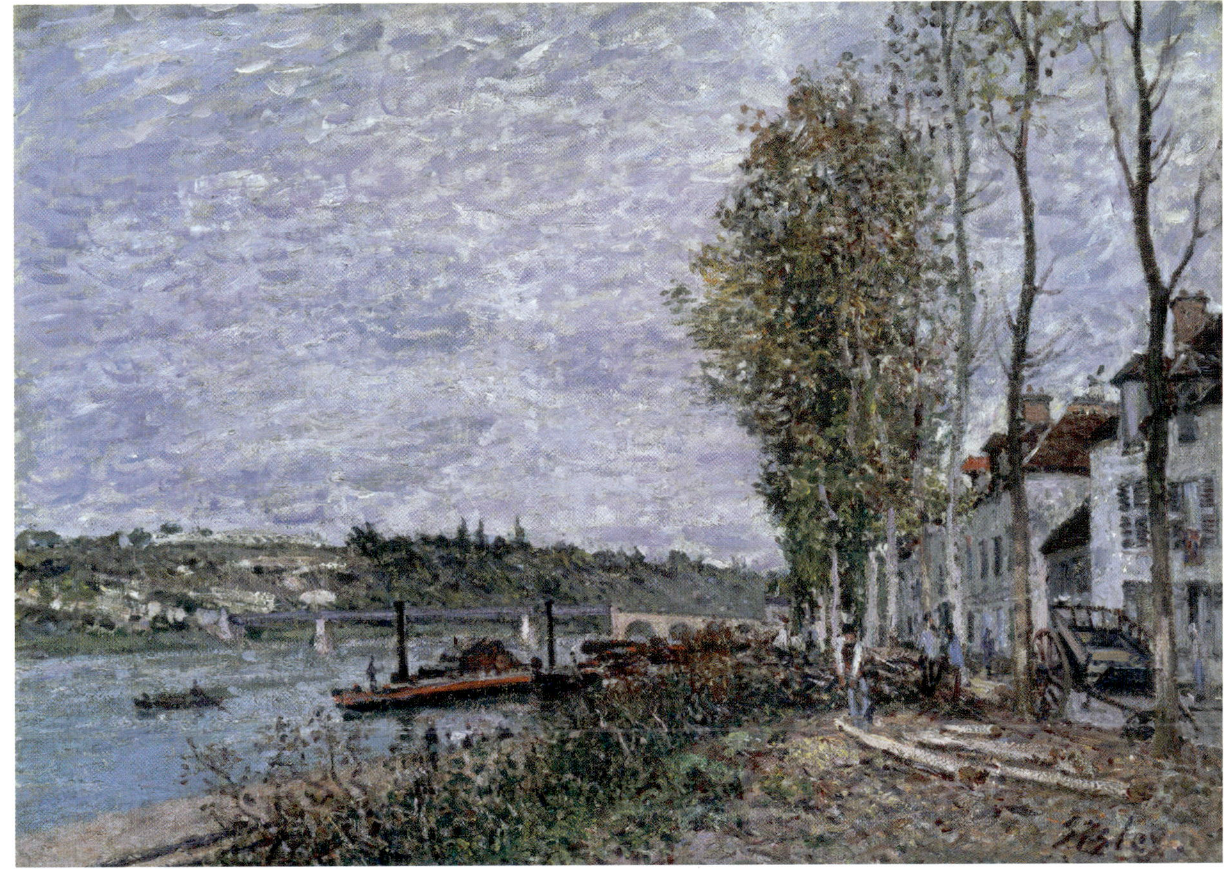

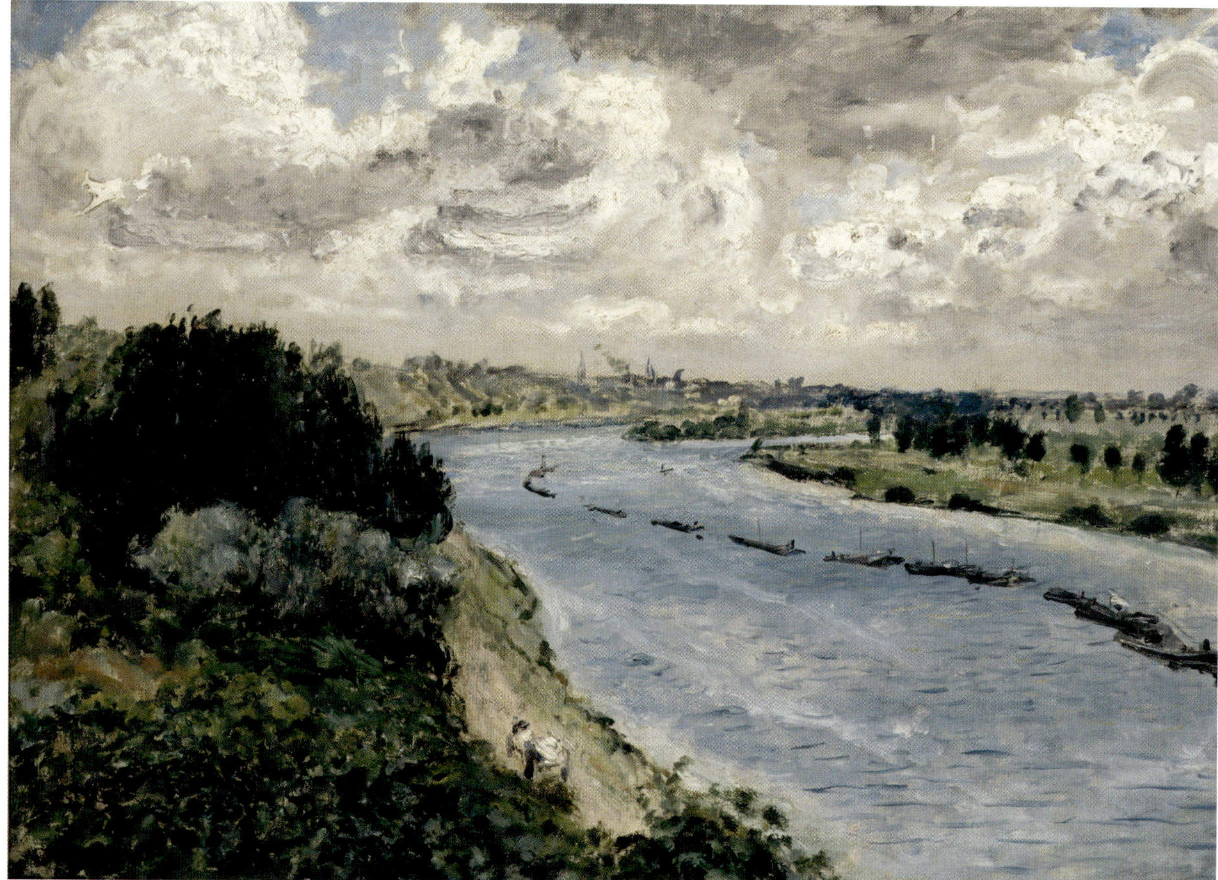

7. Auguste Renoir
Barges on the Seine, 1869
Oil on canvas, 47 × 64 cm (18 ½ × 25 ¼ in.)
Musée d'Orsay, Paris, RF 3667

The gamble Freycinet had taken with his extravagant public spending was a failure, leading the nation further into debt and recession. As one nineteenth-century commentator simply stated, "he made the country poorer while trying to make it richer."[46] The French economist Paul Leroy-Beaulieu later put his opinion more passionately, saying the plan was, "conceived in a moment of hallucination."[47] Freycinet had seen railways and waterways as complementary services when in reality they were competing against each other in a market where the railway would inevitably win.

For centuries the river had been the lifeblood of the city of Paris and the key to the French nation, uniting the wealth of the regions in their capital. As the essential envoys, the barges were to the Seine what the Seine was to Paris, and visually they did not lose that affinity. In Armand Guillaumin's *Quai de Bercy* (cat. 17), for example, the masts of the barges stand tall above the horizon, echoed in the background by the spire of Notre Dame de Paris, each as monumental as the other. The role of the Seine and its waterways as a national and historic symbol was such that it was hard for many, including Freycinet, to conceive of a France in which they played no functional role.[48] While the riverbanks around the city teemed with city dwellers seeking recreation, the economic power of the river paled in significance. Like Joséphine set aside by Napoleon for Marie-Louise of Austria, it became obvious that the railway had taken over the Seine's vital role; although it maintained its place in the nation's heart. After the stock market crash of 1882, Freycinet's opponents took control, bringing work on

8. Alfred Sisley
The Loing at Saint-Mammès, 1882
Oil on canvas,
49.8 × 64.9 cm
(19 ½ × 25 ½ in.)
Museum of Fine Arts, Boston, Bequest of William A. Coolidge, 1993, 1993.44

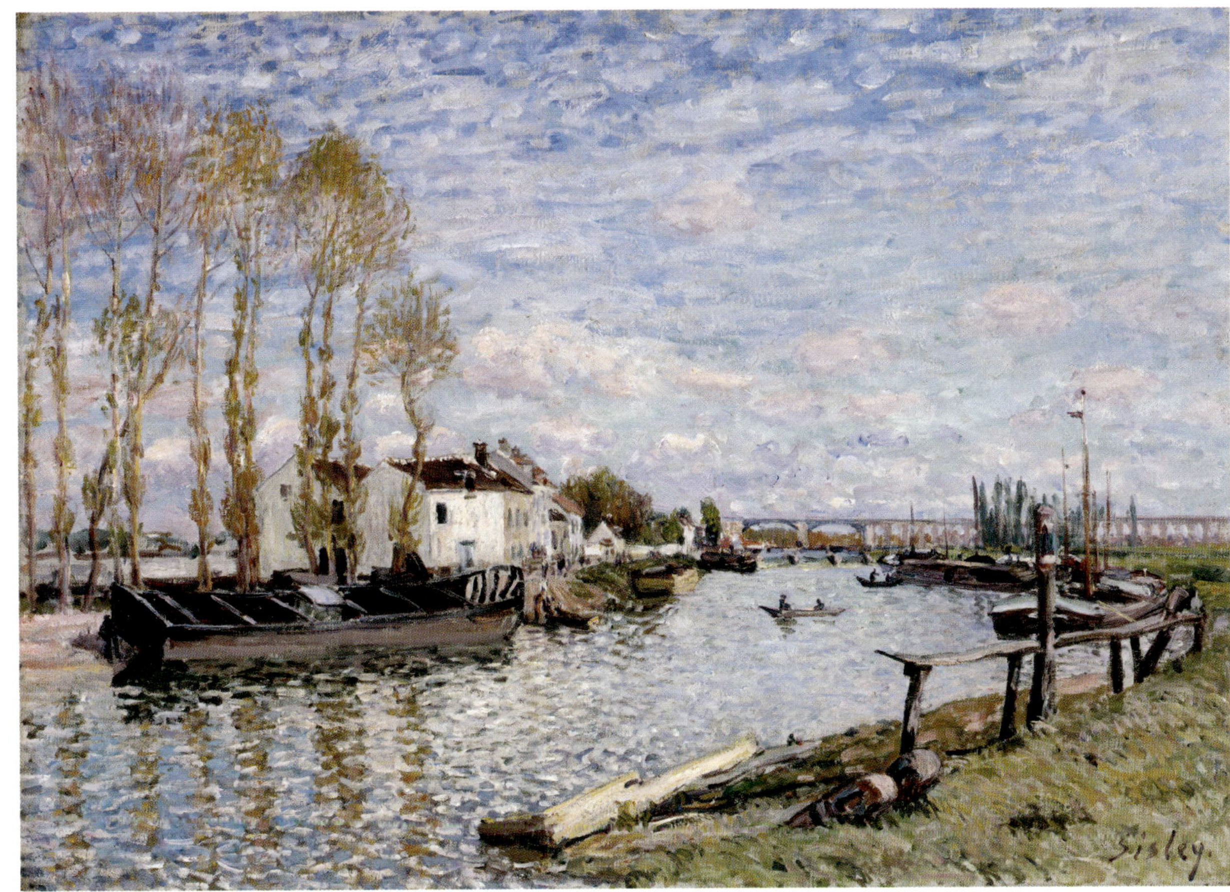

the waterways to a halt.[49] In this context Sisley's *The Loing at Saint-Mammès* (fig. 8), which was painted that same year, makes a pointed comparison. In the foreground the large hulk of a redundant barge is in the process of being stripped, the open beams of its bow corresponding to the thirty-three magnificent arches of the railway viaduct which runs across the background. It represents not just the painting of a moment but the passing of an era.

The lively confrontation of technological man and the natural river, which Sisley had previously revelled in, gave way to a more peaceful form of co-existence. His initial eagerness to depict the active riverside community in the context of the modern industrious nation subsided in favor of the natural and historic beauty of his rural location. He must have perceived that the barges, which had been a potent indicator of the nation's economic strength and Republican centralist policy, were becoming an anachronism to the modern landscape. Sisley no longer painted the steam tugs on the Seine or the convoys going downriver, but focused on the banks of the Loing and the slow waters of the canal. If the river was an analogy for life and death, then Sisley was entering his maturity. He, like the subjects in his paintings, was becoming more disconnected from the capital and settling into the character of Moret and its surroundings. The river, while having lost much of its economic significance, remained a dynamic force in Sisley's art. Ernest Chesneau wrote in a review of the Seventh Impressionist Exhibition in 1882, "he has become the master of the banks of the Seine and its waters..."[50]

[1] Albert Demangeon, "The Port of Paris," in *The Geographical Review*, X : 5 (November 1920), 277–96 at 277.
[2] Ibid., 288.
[3] François Beaudouin et al., *Seine et Marne* (Paris: Christine Bonneton, 1989), 193–94.
[4] Scott Schaefer, "Rivers, Roads, and Trains," in *A Day in the Country: Impressionism and the French Landscape*, exh. cat., Los Angeles County Museum of Art / The Art Institute of Chicago (New York: Harry N. Abrams, 1984–85), 137–73 at 146.
[5] Ibid., 139.
[6] See Philip Nord, *Impressionists and Politics: art and democracy in the nineteenth century* (London & New York: Routledge, 2000), 69ff.
[7] Miss Collin, Governess, *Département de Seine-et-Marne, Arrondissement de Fontainebleau, Canton et Commune de Moret-sur-Loing* (unpublished 1889), 3.
[8] Léon Lhermitte, Edmond Yon and Eugène Lavieille were among the many others.
[9] See Anne L. Cowe, *Community and Nation: The Representation of the Village in French Landscape Painting 1870-1890*, PhD Thesis (Edinburgh 2005), 120ff.
[10] Letter from Sisley to Monet, 21 August 1881, published in "Sisley," *Bulletin des expositions* (Paris: Galerie d'Art Braun, 30 January–18 February 1933), 7.
[11] Abbé Clément, *Saint-Mammès : le village et l'ancien prieuré*, 1900 (Dammarie-les-Lys: Éditions Amatteis, 1985), 171.
[12] Vanessa Manceron, *Saint-Mammès, terre de mariniers, approche ethnologique d'une population et d'une territoire* (Dammarie-les-Lys: musée départemental des Pays de Seine et Marne, 1994), 29.
[13] Although paintings such as *The Small Meadows in Spring: By*, Tate Gallery, London (D391) [*Les Petits prés au printemps–By*] show a figure strolling by the river, it is thought to be Sisley's daughter. And paintings such as *The Seine from the Hills of By* (cat. 34) suggest a quest for isolation and not a sociable excursion.
[14] See Mary Anne Stevens, *Alfred Sisley*, exh. cat. London, Royal Academy / Paris, musée d'Orsay / Baltimore, The Walters Art Gallery (London / New Haven: Yale University Press: 1992), *Fishermen Spreading out their Nets*, 108, cat. 13.
[15] See cat. 26; see also Schaefer, op. cit., 154.
[16] Later attempts to become a French national failed.
[17] Arsène Alexandre, "Days when the struggle is past [Lendemains de Luttes]" in Gustave Geffroy & Arsène Alexandre, *Tableaux... par Alfred Sisley*, studio sale catalogue, Galerie George Petit, 1 May 1899, preface. [Transcribed and translated in Richard Shone, *Sisley* (London: Phaidon Press Ltd. 1992), 220–23, at 222.]
[18] See Virginia Spate, *The Colour of Time* (London: Thames & Hudson, (1992) 2001), 106.
[19] *The Seine at Asnières*, 1873, private collection, France (W. 269); *Barges at Asnières*, 1873, private collection, USA (W. 270); see also Robert Herbert, *Impressionism: Art, Leisure and Parisian Society* (New Haven & London: Yale University Press 1988), 200–01.
[20] Nord, op. cit., 84; and Richard Thomson, *Camille Pissarro: Impressionism, Landscape and Rural Labour* (London: Herbert press, 1990), 56ff.
[21] Clément, op. cit., 172.
[22] Manceron, op. cit., 33.
[23] Jules-Michel Regnault, *Veneux-les-Sablons : Histoire de mon village* (Le Mée-sur-Seine: Lys Éditions Presse 1991), 95.
[24] Rausoir, Tutor, *Commune de Saint-Mammès* (unpublished 1889), 12.
[25]Arthur Baignères, "Le Salon de 1879", *Gazette des Beaux-Arts*, pér. 2 : XX (1879), 35–57 at 44–46.
[26] Jules de Glouvet, *Le Marinier : Au Bord de la Loire* (Turquant: Éditions Cheminements, (1881) 2002), 87.
[27] Manceron, op. cit., 39.
[28] Richard Brettell, "The River Seine: Subject and Symbol in Nineteenth-Century French Art and Literature," in Eliza Rathbone et al., *Impressionists on the Seine: A celebration of Renoir's 'Luncheon of the Boating Party'* (Washington D.C.: Counterpoint in association with the Phillips Collection, 1996), 87–129 at 101.
[29] Schaefer, op. cit., 137–45.
[30] Brettell, op. cit., 113
[31] Letter to Tavernier, 19 January 1892, transcribed in Shone, op. cit., 216.
[32] Geffroy in Geffroy & Alexandre, op. cit., 11, quoted in Shone, op. cit., 80.
[33] Adolphe Tavernier, *L'Atelier de Sisley* (Paris: Bernheim Jeune, 14 December 1907) transcribed in Shone, op. cit., 219.
[34] Alexandre in Shone, op. cit., 222.
[35] One of the main causes of the French defeat in the Franco-Prussian War in 1870 had been the slow mobilization of troops to the border.
[36] Moncure Robinson, *Obituary Notice of M. Chevalier, Read before the American Philosophical Society, May 7, 1880* (Philadelphia, 1880), 6–7, quoted in Cecil O. Smith, Jr. "The Longest Run: Public Engineers and Planning in France," *American Historical Review*, 95:3 (June 1990), 657–92 at 657.
[37] Smith, Jr., op. cit., 682.
[38] Demangeon, op. cit., 284.
[39] Sisley, letter to Monet, 21 August 1881, op. cit., note 10.
[40] See Anne L. Cowe, "Impressions of the Riverside Village: Monet and Sisley at Vétheuil and Saint-

Mammès," in Frances Fowle (ed.), *Monet and French Landscape: Vétheuil and Normandy* (Edinburgh: National Galleries of Scotland, 2006), 16–29 at 21.
[41] Manceron, op. cit., 47–8 and 75–6.
[42] Ibid., 23.
[43] Sisley, letter to Tavernier, January 1892, transcribed in Shone, op. cit., 217–18.
[44] See also Claude Monet, *Chiatte sulla Senna*, private collection, featured in *Monet: i luoghi della pittura* (Treviso: Casa dei Carraresi, 29 September 2001–10 February 2002), cat. 4.
[45] Regnault, op. cit., 91.
[46] Émile Marché, *SICMD* (1883), 28, quoted in Smith, op. cit., 683.
[47] Paul Leroy-Beaulieu, quoted in Smith, op. cit., 684.
[48] Brettell, op. cit., 92–3.
[49] Smith, op. cit., 684.
[50] Ernest Chesneau, "groupes sympathiques, les impressionnistes," *Paris-Journal*, 7 March 1882, quoted in Stevens, op. cit., 283.

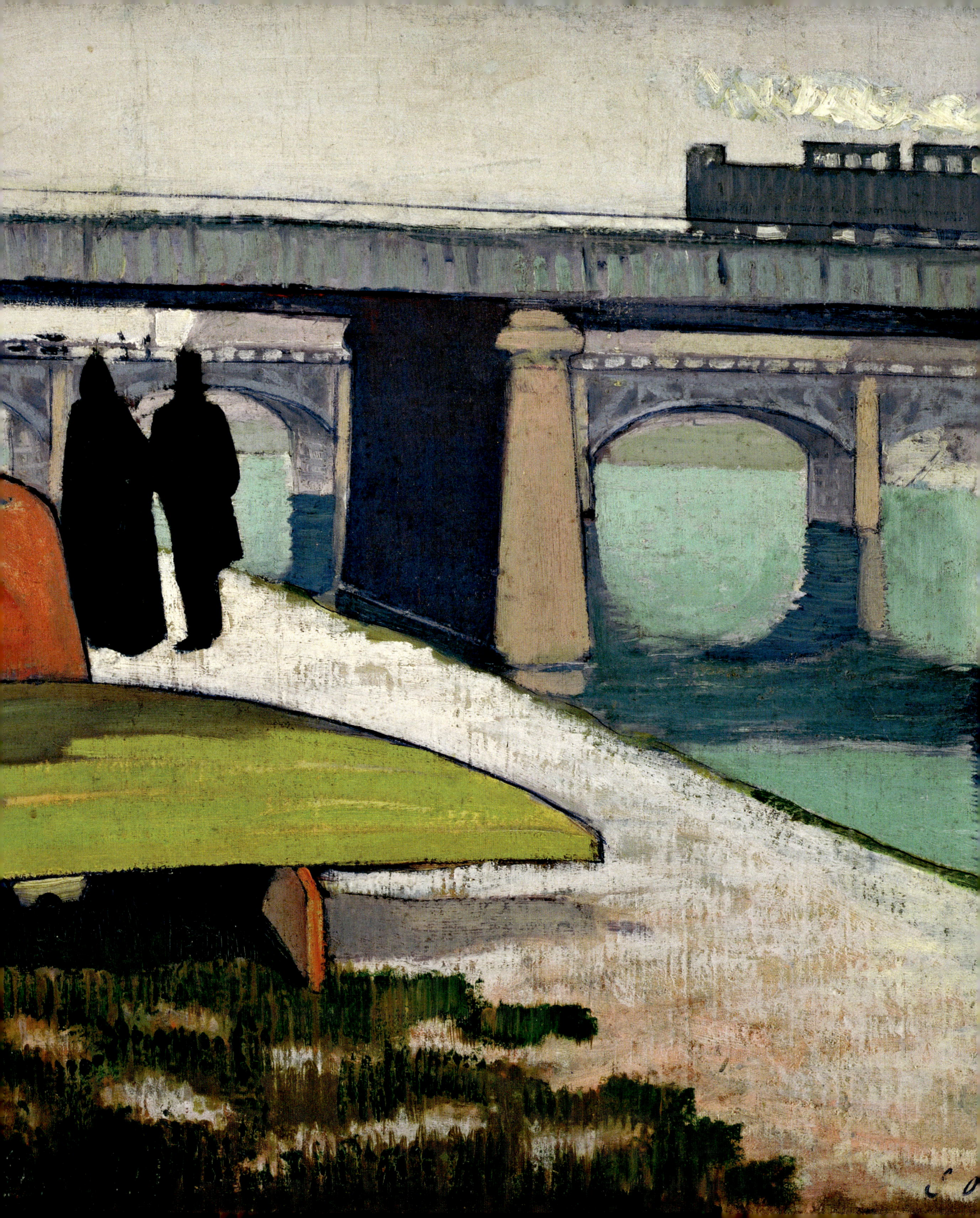

Asnières-sur-Seine. Which Subjects for Which Artists?

DOMINIQUE LOBSTEIN*

"The earliest known document to mention the village [Asnières] is a bull from the year 1158; Anières [*sic*] is mentioned in it with the title of *cure*, which points necessarily to its much more elevated origins." What Jacques-Antoine Dulaure described in these words[1] was an area that no longer exists; on the first territory dependent upon the abbots of Saint-Denis, several localities had over the years become full-fledged communes, such as Gennevilliers, while most of the land had passed from the hands of the Church to those of the aristocracy. The seventeenth century was a flourishing period in which fine residences sprung up, built by the duchess of Brunswick, the prince palatine of Bavaria and his wife Anne Gonzague of Clèves, or later by the marquis Voyer d'Argenson, before the Revolution put an end to the expansion and the village lost part of its splendour. This downturn did not last long, however, and the construction of several bridges restored some lustre to the place, which in 1838 was described as follows: "Asnières-sur-Seine. Village situated 2 leagues from Saint-Denis and 2 leagues from Paris. Pop. 519 inhabitants. It is well built, in a pleasant position, on the left bank of the Seine, which is crossed by a newly constructed bridge. One can admire the public square planted with trees in staggered rows, as well as a beautiful castle and several pretty country houses."[2] The author of these lines, Pierre Girault de Saint-Fargeau, could have completed his description by mentioning not one, but the several bridges serving the village. The first, in fact, was built in 1826, a toll bridge for road and foot traffic, which was joined by a railway bridge in 1836–37. Asnières was the first stop after Paris in the direction of Saint-Germain-en-Laye from 26 August 1837, and of Versailles Rive droite from 2 August 1839. Damaged in 1848, the wooden railway bridge was rebuilt in 1852 by the engineer Eugène Flachat, who designed a 165-metre-long[3] metal structure that was also used for the line between Asnières and Argenteuil, inaugurated in 1851.

The charming village—despite what Eugène Sue may have said about it in the *Mystères de Paris*, published in 1843,[4] which made part of the city a frightening den of thieves—soon

Émile Bernard
Iron Bridges at Asnières
(detail), see fig. 6 p. 48

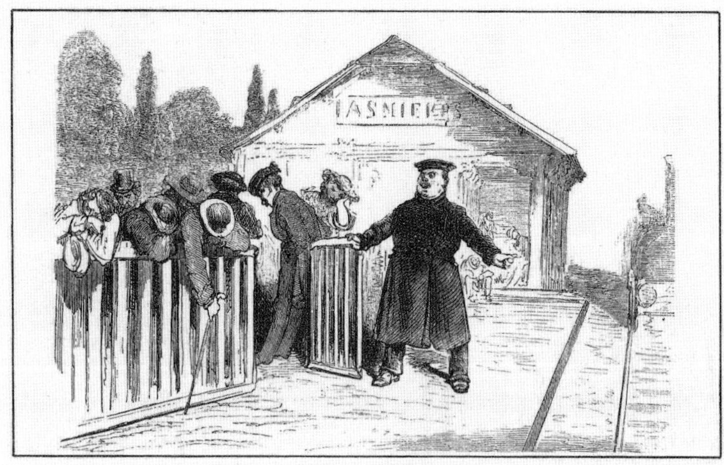

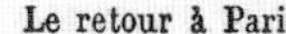
Le retour à Paris

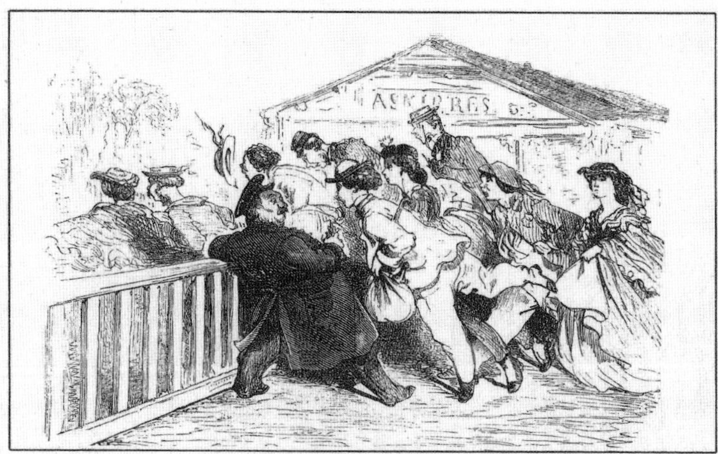
L'arrivée à Asnières

1. Gustave Doré, *The Return to Paris*, in Émile de la Bédollière, *Histoire des environs du Nouveau Paris*, Paris, Barba, 1861

2. Gustave Doré, *Arriving at Asnières*, in Émile de la Bédollière, *Histoire des environs du Nouveau Paris*, Paris, Barba, 1861

began, benefitting from the presence of the railway, to develop in various ways, suddenly attracting factories (generally, thanks to the desire for the conservation of the place, small transformation or luxury industries, such as the factories that Louis Vuitton built here in 1859, rather than the heavy industries such as those that would develop in the communes situated on the other side of the Seine, like the gas plant which opened in Clichy in 1875[5]), but also vacationers, for whom various sources of entertainment were created.[6] The 1850s saw the foundation of a rowing club,[7] which went on to establish water festivals and a swimming school, while the castle grounds hosted public balls that were called "Folies-Asnières," depicted in a lithograph by A. Provost.[8] Attractions which did not seduce everyone if we are to believe Jules Claretie, comparing the town to Richmond: "There is Asnières, a richer and larger Asnières, but Asnières without the *je ne sais quoi* of stylishly Parisian that makes it charming, when it is not invaded, everyone says, by its ghastly Sunday population."[9]
Thirty years after the brief description by Girault de Saint-Fargeau, one of the first authors of popular tourist guides, Adolphe Laurent Joanne, was more loquacious, though he, too, began with a figure (the population had now reached 5,455 inhabitants) and concluded as follows: "In the past few years in Asnières and on the nearby hills a large number of houses labelled as villas have been built, affecting all the forms of architecture."[10] Various establishments to welcome visitors had sprung up: the Hôtel Cassegrain or de la Marine "near the bridge," and the Café de la Terrasse. Closer to nature than Paris, without being too far from the city, and less expensive, the town had managed to attract all sorts of people: factory-workers who found employment there, tradesmen, the bourgeoisie from Paris who could build convenient holiday homes, but also, in the guise of tourists, "passers-by, groups of male and female friends, painters and artists of sorts, mysterious women known only by their first names, teenagers from Grenelle, unemployed *lorettes*."[11] Some of the artists who frequented these festivities had taken up residence locally. A few of them were so easy to spot that they were given pride of place at the Salon (see Appendix). While these men exerted a pull on other artists, it is evident that Asnières was never as attractive as other towns on the outskirts of Paris recently served by the railway, especially Sèvres, which suddenly attracted many artists and was the subject of numerous works, not to mention the more distant Barbizon, whose success never waned throughout the period.
The landscapes of Asnières and the surrounding area that inspired painters, drawers, engravers and lithographers do not seem to have offered picturesque subjects and barely aroused the interest of the artists resident in Asnières who were admitted to the official event. From 1868 to1886, in fact, only one such artist took the town as the subject for a painting, the Italian Felipe

3. Jean-Alfred Taiée
Asnières, 1872
Engraving,
13.5 × 21.7 cm
(5 ¼ × 8 ½ in.)
Bibliothèque nationale de France, Cabinet des Estampes, Paris, EF 566(2). Fol

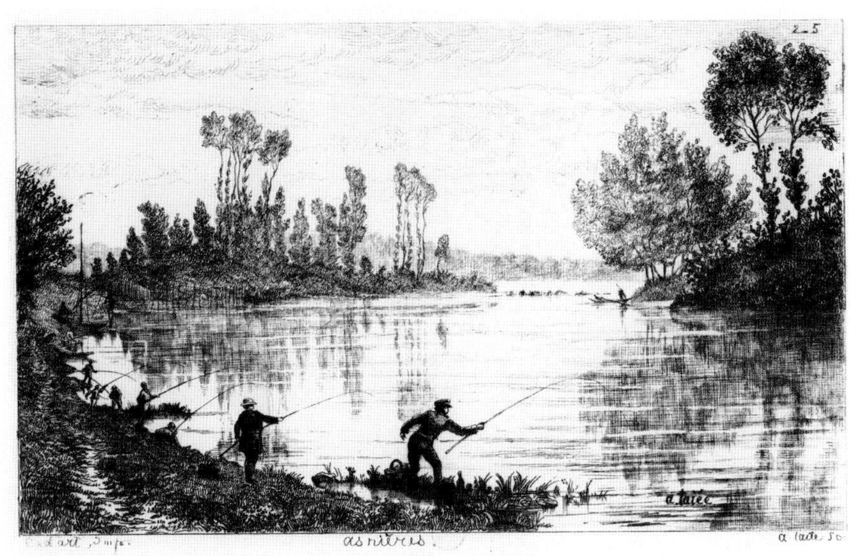

Liardo in 1883. However, a few other rare artists did take inspiration from the town. In 1870, Louis Latouche (1829–84), born in la Ferté-sous-Jouarre, and resident in Paris, sent under numbers 1600 and 1601 *The Bridge at Asnières* (current location unknown) and *The Seine at Asnières* (current location unknown); and Luigi Loir (1845–1916), born in Goritz, Austria, and resident in Neuilly, *View near Asnières, gouache* (no. 3744). At the 1872 Salon Latouche also presented, under the number 940, *The Maison de Lavoignat, Asnières; The Island of Grande Jatte* (current location unknown), while one of the eleven etchings by Jean-Alfred Taiée in the series *Paris et ses environs* (no. 2057) depicted Asnières (fig. 3). Rejected by the 1873 Salon, Latouche's *A Hut at Asnières (the Island of Grande Jatte)* (current location unknown) was presented under the number 46 at the Salon des Refusés. When this devotee of the banks of the Seine turned towards other subjects and other places, mentions became fewer and finally disappeared, even if we include less precise place descriptions, as, in 1874, Ernest Émile Armand-Delille's painting entitled *View of the Seine, near Asnières (Seine)* (no. 39, current location unknown). There was no mention in the following years, and it is only possible to cite exceptional mentions like *The Seine at Asnières* (no. 1915, current location unknown) by Octave Saunier at the 1877 Salon or *The Quay at Asnières during the Flood of 1883* (no. 1524, current location unknown) by the Italian Liardo, his Christian name gallicized to Philippe by the authors of the catalogue of the 1883 Salon de la Société des artistes français.

These meagre results oblige us to address the question of the lack of interest shown by artists towards the small town. Various explanations are possible: it did not possess any remarkable "natural" sites, no woods, forests, or ponds, not even a market, which might have provided settings for the original compositions much loved by the members of the jury of the official exhibition, and its castle, now an outdoor cafe, offered neither the interest of a "view" nor the romantic appeal of a ruin. None of the inhabitants of the village seems to have been blessed with the slightest renown that might have encouraged artists to immortalize them for posterity, and none of them, probably, were rich enough or proud enough of their place of residence to have themselves portrayed at the Salon. At that time Asnières was, in fact, a modern town without any picturesque appeal for artists steeped in tradition,[12] but it was precisely this relative modernity, these occupations and amusements, more important than the place in which they unfolded, that would inspire the Impressionists and their successors.

During this time various artists outside the established institutional circuits enjoyed staying in[13] or representing Asnières. The first, who we may count as among the harbingers of the *Nouvelle Peinture*, were the painters and drawers Adolphe Félix Cals,[14] and Charles-François Daubigny, also an engraver, who at the end of the 1850s had portrayed himself in his boat-cum-studio on

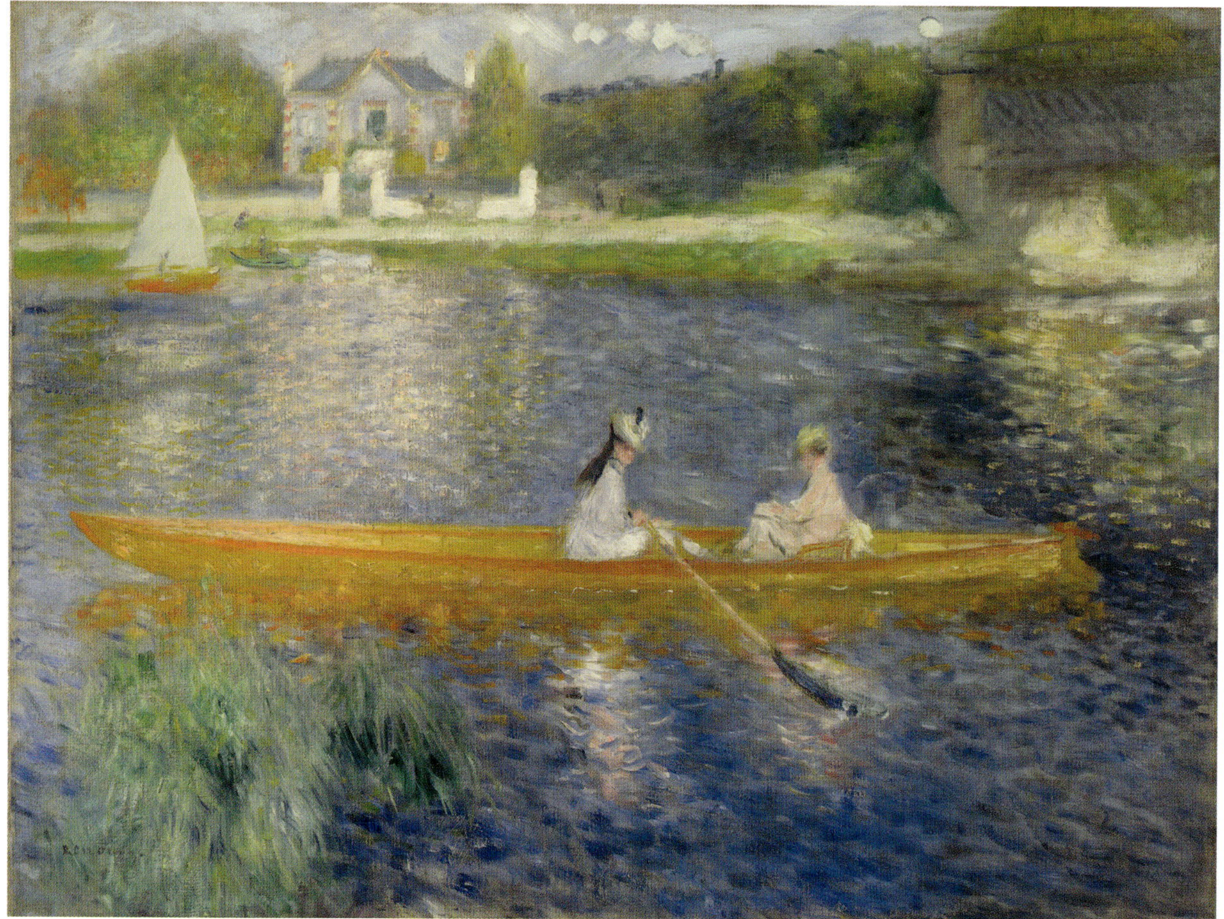

4. Auguste Renoir
The Skiff (La Yole), 1875
Oil on canvas,
71 × 92 cm
(28 × 36 ¼ in.)
The National Gallery,
London, NG6478

the banks of the Seine, choosing Asnières as the starting point of his journey, with a pen-and-ink drawing (musée du Louvre, Cabinet des Arts graphiques, Paris, RF 5312) that was the source of the first plate of his album *Voyage en bateau*, published in 1862 by Cadart. But it was with the following generation, which would soon be labelled with the name "Impressionists," and even more so with those that came on their heels, the post- and neo-Impressionists, that the representation of Asnières in painting would become more celebrated.

The number of Impressionist depictions is not as large as Asnières' subsequent fame would suggest. There were certain special characteristics of the town during the 1870s, the period in which painters visited regularly for their pleasure, that justified these rare representations, while other places in the Parisian banlieue, often those where they resided, inspired far more illustrations.

In Asnières Renoir saw a place of amusement, as is shown by his painting *The Skiffs (La Yole)* (1875, The National Gallery, London) (fig. 4) and the preparatory studies, while Monet saw the town above all as a place of work, as is shown by the painting and the sketch *Seine at Asnières* (1873), both in private collections,[15] or his exceptional depiction of the *The Coal-Dockers* (c. 1875, musée d'Orsay, Paris) (cat. 13), which, although it is situated on the quay opposite Asnières, carefully details the road bridge that would appear later in the work of other painters. While Camille Pissarro seems never to have visited the banks of the river in Asnières,[16] Alfred Sisley must have visited the environs, without representing the city;[17] see, for example, his view of the nearby *The Island of Saint-Denis* (1872, musée d'Orsay, Paris). All this would change very quickly, and depictions of the town grew in number with the later exhibitors at the Impressionist exhibitions,[18] who were also the founders and leading lights of the new Expositions de la Société des artistes indépendants, from 1884 onwards, mainly due to reasons of friendship. Members of the family of Paul Signac resided in Asnières, in fact, and thanks to his friendly relations with some of his contemporaries the place of his first artistic attempts also became popular with them.

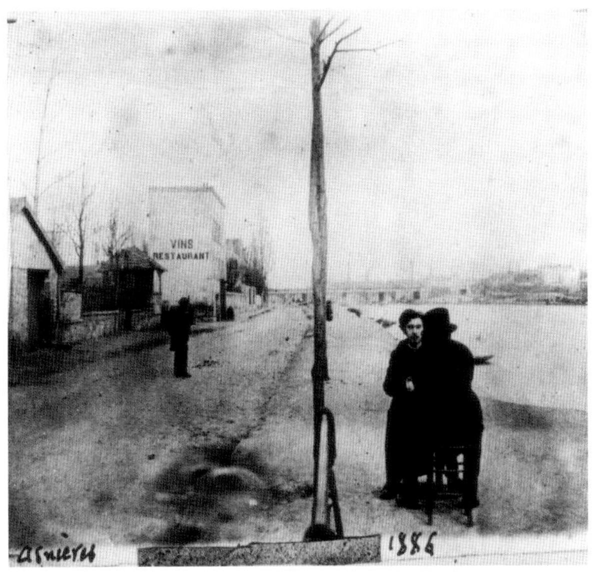

5. Anonymous, *Photograph of Émile Bernard and Vincent van Gogh (seen on the back), Asnières,*1886 Van Gogh Museum, Amsterdam, Tralbaut 258

While Signac's first dated painting (December 1881), soberly entitled *Landscape with Boat*[19] (Private collection, Saint-Martin-la-Garenne), seems to have been situated in Asnières, the fifth (April 1882), entitled *Study at Asnières (Wash House)* (Suzuki Fine Art Corporation, London; Cachin, 5), was certainly so, as were the following numbers, 6 to 9 in the *Catalogue raisonné*. Signac now regularly painted and drew views of Asnières, where the great lover of boats generally depicted the river[20] and its banks, sometimes the Asnières side, sometimes the Clichy side,[21] until his more remarkable pointillist works *Stern of the Tub, Opus 175*[22] (1888, *Auction Sale*, New York, Christie's, 9 May 2007, no. 35; Cachin 161) and *Bow of the Tub, Opus 176* (1888, Private collection, Switzerland; Cachin 162) (cat. 43). Following him, his friends also came to the place: Georges Seurat, Émile Bernard and Vincent Van Gogh, who in turn would leave their impressions of the Seine and its bridges.

Of Seurat, who died too young after producing several "manifesto-paintings" of what would be called neo-Impressionism, one work and its many preparatory studies,[23] sketches and drawings in Conté crayon, have a link with Asnières: *Bathers at Asnières* (1883–84, The National Gallery, London). Here he seems to reflect certain passages from *Manette Salomon* by the Goncourt brothers, published in 1868 by Lacroix et Verboeckhoven.[24] The town expanded rapidly, however, and in 1886 the artist chose to set up his easel on the island of La Grande Jatte, which at the time was part of the commune of Courbevoie and which now lies on the border between the communes of Neuilly and Levallois. There he painted his *A Sunday Afternoon on the Island of La Grande Jatte* (1884–86, The Art Institute of Chicago) (fig. 8 p. 24), a resort that was also a source of inspiration for another neo-Impressionist absent from Asnières, Charles Angrand.[25]

The most famous painting by Émile Bernard, now at the Museum of Modern Art in New York, is *Iron Bridges at Asnières* (1887) (fig. 6). Van Gogh was not content with the view of the river depicted in the various versions of the bridges over the Seine at Asnieres (1887, The Foundation E.G. Bührle Collection, Zurich[26] (fig. 7) or De Menil Collection, Houston; La Faille 240), but also depicted a few of the town's main places of interest; on several occasions he painted the recent improvements made to the park called "Voyer d'Argenson," such as *Corner in Voyer d'Argenson Park at Asnières* (1887, Yale University Art Gallery, New Haven, Connecticut; La Faille 276) or the *Courting couples in the Voyer d'Argenson Park in Asnières* (1887, Rijksmuseum Vincent Van Gogh, Amsterdam; La Faille 314), and various restaurants: *Restaurant Rispal at Asnières* (1887, Henry W. Bloch Collection, Shawnee Mission, Kansas; La Faille 355) or *The Restaurant de la Sirène at Asnières* (1887, University of Oxford-Ashmolean Museum, Oxford; La Faille 312) (fig. 8).

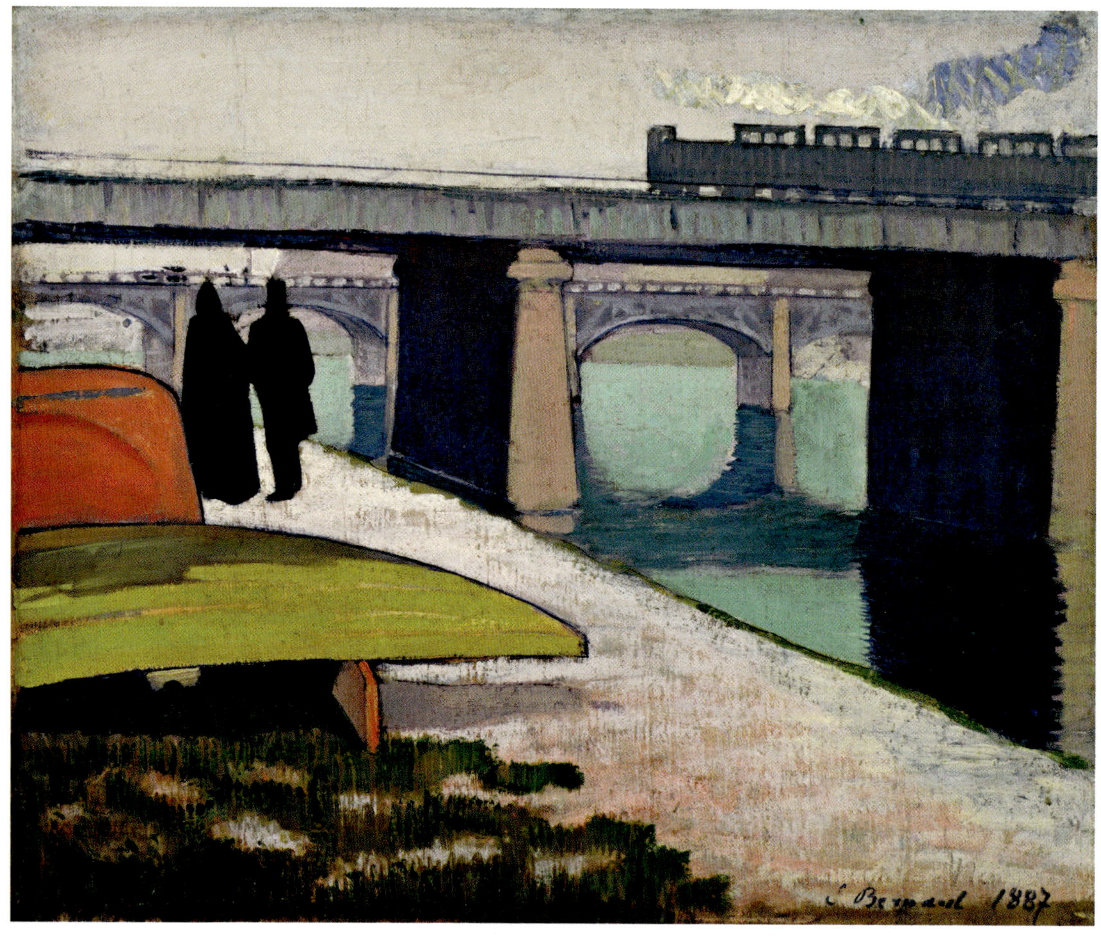

6. Émile Bernard
Iron Bridges at Asnières, 1887
Oil on canvas,
45.9 × 54.2 cm
(18 ⅛ × 21 ⅜ in.)
The Museum of Modern Art, New York

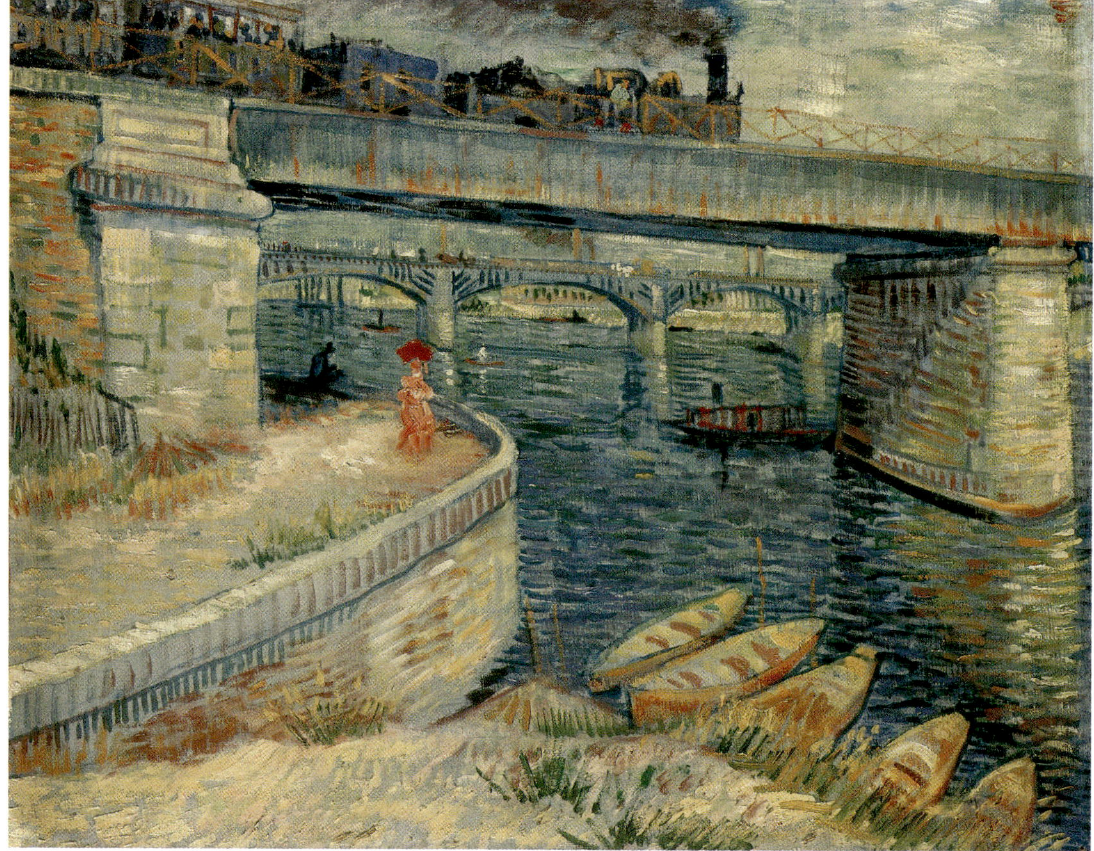

7. Vincent Van Gogh
Bridges across the Seine at Asnières, 1887
Oil on canvas,
52.5 × 65 cm
(20 ¾ × 25 ½ in.)
The Fondation E.G. Bührle Collection, Zurich, De la Faille 301

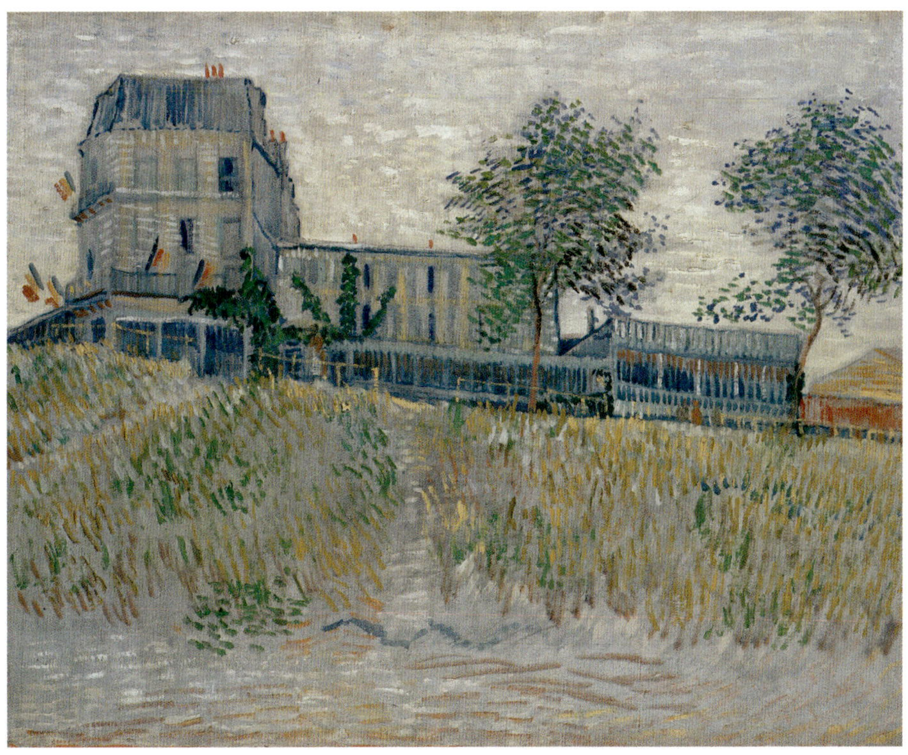

8. Vincent Van Gogh
Restaurant de la Sirène at Asnières,
summer 1887
Oil on canvas,
52 × 64.4 cm
(20 ½ × 25 ¼ in.)
University of Oxford-Ashmolean Museum,
Oxford, Bequest of M. Erich Alport,
1972, WA1972.18

It was therefore with these "moderns" and over a short lapse of time, the 1870s and the 1880s, that artists took possession of Asnières in order to represent it. They were no longer in search of the picturesque, but of the contemporary, and of an art shorn of any academic temptations. This well-preserved and easily accessible corner of the Parisian banlieue where one could be among friends (fig. 5) provided them with what their predecessors had not been able to find... but this improved situation was not to last long, ended by other movements such as Naturalism and Symbolism, the former exploring more provincial regions that had retained their rural character, the latter choosing the territories of the spirit where they looked for new esoteric speculations. Asnières was able to return to its previous life, following its protected growth; it would always welcome artists who, however, paid little homage to its hospitality.

APPENDIX

List of artists, painters, drawers, and engravers present at the Salon and then at the Salon de la Société des artistes français, declaring their place of residence as Asnières from 1868 to 1886.

1868:
Painting:
FÜHR (Charles), born in Bayonne (Basses-Pyrénées), pupil of Feuillet. Asnières (Seine-et-Oise [*sic*][27]), rue des Petites Couronnes, 11. [no. 2898; no. 4185]

1869:
Painting:
BONCZA TOMACHEVSKI (Jules), born in St Petersburg. Asnières (Seine), rue de Nanterre, 5. [no. 263]
CLAUDE (Eugène), [1841–1922], born in Toulouse. Asnières (Seine), rue d'Argenteuil, 40. [nos. 491–492]
Lithography:
FÜHR (Charles), born in Bayonne (Basses-Pyrénées), pupil of Feuillet. Asnières (Seine), rue des Petites Couronnes, 11. [nos. 4197–4198]
LAMY (Pierre-Auguste), born in Paris. Asnières (Seine), rue Traversière, 6. [nos. 4203–4204]

1870[28]:
Painting:
CLAUDE (Eugène), born in Toulouse. Asnières (Seine), rue d'Argenteuil, 40. [nos. 576–577]

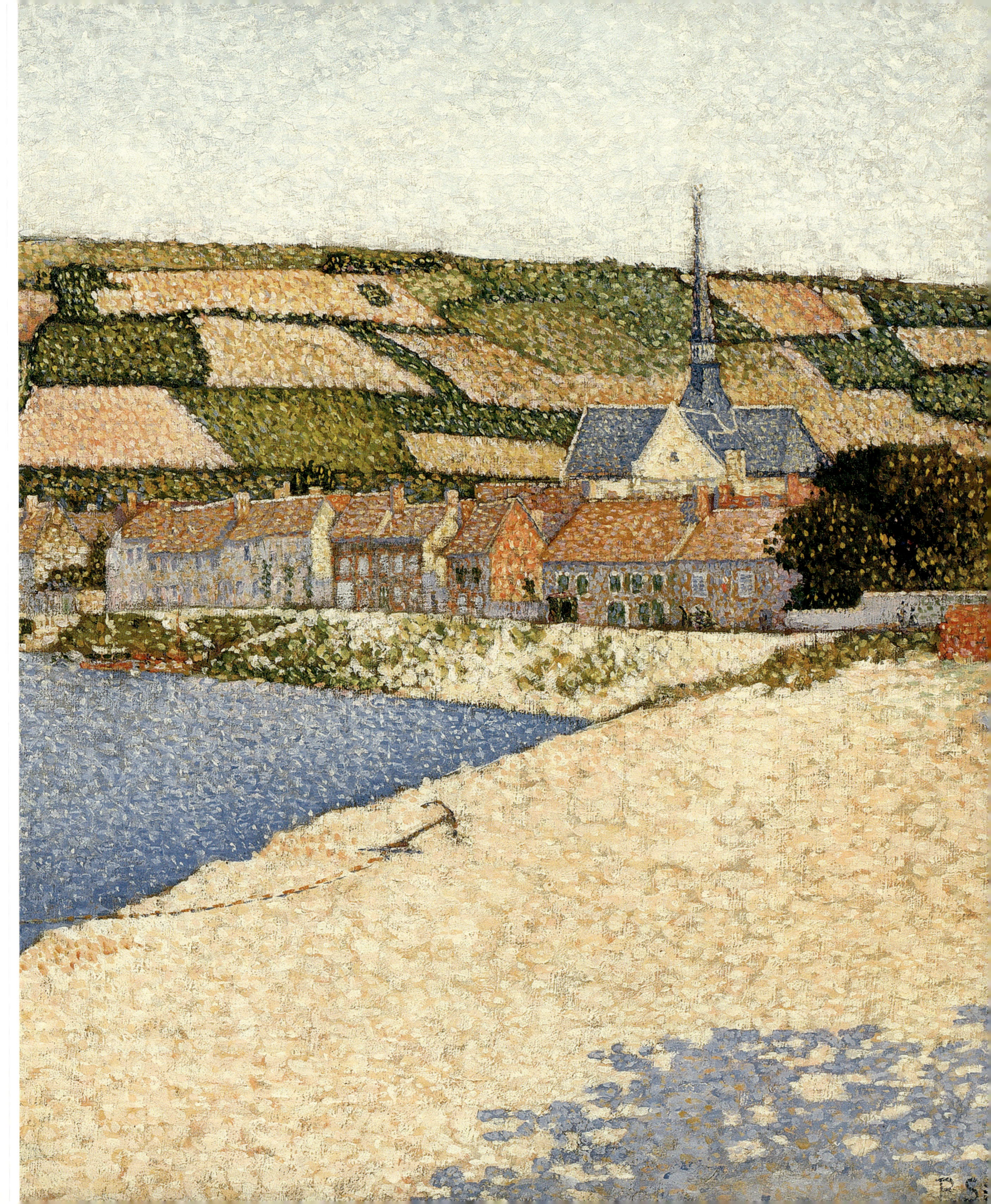

Paul Signac and Félix Vallotton in Les Andelys

VANESSA LECOMTE

"It is more pleasant to see this town [Les Andelys] within the landscape framing it than to visit its interior..."[1] This is how the village of Les Andelys, situated in the meanders of the Seine valley some forty kilometres from Rouen and a hundred from Paris, was described by Charles Nodier in 1836. The main attraction lay in the picturesque ruins of the Château-Gaillard, as shown in the vignette by Foussereau accompanying the text. This view looking downstream towards the church of Saint-Sauveur and Petit-Andely beneath the fortress of Château-Gaillard was to become one of the best known. The Château-Gaillard was built by Richard the Lion Heart, king of England and duke of Normandy, in 1196 to control shipping on the Seine and protect Rouen. As Girault Pierre de Saint-Fargeau wrote, "The history of Les Andelys conjures up the strongest memories of the days of chivalry. It was one of the principal theaters of the exploits of Philippe-Auguste and Richard the Lion Heart. All the memorable events of that great era are, however, bound up with the tragic annals of the château Gaillard, whose majestic ruins tower over the course of the Seine and Petit-Andely."[2] The view of the Château-Gaillard drawn from life by Rauch is not radically different from that of his predecessor. Joseph Morlent devoted a chapter of his *Voyage historique et pittoresque de Rouen à Paris sur la Seine, en bateau à vapeur* to Les Andelys and the Château-Gaillard in 1836: "Here is the fortress, a place of pilgrimage for artists, antiquarians and historians; here is the Château-Gaillard [...] Greetings to these crumbling battlements, to these old ruined towers! Greetings to these majestic rocks, from which the melancholy traveller will be able to meditate on the quarrels of the kings, the frailty of our monuments and the imperishable permanence of those raised by nature all at the same time!"[3] Of the five engravings that illustrate the work, one is devoted to the view from Petit-Andely dominated by the imposing ruins of the Château-Gaillard, where one can notice the church of Saint-Sauveur and a steamboat on the winding course of the river. This viewpoint was later taken up by Morel-Fatio to illustrate the guide-

Paul Signac
Hillside from Downstream, Les Andelys (detail),
see fig. 3 p. 58

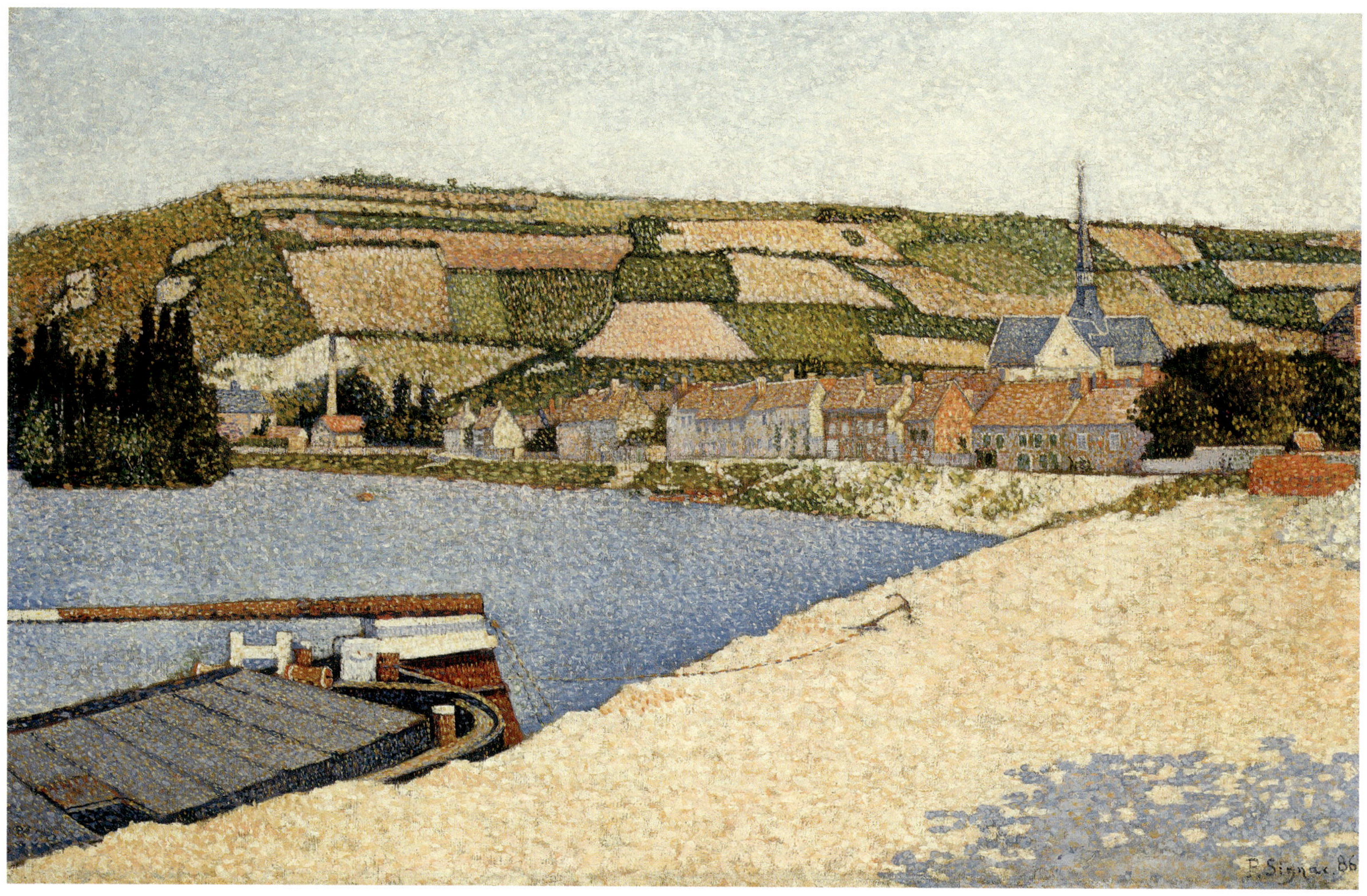

3. Paul Signac
Hillside from Downstream, Les Andelys, September 1886
Oil on canvas,
60 × 92 cm
(23 ¾ × 36 ¼ in.)
The Art Institute of Chicago, through prior gift of William Wood Prince, 1993.208

artistes indépendants[19] from 21 August to 21 September 1886 and aroused the interest of Félix Fénéon. Struck by the "polychromatic verve"[20] of these river landscapes, the critic made this observation: "The most recent ones are also the most luminous and complete. The colors provoke each other to mad chromatic flights—they exult, shout! And the Seine flows on, and in its waters flow the sky and the vegetation along the riverside beneath a sun that sets the ruins perched on high ablaze—*The Château-Gaillard from my window*—and tears the faint shadows of bushes to shreds—*The Port Morin*. [...] The vision of this painter has refined itself to a remarkable degree in the space of a few months."[21] *Les Andelys, The Washerwomen*[22] (fig. 5), painted in August 1886, was exhibited at the Salon de la Société des artistes indépendants in the spring of 1887 together with another three paintings of Les Andelys, including *Hillside from Downstream, Les Andelys* (fig. 3).[23] Signac's fidelity to the topography of the location can be gauged on the basis of a later picture postcard with a view from practically the same point (fig. 4). Grounded on the use of pure colors and the artist's beloved contrasts—between the orange of the riverbanks and the geometric façades of the houses and the blue of the sky and the river, and between the green of the vegetation and the purple of the tiled roofs—the compositions bear witness to the liberties taken with respect to color. Gustave Kahn made this observation about the canvases: "This colorist delights in placing colors beside one another so as to dazzle. [...] Signac perpetually returns to bends in the river full of wooded isles, reflected trees, closely huddled houses, peasant women washing, sparkling patchworks of cultivated field. It is the blaze of the Mediterranean sun that is fixed in these landscapes, imbued with the joy of things and illustrated with fantasies of light."[24] The critic Jules Christophe described them as "powerful and joyous but

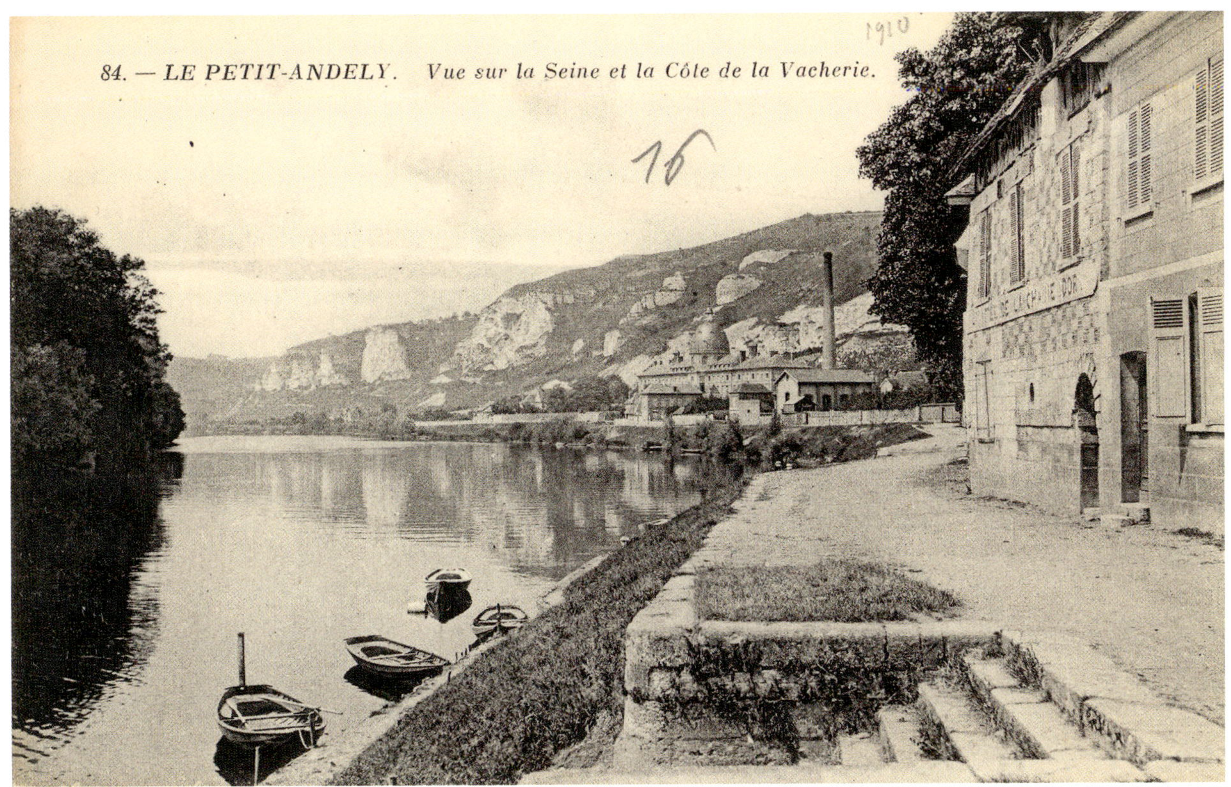

4. *Le Petit Andely – View of the Seine and the Côte de la Vacherie*
Postcard
Archives départementales de l'Eure, Évreux, 8 Fl 16/700

5. Paul Signac
Les Andelys, The Washerwomen,
August 1886
Oil on canvas,
60 × 93 cm
(23 ¾ × 36 ¾ in.)
Private collection on long term loan at the National Gallery, London

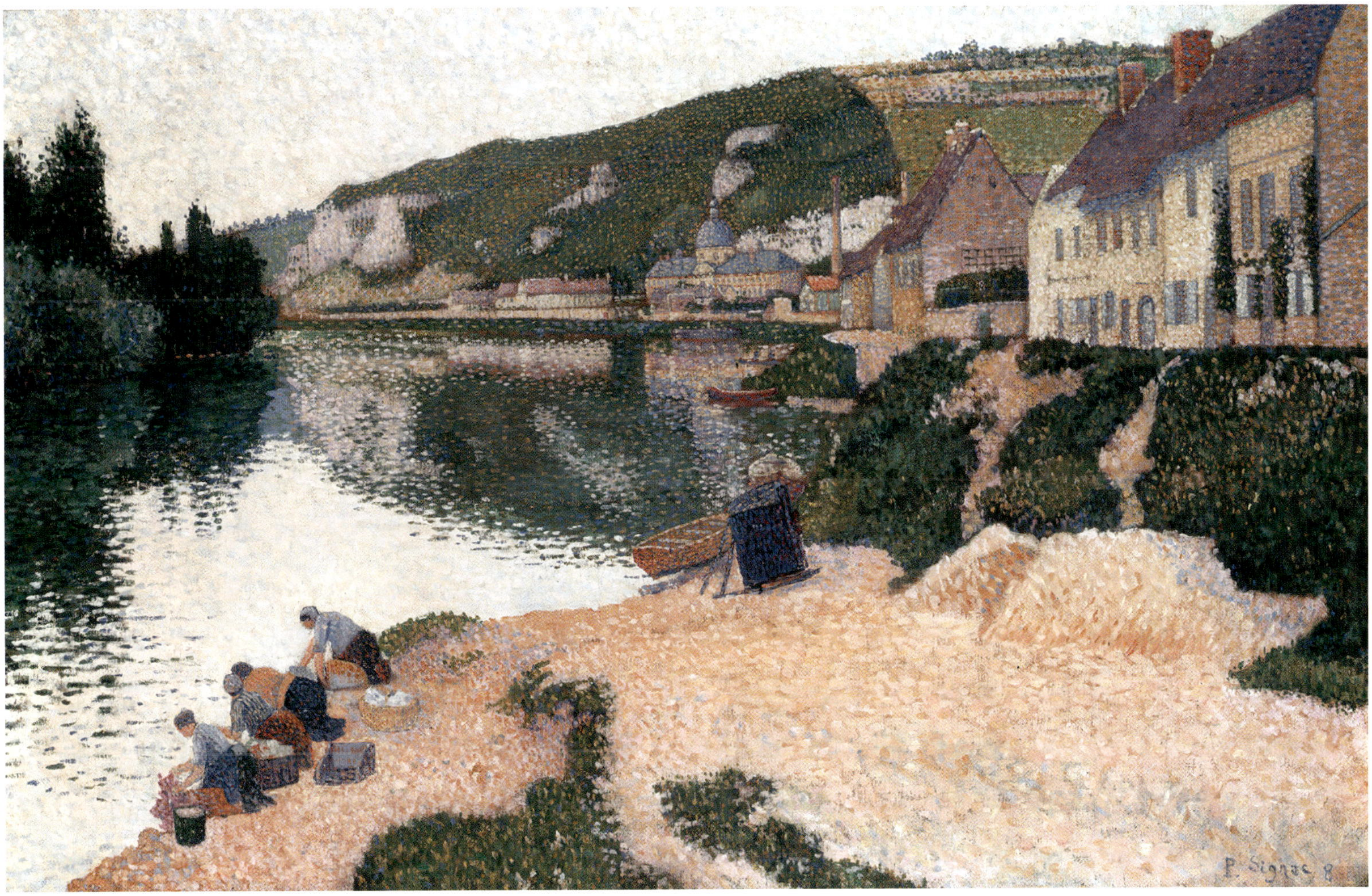

slightly Africanized."[25] Fénéon wrote in *L'Émancipation sociale* about the "frenzied triumph of the sun"[26] and [Paul Alexis] Trublot had this to say in *Le Cri du peuple*: "Signac's vision is brightly colored and very powerful while remaining harmonious. [...] *Scenes in Les Andelys* gleam in the sun. In short, it's very striking."[27] Jean Le Fustec raised this question: "Is there not, however, a contradiction between some of these works, where the palette is so concrete, and those where we are denied any indications?"[28]

The importance of this stay in Signac's artistic development has been widely remarked, and it is hardly surprising, as Marina Ferretti Bocquillon rightly notes, that most of the canvases of this series were offered to people close to the artist, who did not want them to be scattered on the market.[29]

Signac stayed at the Caplain house in Petit-Andely, not far from Giverny, from 15 July to 15 October 1921. In a letter to Fénéon, he rejoiced over a visit from Claude Monet, who acquired seven of his watercolors: "I've been feeling lousy. The river climate doesn't agree with me, but the town is very beautiful and I enjoy working: watercolors and 3 canvases of 30 – *so* [*illegible*] I won't beat Dufy's record production. I had an encouraging visit from Monet, who wanted some watercolors."[30] He devoted two canvases to Petit-Andely: *Le Petit Andely (aval)* (August–September, T. Kakinuma Collection, Tokyo, FC 548) and *Les Andelys, Château-Gaillard* (Private collection, FC 547). When Signac exhibited *Les Andelys, Château-Gaillard* at the Salon des indépendants the following year, Gustave Kahn was outspoken in his admiration: "Signac, the glory of the Salon des indépendants. The *Port of La Rochelle* and the *petit Andely* of Paul Signac will figure among his best canvases. The most intuitive of painters, the quick-sighted visionary attested by his watercolors and drawings, can change—a splendid aesthetic phenomenon—into a perfect architect of light and a whole quivering life of decoration takes shape without solidifying, with powerful serenity, in a simultaneously precise and magical impression."[31]

Signac returned to the Caplain house at Petit-Andely, where he went sailing as in Herblay and Saint Tropez, from 11 July to 12 October 1923 and planned to visit Claude Monet, the painter he "admired most in the world."[32] A letter written to Fénéon on 13 August describes how he spent his days painting: "It's hot. I paint with watercolors on the banks of the river in the morning and oils in the covered playground of the nursery school in the afternoon. If you didn't loathe the countryside, you'd be welcome to spend a Sunday with us on the Seine. We'd go sailing, as in Herblay and St Tropez!"[33] This second stay resulted in two canvases—*Les Andelys, The Lime Tree* (Private collection, Great Britain, FC 559) and *Les Andelys, Morning, Summer* (Private collection, FC 557)—and a series of watercolors. As he wrote to Fénéon on September 18: "We've just had a quick drive along the estuary in my nice little Renault 6HP. It handles like a Japanese paintbrush. There's always room for you. Return to Paris on 12 October: 2 canvases of Les Andelys and about 60 watercolors: Groix, Lorient, Les Andelys, Quillebœuf, Honfleur, Rolleboise. Etc."[34] *Les Andelys, Morning, Summer* was exhibited at the Salon des artistes indépendants in 1924. Gustave Kahn described it as conjuring up "all the joyous opulence of this beautiful landscape on a sunny day"[35] and Robert Rey wrote that his canvases "sparkle like the dew in the rising sun. Never has light been handled in more scintillating and crystalline fashion."[36]

6. Félix Vallotton
Memory of Les Andelys, 1916
Oil on canvas, 114 × 146 cm (45 × 57 ½ in.)
Private collection

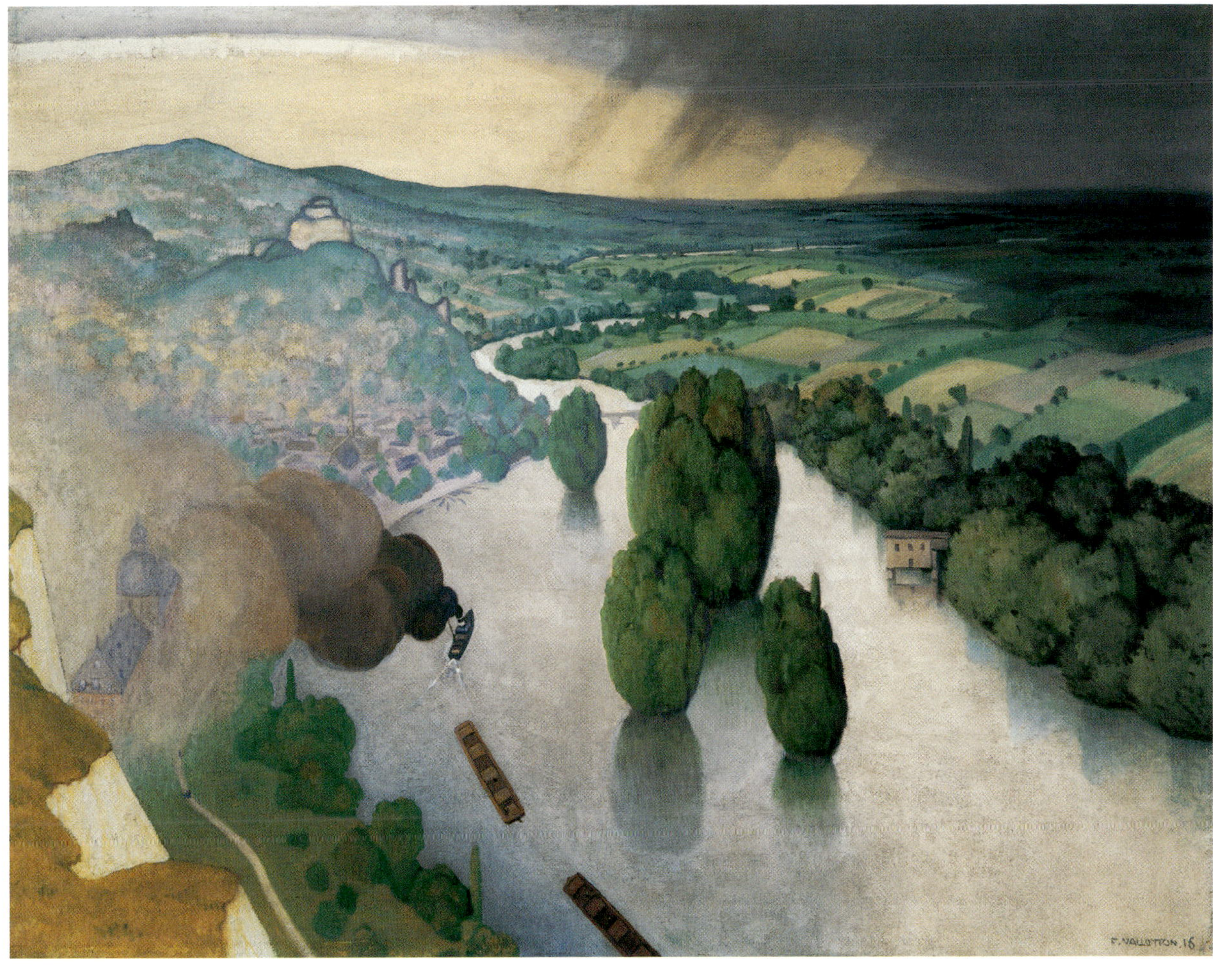

The town of Les Andelys, Poussin's native land, occupies a particularly important place in the work of Félix Vallotton, who first stayed there for about eight days in September 1916 and was enchanted by the discovery. As he wrote in his journal on 6 September, "Have been in Les Andelys for two days and its charm exceeds all my expectations. I like everything about it, the structure of the terrain, the arrangement of the rocks masses and the cut of the river with its lush and shaded banks. There is nothing to spoil the view, no clumsy buildings and misbegotten villas. And then the great procession of barges, whose slowness fits in so well with the majesty of surroundings. I relish all this to the full and would like to spend weeks here."[37] He described it a few days later as an "admirable town, one of most beautiful I know"[38] and then as "one of the most perfect landscapes that I know and that can exist" in a letter of 24 September 1916 to Hedy Hahnloser.[39] Vallotton noted down the emotions experienced in his journal like memoranda. The following lines appear to have inspired his *The Seine near Les Andelys, Pale Sun* (Banque cantonal vaudoise, BCV-ART Collection, Lausanne, CR 1150, LRZ 1088): "A splendid day with a moonlit evening on the banks of the Seine as its apotheosis. The enchantment of heavy masses of greenery sprinkled with phosphorescent light, quivering and almost fluid in a distant and softly subdued setting, more musical than sculptural. I was deeply moved."[40] On his return to his studio in Paris during the second half of September, Vallotton referred in his journal to the sketchbook studies[41] made at the time of his stay in Les Andelys and stated his intention to make use of them: "I am trying to make something out of my sketches while the impressions are still fresh."[42] He referred on 2 October to "two or three paintings" perpetuating the memory of Les Andelys.[43] The *Livre de raison*, where he kept a record of his paintings, lists five works, one on the plain of Les Andelys (*Storm Gathering, Les Andelys*, Private collection, Paris, CR 1148, LRZ 1085) and four on the banks of the Seine (*The Seine near Les Andelys*, Private collection, CR 1149, LRZ 1086; *The Seine near Les Andelys, Pale Sun*, Banque cantonale vaudoise, BVC-ART Collection, Lausanne, CR 1150, LRZ 1088; *The Seine near Les Andelys, Morning Sunshine*, Private collection?, Geneva, CR 1151, LRZ 1089; *Memory of Les Andelys*, Private collection, Paris, CR 1152, LRZ 1090).

The review in *L'Art décoratif* of the exhibition at the Galerie Druet in 1912 criticized the "photographic tendency" of Vallotton's landscapes.[44] As Marina Ducrey rightly points out, Félix Vallotton constantly varied and combined his techniques in these canvases: painting in nature, on the basis of preparatory sketches drawn from life or using photographs.[45] The recent publication of the *Catalogue raisonné* revealed a picture postcard of the banks of the Seine at Petit Andely annotated by Vallotton unquestionably in the period around 1916 (fig. 7). There does not seem to be other material of this type. The possibility therefore cannot be ruled out that Vallotton made use of photographic postcards for the transposition onto canvas back in the studio. These images aimed at tourists did indeed undergo marked development during the first decade of the twentieth century. The same spot was to be depicted from different viewpoints in several paintings of Les Andelys, including *The Seine near Les Andelys* (1916), *The Seine near Les Andelys, Morning Sunshine* (1916), *The Seine at Les Andelys, Evening* (1924, CR 1596, LRZ 1499) and *The Seine at Les Andelys* (1924, CR 1602, LRZ 1505), which were also based on preparatory sketches in pencil drawn from life according to nature, the existence of which is a known fact. On the postcard as on the studies, a numbered code specifies the choice of colors while notes on the back or in the margins express the painter's subjective vision and very often indicate the hour of day when the landscape was observed. It is, however, sufficient to compare the paintings of Les Andelys with the postcard to gauge the extent to which the subject was interpreted and how far it is Vallotton's composition. He did indeed make some changes, including the chosen view of a limited portion of the river, the condensation of the masses of dark green vegetation on the island and the colors. As was his normal practice, Vallotton did not scrupulously include all the details but deliberately omitted the factory, the Saint-Jacques hospital, the church of Saint-Sauveur and the barge.

Vallotton's depiction of the landscape is thus related to a distancing with respect to reality, a conception indissolubly linked with Poussin. As he wrote in his journal on 7 September after a visit to the town museum, "I have just seen Poussin's Coriolan. It is wonderful, like a magnificent piece of organ music. The colors ring out in the delimited forms like a full peal of bells and the whole attains harmony in an ensemble that is powerful, ample and gentle. A fine lesson [...] I am turning ideas over in my mind with great intensity."[46] It is therefore hardly surprising that he should implicitly refer to the concept of the "historical landscape" in his journal. While working on the Les Andelys series, he considered a highly revealing question: "I dream of a type of painting detached from all literal respect for nature. I would like to re-create landscapes with the sole aid of the emotion they have aroused in me, some evocative outlines, one or two details chosen with no superstitious precision as regards time of day or lighting. This would be essentially a kind of return to the famous 'historical landscape'. Why not?"[47] He was still more specific a few days later: "I have just finished a large landscape, which will

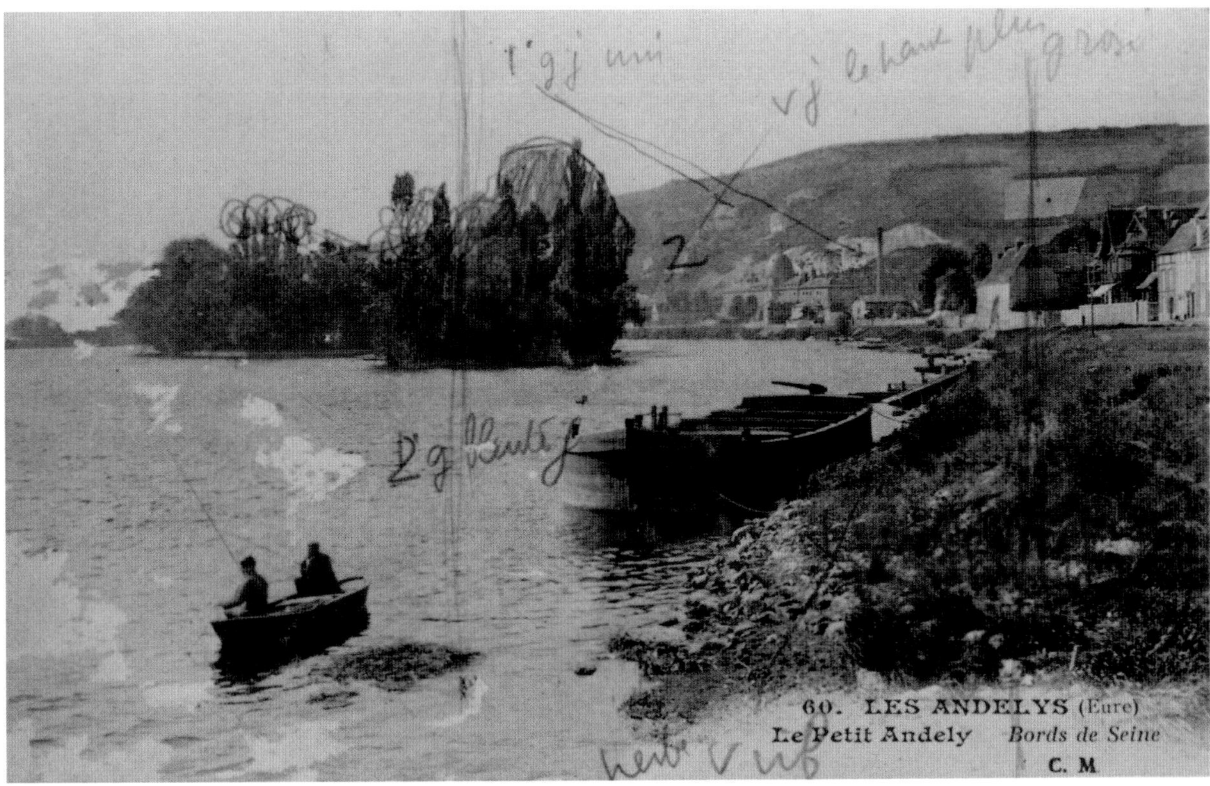

7. *Les Andelys (Eure). Le Petit Andely. Banks of the Seine*
Postcard annotated by Félix Vallotton, 1916
Private collection

unquestionably end the Andelys series. It gave me the greatest pleasure. Not being obsessed with the precise recollection of nature, I had a free hand and was thus able to relax a little. I consider the result interesting."[48] The landscape to which he refers is in all probability the large *Memory of Les Andelys* (fig. 6), described as follows in the *Livre de raison*: "*Memory of Les Andelys*. The Seine and its banks, varied effects, rain and sun, reconstructed landscape." It was just two years later that Vallotton first used the term *paysage composé* in the *Livre de raison* in connection with four works. *Memory of Les Andelys* provides a perfect example in this connection. The painter's recollection of Les Andelys reappears in this large painting recomposed from memory in his studio in Paris without the aid of any preparatory document and shielded from any "precise remembering of nature" that he may have retained. This panoramic view of the entire valley of the Seine from a rocky slope juxtaposes deliberately divergent meteorological effects and viewpoints: the plain with geometrical fields and a threatening rainstorm effect in the distance on the right, while Les Andelys is bathed in pale sunlight at the bottom on the left. The blue dome of the hospital disappears behind a dense cloud of black smoke from a steamboat. Similar views are to be found in many sketches and postcards of the period.[49]

A "picturesque drive back"[50] from Honfleur on 28 October 1917 was in all probability the origin of *Morning Mist at Les Andelys* (Private collection, Switzerland, CR 1200, LRZ 1134), which Vallotton painted in the studio on his return to Paris on the basis of a sketch, the existence of which has been established. He made this note in his journal about ten days later: "Painted two small canvases of Les Andelys and Mantes. Work done while waiting. As for everything else, it's foggy."[51]

Vallotton returned to Les Andelys for just under a week in June 1924 and made a dozen sketches. As he wrote to his brother on his return to Honfleur, "I hope to get down to work with no delay, which is something necessary in any case if I am to retain the freshness of my impressions."[52] Vallotton produced nine paintings of the town and its historical buildings, the hospital of Les Andelys, the ruins of the Château-Gaillard and the banks of the Seine. *Les Andelys, Evening* and *Morning at Les Andelys* were presented at the Salon d'automne of the same year and criticized by du Colombier: "As for the landscapes, it is best to acknowledge just how disappointing they are. It is as though this highly knowledgeable artist Félix Vallotton felt the need to immerse himself in naivety and went looking for this naivety not in nature itself, but in the simultaneously folksy and artificial ingenuousness of a Douanier Rousseau, who sees nature in the form of a colored picture postcard."[53]

[1] Charles Nodier, *La Seine et ses bords* (Paris: M. A. Mure de Pelanne, 1836), 137. The name Les Andelys designates two towns separated by a roadway, Grand Andely and Petit-Andely, the latter located on the banks of the Seine. According to Jacques-Antoine Dulaure, the name appears to derive from *ande*, meaning town or territory, and *lis*, edge or border. *Histoire physique, civile et morale des environs de Paris, depuis les premiers temps historiques jusqu'à nos jours* (Paris: Furne et Cie, 1838, Vol. II, 2nd Edition), 570.

[2] Girault Pierre de Saint-Fargeau, *Guide pittoresque du voyageur en France, Routes de Paris à Rouen et au Havre*, Département de l'Eure (Paris: Firmin Didot Frères, L. Hachette, 1838), 11–12.

[3] Joseph Morlent, *Voyage historique et pittoresque de Rouen à Paris, sur la Seine, en bateau à vapeur* (Rouen: Édouard Frère, 1836), 60.

[4] Jules Janin, *La Normandie* (Paris: Ernest Bourdin, 1843); Jules Janin, *Voyage de Paris à la mer* (Paris: Ernest Bourdin, 1847), 38; Eugène Chapus, *De Paris au Havre*, Département de l'Eure (Paris: L. Hachette, 1855), 55.

[5] A sketch in pen and ink entitled *The River Crossing below Château-Gaillard* (1827–29?) presents a similar view. Reproduction in Ian Warrell, *Turner on the Seine* (London: Tate Gallery Publishing, 1999), 196: fig. 179 (cat. 35).

[6] Leitch Ritchie, *Wanderings by the Seine, from Rouen to the Source*, London, Longman Rees, Orme Brown, Green and Longman, 1835, and *Wanderings by the Seine*, London, Longman Rees, Orme Brown, Green and Longman, 1834, which follows the course of the Seine from its mouth to Rouen. The albums, designed as gift books, were published in pocket format at the end of the previous year. For Turner and the Seine, see

in particular Warrell, *Turner et la Seine*, op. cit., esp. 196–202. See also Diederik Bakhuÿs, "Artistes et antiquaires britanniques en Normandie à l'époque romantique," *Voyages pittoresques, Normandie 1820-2009*, Rouen, musée des Beaux-Arts, Le Havre, musée Malraux, Caen, musée des Beaux-Arts (Milan: Silvana Editoriale, 2009), 65–81.

[7] The picturesque character of the location inspired many other artists and writers, including Victor Hugo, Paul Huet, Charles-François Daubigny (*Château-Gaillard, Les Andelys*, 1877, musée d'Orsay, Paris, RF 3782) and Théodore Rousseau. See in particular Dominique Pitte, Sophie Fourny-Dargère and Paola Calderoni, *Château-Gaillard : découverte d'un patrimoine*, Vernon, musée municipal A.-G. Poulain, Vernon, 1995.

[8] Leitch Ritchie, *Rivers of France*, John MacCormick, London, 1837. Leitch Ritchie writes as follows:
"To obtain even a faint idea of this remarkable place, it is necessary to pursue laboriously the traces of the varnished towers, and even to conjecture, by analogy, the course of the walls, the ruins of which are now entirely covered by successive deposits of the soil. Standing on the loftier hill behind, the scene of mingled grandeur and desolation is inconceivably fine. It is from this point that Turner has taken his view.
The principal portion of the ruins in front consists of the walls of the citadel; and, within this circle, those of the Donjon tower. On the right below is the town of Petit Andeli [*sic*], and the course of the Seine; while on the left a similar sweep of the river assists in forming the peninsula of Bernieres."

[9] *Journal*, November–December 1897, Archives Signac, quoted in Marina Ferretti Bocquillon, *Paul Signac* (Martigny: Fondation Pierre Gianadda, 2003), 178.

[10] Archives Signac, quoted in John Rewald, "Extraits du Journal inédit de Paul Signac III, 1898-1899," *Gazette des Beaux-Arts*, July–August 1953, 32. For Signac and Turner, see in particular Marina Ferretti Bocquillon, " The Artist of Whom I Think Most Often is Turner", *Signac Watercolors* (Paris: Vilo International, 2001), 66–73. A sketchbook from the Cabinet des Arts graphiques of the musée du Louvre containing the watercolor studies of Turner's works in The National Gallery executed by the artist during his stay in London in the spring of 1898 is now at the musée d'Orsay.

[11] Paris, April 1898, John Rewald, "Extraits du Journal inédit de Paul Signac II, 1897-1898," *Gazette des Beaux-Arts*, April 1952, 279. English translation on p. 302.

[12] 29 March 1899, John Rewald, "Extraits du Journal inédit de Paul Signac III, 1898-1899," *Gazette des Beaux-Arts*, July–August 1953, 51–52. English translation on p. 78.

[13] Drawing in pen and ink with the annotation "*D'après Turner*," (After Turner) 19.2 x 15.5 cm, published in Ferretti Bocquillon, op. cit., 179, cat. 81.

[14] See the letter from Camille Pissarro to Lucien, Paris, Wednesday [first half of June 1886], published in Janine Bailly-Herzberg, *Correspondance de Camille Pissarro, 1886-1890* (Paris: Éditions du Valhermeil, Vol. 2, 1986), 54, no. 339.
Ten canvases were painted during this first stay: *Les Andelys. The Riverside*, August (musée d'Orsay, Paris, FC 128), *Hillside from Downstream, Les Andelys*, September (The Art Institute of Chicago, FC 125), *Les Andelys, The Island of Lucas*, June–July (Private collection, FC 119), *Les Andelys, Château-Gaillard*, June–July (William Rockhill Nelson Gallery, Kansas City, FC 120), *Les Andelys. Setting Sun*, August (present location unknown, FC 121), *Les Andelys, Port Morin*, June–July (United States, Private collection, FC 122), *Les Andelys, Bathing*, August (Private collection FC 123), *Les Andelys, The Washerwomen*, August (Private collection, Paris, FC 124), *Les Andelys, The Quay* (Norton Simon Museum of Arts, Los Angeles, FC 126), *Les Andelys, The Bridge*, September (Ise Cultural Foundation, Tokyo, FC 127).

[15] Signed autograph letter from Georges Seurat to Paul Signac, 25 June 1886, Archives Signac, quoted in Marina Ferretti Bocquillon, *Signac 1863-1935* (New York: The Metropolitan Museum of Art, 2001), 121. I wish to express my particular gratitude to Françoise Cachin who allowed me to consult the Signac Archives and to retranscribe the letters cited in this text.

[16] Signed autograph letter to Lucien Pissarro dated 24 July 1886 (Ashmolean Museum, Oxford). I wish to thank Colin Harrison, curator, for making the whole of this letter available to me.

[17] Signed autograph letter with no indication of place or date [summer 1886] quoted in *Archives de Camille Pissarro*, Hôtel Drouot auction, Friday 21 November 1975, Paris, M. Castaing, 1975, lot no. 166 (Étienne et Antoine Ader, Jean-Louis Picard, Jacques Tajan).

[18] Signed autograph letter from Lucien Pissarro to Camille Pissarro, Le Petit Andely, Sunday, mid-August 1886, published in Anne Thorold (ed.), *The Letters of Lucien to Camille Pissarro, 1883-1903* (Cambridge: Cambridge University Press, Department of Western Art, Ashmolean Museum Oxford, 1993), 69.

[19] Namely *Les Andelys, Château-Gaillard, Les Andelys, The Island of Lucas, Les Andelys, Port Morin* and *Les Andelys, Bathing*.

[20] Félix Fénéon, "IIe Exposition de la Société des Artistes Indépendants," *Les Impressionnistes en 1886* (Paris: publications de La Vogue, 1886), 39.

[21] Félix Fénéon, "L'Impressionnisme aux Tuileries," *L'Art moderne* (Brussels), 19 September 1886, 301.

[22] Related works: drawing in Comté crayon, 1886, 23 x 0.5 cm, Private collection; color lithograph, Les Andelys, 1895, 30.3 x 45.3 cm (printer: Auguste Clot, publisher: Gustave Pellet), reproduction in E. W. Kornfled & P. A. Wick, *Catalogue raisonné de l'œuvre gravé et lithographié de Paul Signac* (Berne: Éditions Kornfeld et Klipstein, 1974), no. 10.
[23] The others were *Les Andelys. The Bridge* and *Riverbank, Les Andelys*.
[24] Gustave Kahn, "La Vie Artistique," *La Vie moderne*, 9 April 1887, 230, quoted in Ferretti Bocquillon, *Signac 1863-1935*, op. cit., 122.
[25] Jules Christophe, "Les Évolutionnistes du Pavillon de la Ville de Paris," *Journal des artistes*, 24 April 1887, no. 16, 123.
[26] Félix Fénéon, "L'Impressionnisme," *L'Émancipation sociale* (Narbonne), 3 April 1887, 67.
[27] [Paul Alexis] Trublot, "À Minuit. L'Exposition des Artistes Indépendants," *Le Cri du peuple*, 26 March 1887, 3.
[28] Jean Le Fustec, "Exposition des Artistes Indépendants," *Journal des artistes*, 10 April 1887, no. 14, 108.
[29] Marina Ferretti Bocquillon, *Le néo-impressionnisme : de Seurat à Paul Klee*, exh, cat. (Paris: Éditions de la Réunion des musées nationaux / musée d'Orsay, 2005), 52. Signac offered *Les Andelys, The Island of Lucas* to the writer Charles Torquet, *Sunset, Les Andely* to Félix Fénéon, *Les Andelys. Port Morin* to Léon Lemonnier, *Les Andelys, Bathing* to Camille Pissarro and *Riverbank, Les Andelys* to his mother Héloïse Signac as well as *Les Andelys, The Quay* to the painter Adolphe Albert, *Les Andelys, The Bridge* to Léon Lemonier and *Hillside from Downstream, Les Andelys* to Alexandre Charpentier.
[30] Signed autograph letter from Paul Signac to Félix Fénéon [12 July 1921]: "How delighted I would be to see you before our imminent departure for Les Andelys" (Archives Signac). See the letter from Signac to Louis and Juliette Cambier dated 29 October 1921: "Claude Monet just bought 7 watercolors from me," Paris, The Librairie des Neuf Muses, March 1991, Catalogue, no. 189, quoted in Ferretti Bocquillon, "Watercolors Rise to Fame," *Signac Watercolors*, op. cit., 62 and note 46, 140. Four of these watercolors are now at the musée Marmottan Monet (Bequest of Michel Monet, 5032, 5046, 5058, 5074).
[31] Gustave Kahn, "Art. L'exposition des Indépendants," *Mercure de France*, 1 March 1922, 487.
[32] Signed autograph letter to Claude Monet, 4 May 1923, quoted in *Précieux manuscrits et lettres autographes*, Hôtel Drouot auction, 24 January 1972, Paris, Mrs. J. Vidal-Mégret, 1972, lot no. 219 (Maurice Rheims and René Laurin). See also the signed, autograph letter to Claude Monet of 22 September 1923, quoted in *Autographes de peintres*, Hôtel Marcel Dassault auction, 22 June 2001, Paris, T. Bodin, 2001, lot no. 108 (Francis Briest and Thierry Bodin).
[33] Signed autograph letter from Signac to Fénéon, 13 August [1923], Archives Signac.
[34] Signed autograph letter to Signac to Fénéon, [18 September 1923] Petit Andely, Archives Signac.
[35] Gustave Kahn, "Art. Les Indépendants," *Mercure de France*, 1 March 1924, 479.
[36] Robert Rey, "Le Trente-Cinquième Salon des Indépendants," *Art et Décoration*, March 1924, 79.
[37] Gilbert Guisan and Doris Jakubec, *Félix Vallotton. Documents pour une biographie et pour l'histoire d'une œuvre, Journal 1914-1921* [III.] (Lausanne/Paris: La Bibliothèque des Arts, 1973), 126. Vallotton mentioned his departure for Les Andelys in his journal on 2 September "We'll meet in Rouen to set off for Les Andelys and stay about a week. I'm haunted by ideas for paintings but it's all unorganized." In Gilbert Guisan and Doris Jakubec, op. cit., 125.
[38] Letter of 15 September 1916 (Fonds Félix Vallotton, Bibliothèque cantonale et universitaire, Lausanne), quoted in Marina Ducrey, "Biographie," *Félix Vallotton 1865-1925, l'œuvre peint* [I] (Zurich/Lausanne: Institut suisse pour l'étude de l'art, Fondation Félix Vallotton, Lausanne. Milan: 5 Continents Editions, 2005), 63.
[39] Gilbert Guisan and Doris Jakubec, op. cit., 126.
[40] Ibidem.
[41] I wish to thank Marina Ducrey in particular for providing me for documentary purposes with photocopies of the eleven preparatory sketches for the paintings of 1916, 1917 and 1924.
[42] 17 September, quoted in Gilbert Guisan and Doris Jakubec, op. cit., 126.
[43] Gilbert Guisan and Doris Jakubec, op. cit., 127–28.
[44] N. S. "À travers les expositions. Exposition de Félix Vallotton (Galerie Druet)," *L'Art décoratif* (Paris), 5 February 1912, 4.
[45] For the pratice of amateur photography, see Marina Ducrey, "Vallotton à Honfleur et en Normandie," *Félix Vallotton (1865-1925), Honfleur et la Normandie* (Honfleur: Musée Eugène Boudin, 1999), 8–30, and *Félix Vallotton 1865-1925, l'œuvre peint*, I. A crucial work in this connection is Isabelle de la Brumière and Philippe Grapeloup-Roche, "Vallotton and the Camera. Art and the Science of Photography," *Apollo*, no. 388, June 1994, 18–23.
[46] 7 September, quoted in Gilbert Guisan and Doris Jakubec, op. cit., 126.
[47] 5 October, quoted in Gilbert Guisan and Doris Jakubec, op. cit., 128. For the concept of the "historical landscape" associated with Nicolas Poussin, see Jean-Baptiste Deperthes, *Histoire de l'art du paysage*

depuis la Renaissance des beaux-arts jusqu'au XVIIIe siècle (Paris: Le Normant, 1822).
[48] 9 October, quoted in Gilbert Guisan and Doris Jakubec, op. cit., 129.
[49] See in particular Jules Camus (for the Sidrot or Berthaud studio, Évreux), *Les Andelys (Eure). Ruines du Château-Gaillard (XIIe siècle)*, vers 1865, proof on albumin paper, in *La Normandie monumentale et pittoresque* [Vol. III] (Eure, Alexis-Guislain Lemâle, Le Havre, 1896, Vol. 1, pl. 30, 177), musée d'Évreux, AI1656. The Archives départementales de l'Eure, Évreux, hold several picture postcards with views of the Seine from the Château-Gaillard.
[50] Gilbert Guisan and Doris Jakubec, op. cit., 176.
[51] Ibid., 177.
[52] Letter of 28 June, quoted in Marina Ducrey, *Félix Vallotton. His Life, His Technique, His Paintings* (Lausanne: Edita, 1989), 146. The works produced during this stay include *Les Andelys, Evening* (Private collection, Switzerland, CR 1594, LRZ 1497), *The Seine at Andelys, Evening* (Private collection, France, CR 1596, LRZ 1499), *Evening at Andelys* (musée des beaux-arts, La Chaux-de-Fonds, CR 1598, LRZ 1501), *The Seine at Andelys, Full Sun* (Private collection, Switzerland, CR 1599, LRZ 1502), *Morning at Les Andelys* (Private collection, Switzerland, CR 1601, LRZ 1504), *The Seine at Les Andelys* (Private collection, Switzerland, CR 1602, LRZ 1505), *Les Andelys and the Château Gaillard* (musée municipal A.-G. Poulain, Vernon, CR 1595, LRZ 1498), *The Dome of the Hospital at Les Andelys* (Private collection, United States, CR 1597, LRZ 1500), *The Château Gaillard* (musée cantonal des beaux-arts, Lausanne, CR1600, LRZ 1503).
[53] Pierre du Colombier, "Arts. Le Salon d'Automne. Peinture," *L'Opinion. Journal de la semaine* (Paris), 7 November 1924, no. 74, 13.

catalogue

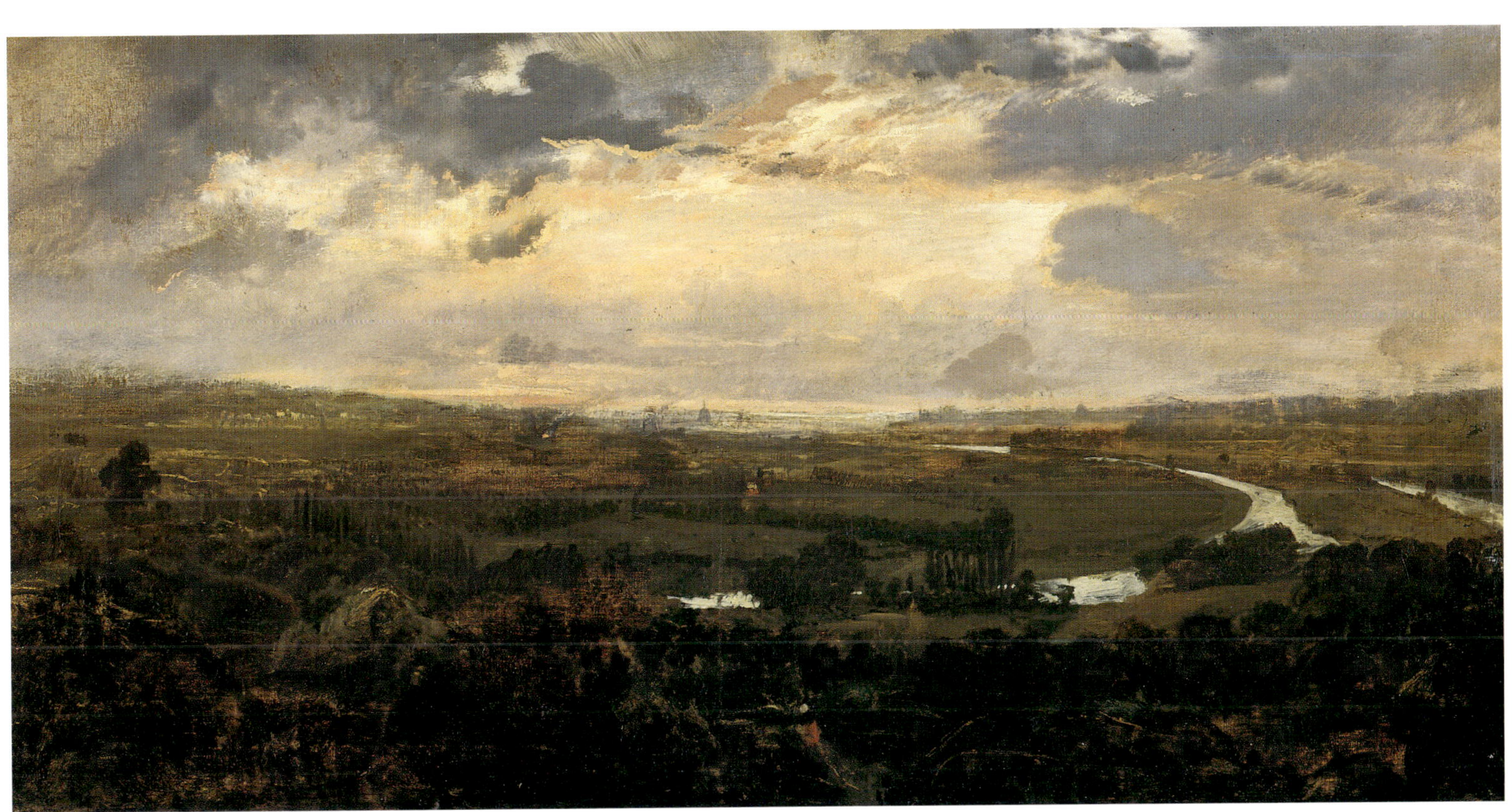

1. Théodore Rousseau

Paris from the Saint-Cloud Terrace, 1832–33
Oil on canvas, 61 × 115 cm (24 × 45 ¼ in.)
Signed lower left, MS 106
Musées royaux des Beaux-Arts de Belgique, Brussels, 4306

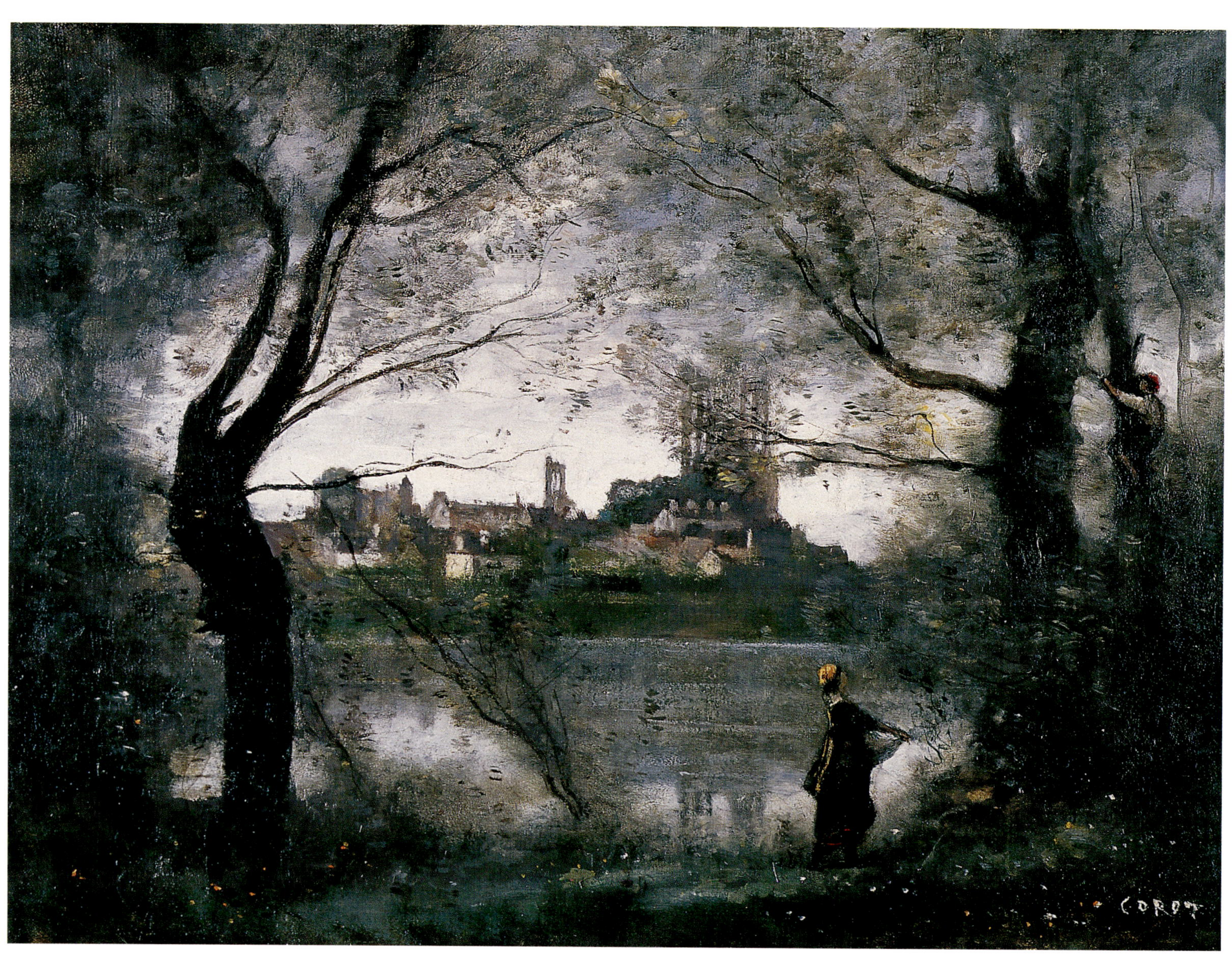

4. Camille Corot

Mantes, View of the Cathedral and the Town through the Trees, Evening or *Mantes, Gathering Mistletoe*, c. 1860–65
Oil on canvas, 42.7 × 55.8 cm (16 ¾ × 22 in.)
Signed lower right
Musée des Beaux-Arts, Reims, 887.23.2

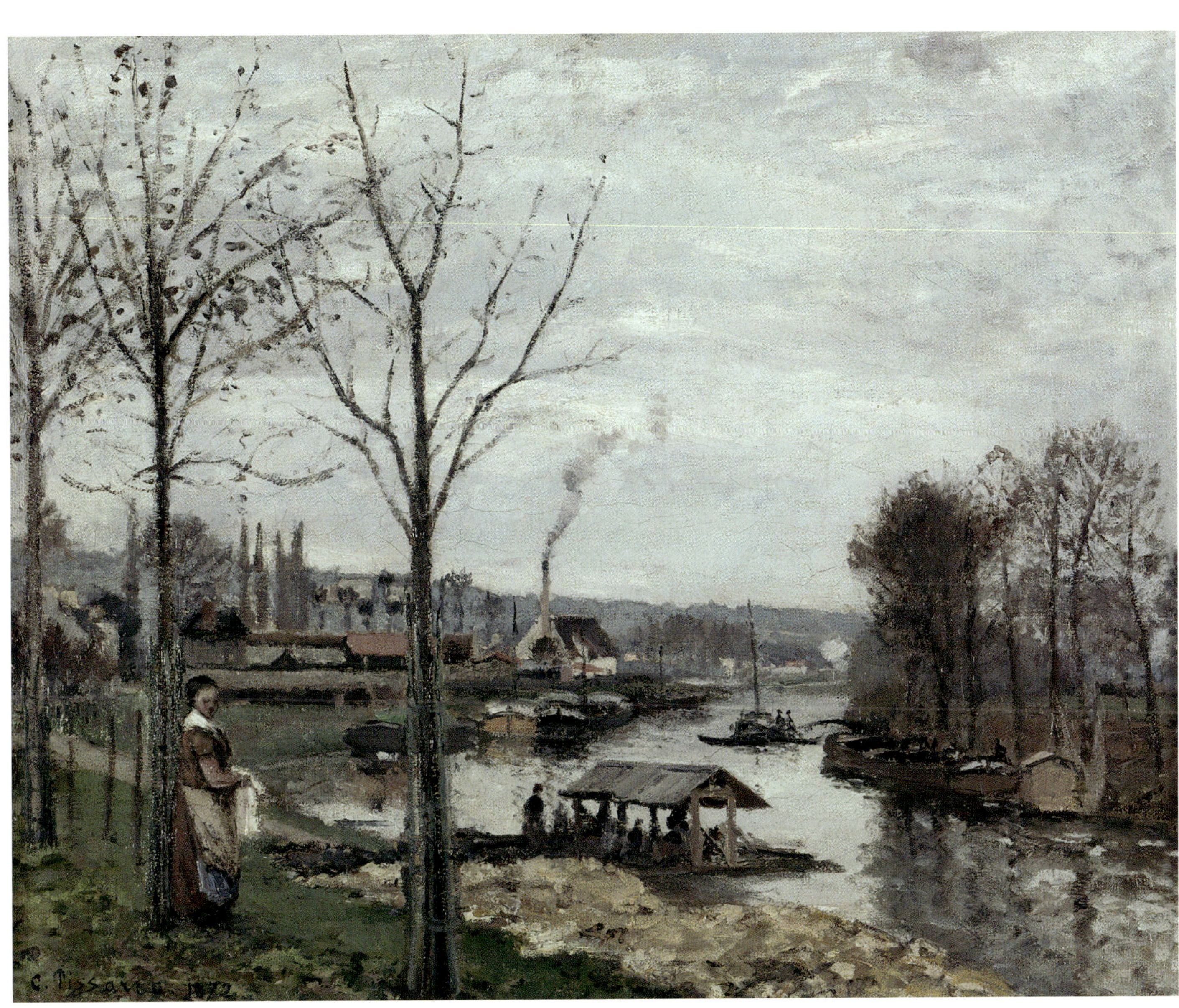

5. Camille Pissarro

The Seine at Port-Marly, the Wash House, 1872
Oil on canvas, 46.5 × 56 cm (18 ¼ × 22 in.)
Signed and dated lower left, P et D-RS 229
Musée d'Orsay, Paris
Bequest of Gustave Caillebotte, 1894, RF 2732

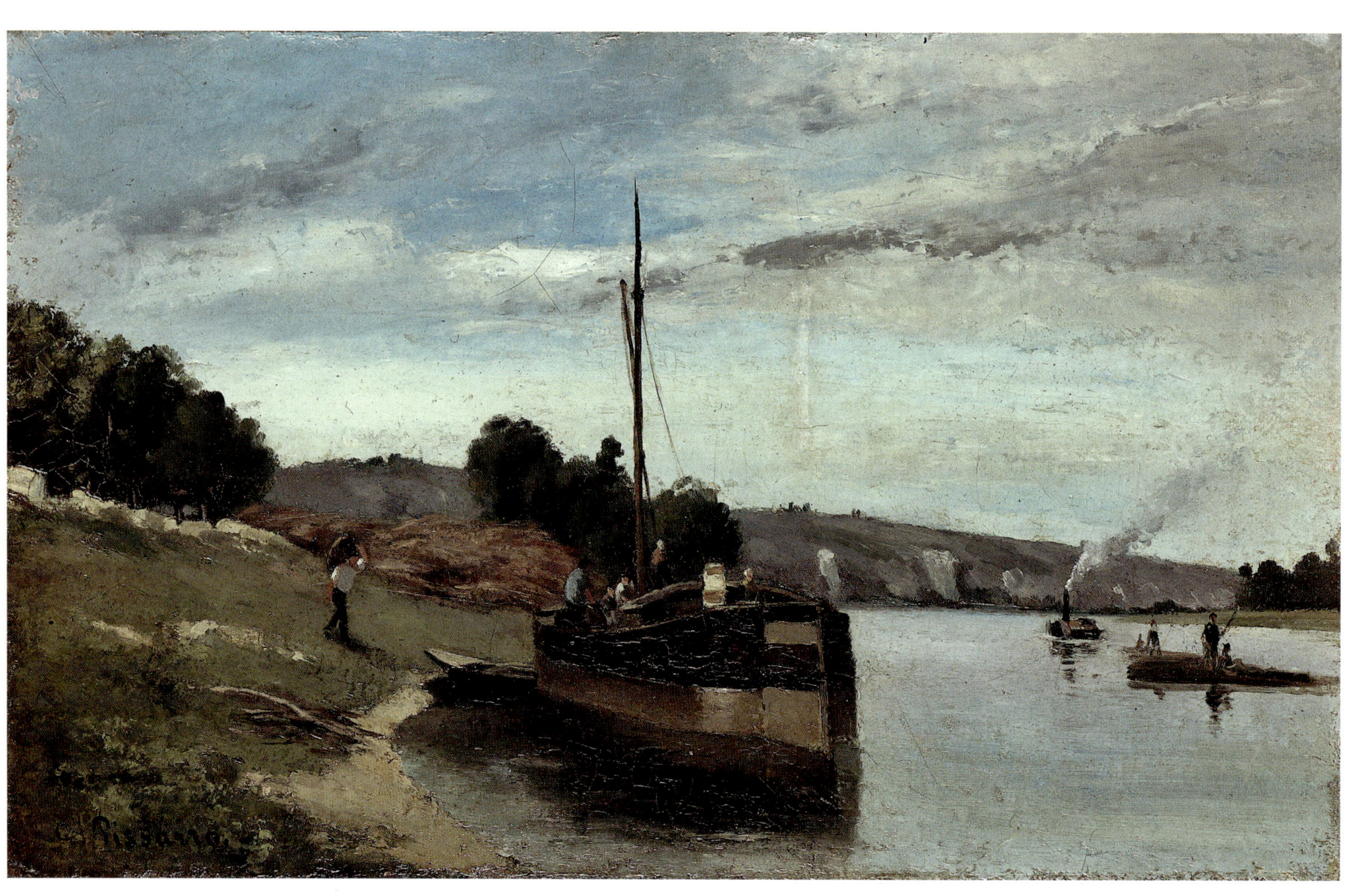

6. Camille Pissarro

Barge on the Seine, c. 1863
Oil on canvas, 46 × 72 cm (18 ¼ × 28 ¼ in.)
Signed lower left, P et D-RS 79
Musée Camille Pissarro, Pontoise, P.1980.3

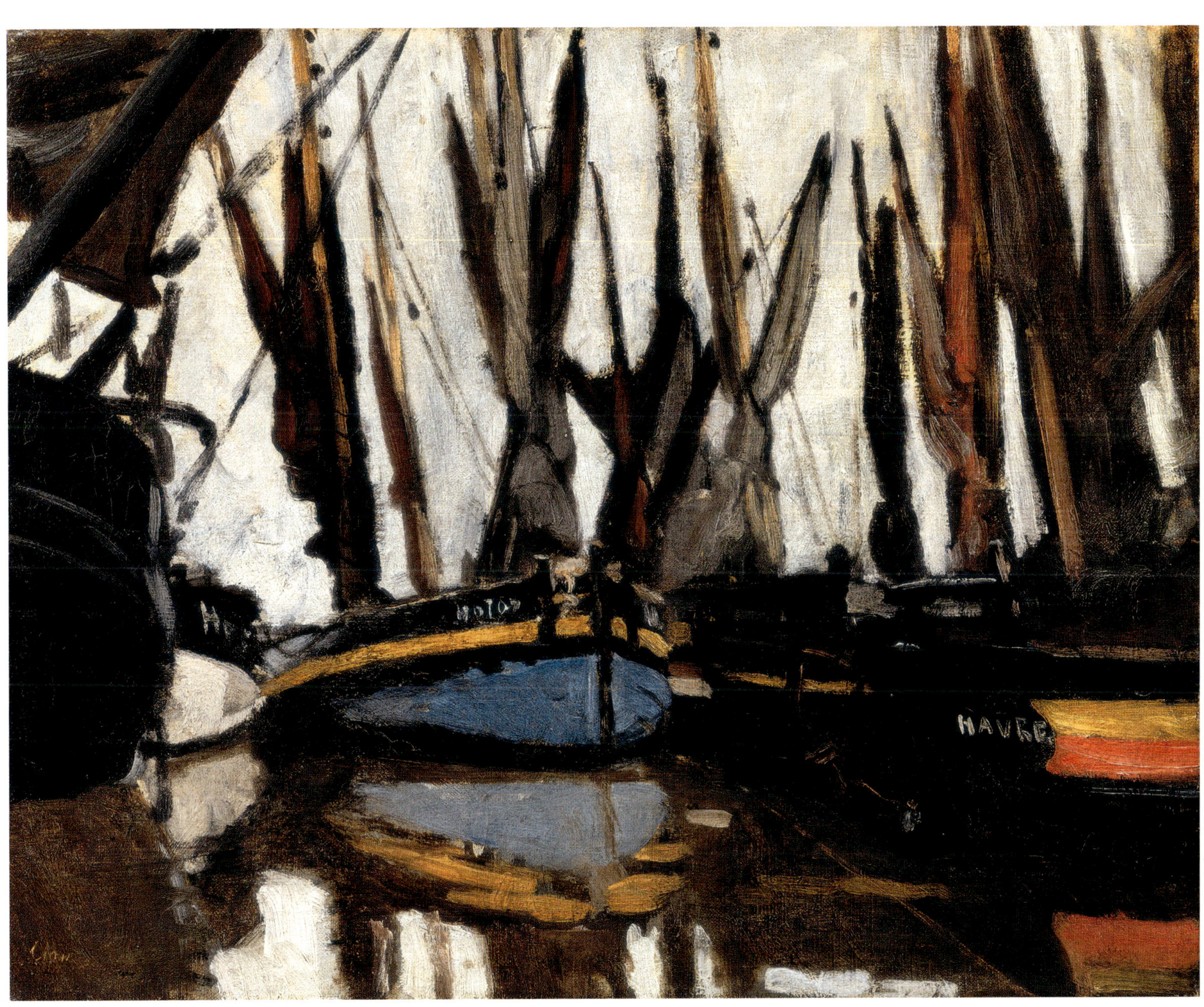

7. Claude Monet

Fishing Boats, Honfleur, 1866
Oil on canvas, 46 × 55 cm (18 × 21 ¾ in.)
Unsigned. Partial signature lower left « *Clau* », W76
Private collection, on long term loan at the Van Gogh Museum, Amsterdam

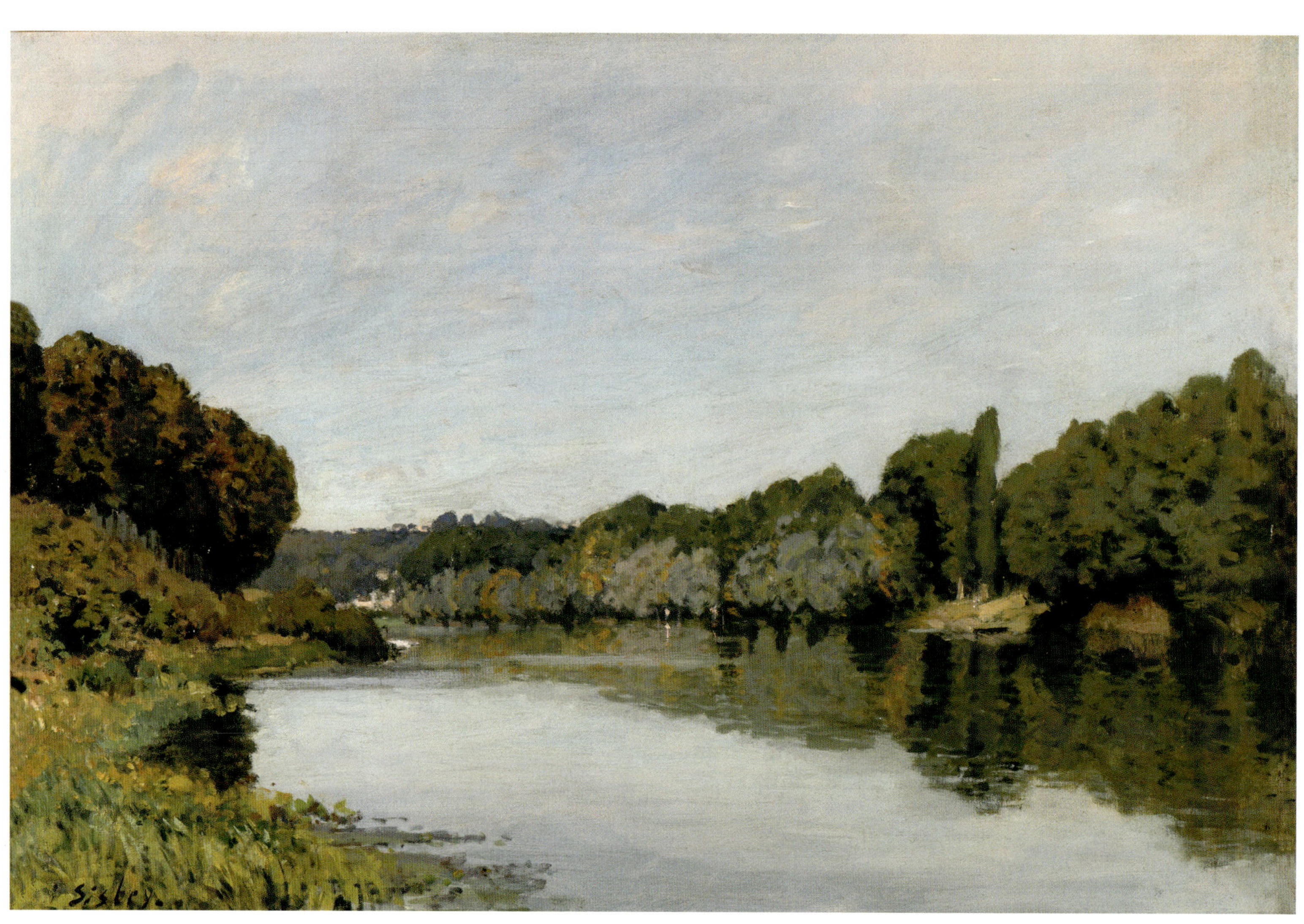

8. Alfred Sisley

The Seine at Bougival, 1873
Oil on canvas, 46 × 65.5 cm (18 ¼ × 25 ¾ in.)
Signed lower left, FD 87
Musée d'Orsay, Paris, work recovered after the Second World War and entrusted to the musées nationaux, MNR 208

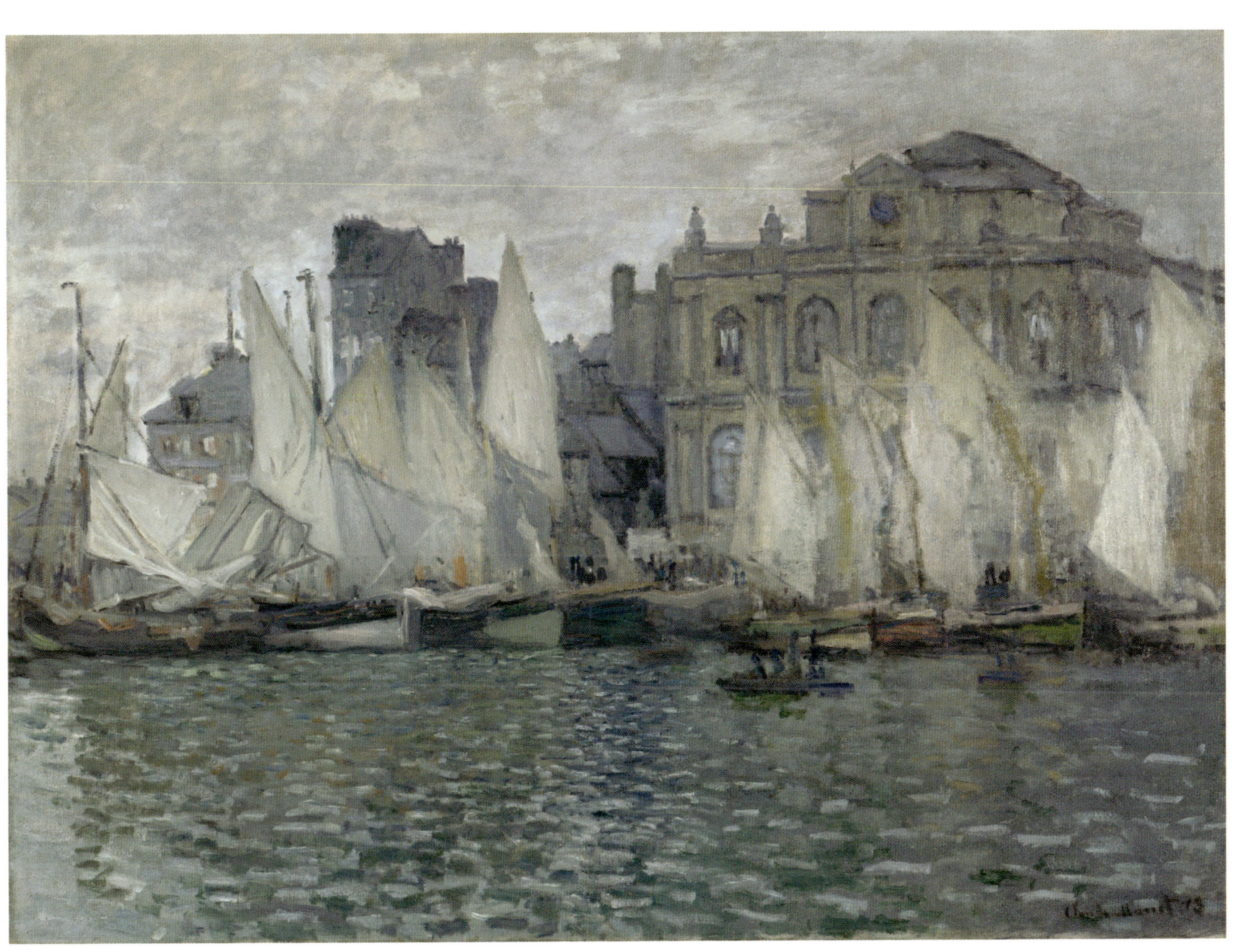

9. Claude Monet

The Museum at Le Havre, 1873
Oil on canvas, 75 × 100 cm (30 × 39 ½ in.)
Signed and dated lower right, W261
The National Gallery, London
Bequest of Helena and Kenneth Levy, 1990, NG6527

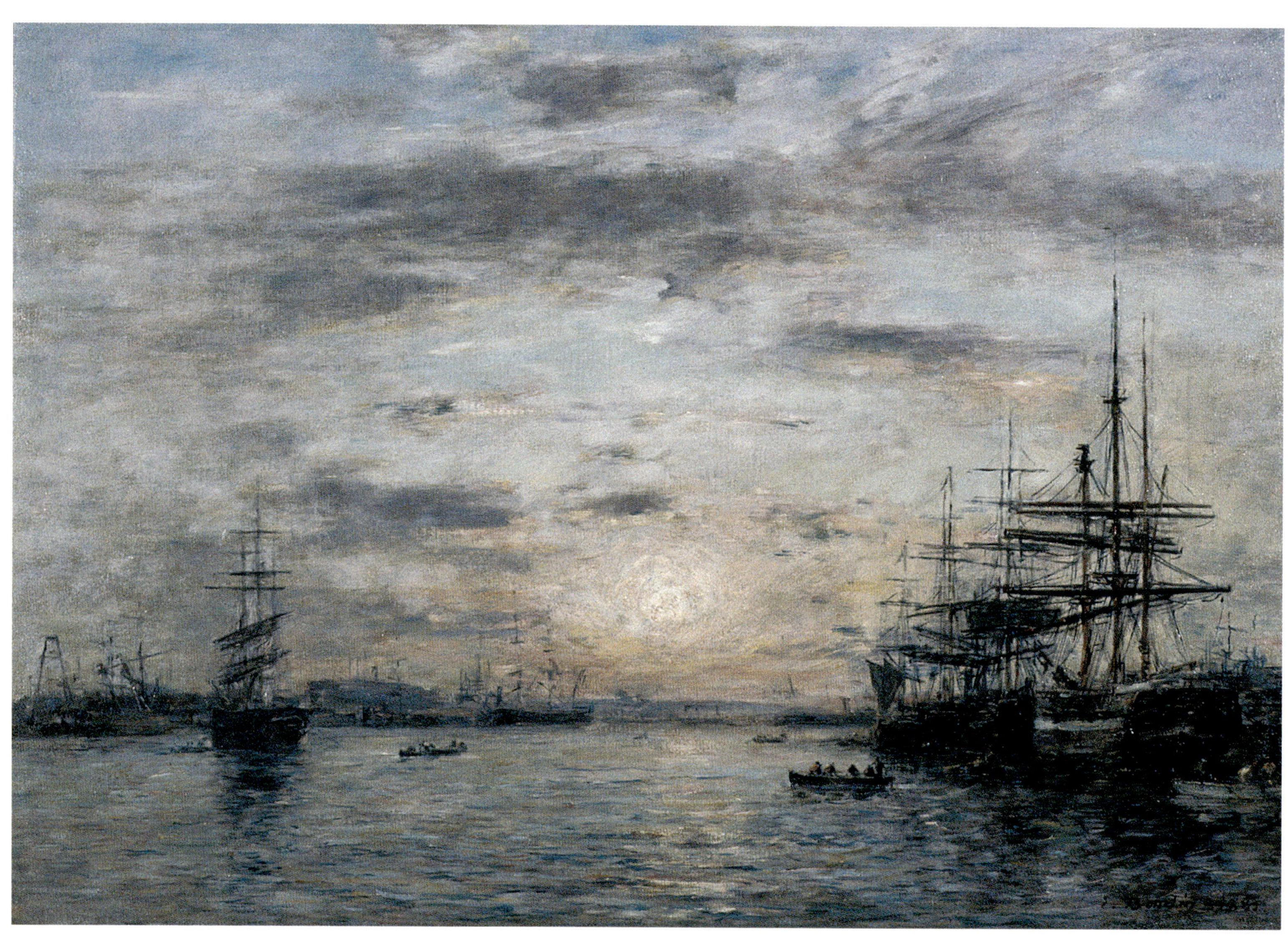

10. Eugène Boudin

Le Havre, Bassin de l'Eure, 1885
Oil on canvas, 65 × 90 cm (25 ½ × 35 ½ in.)
Signed and dated lower right, S 1939
Musée d'Art, Histoire et Archéologie, Évreux, 7859

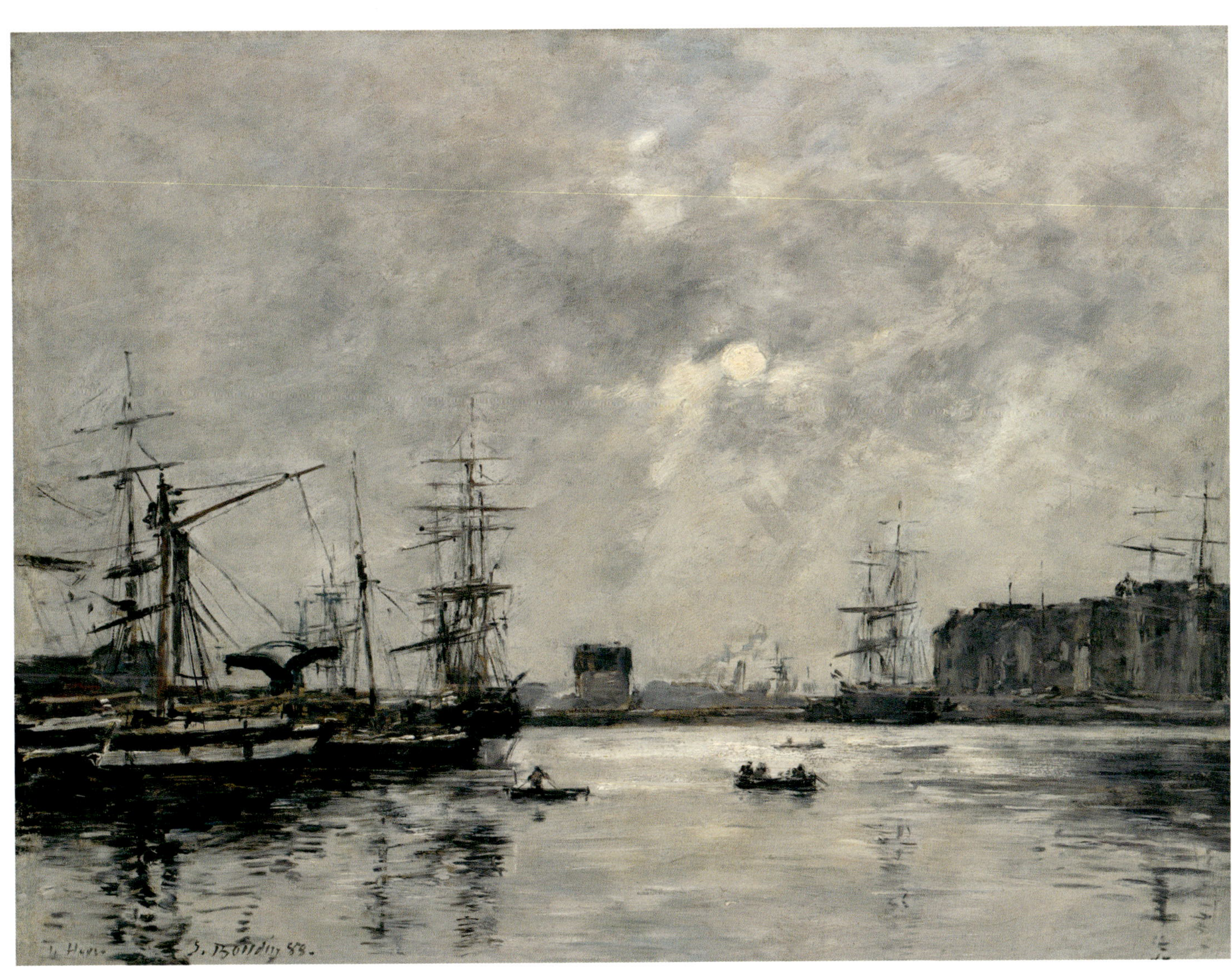

11. Eugène Boudin

Port of Le Havre, Bassin de la Barre, 1888
Oil on panel, 32 × 41 cm (12 ½ × 16 ¼ in.)
Signed and dated lower left
Musée d'Orsay, Paris
Bequest of James N.B. Hill, 1978, RF 1978-19

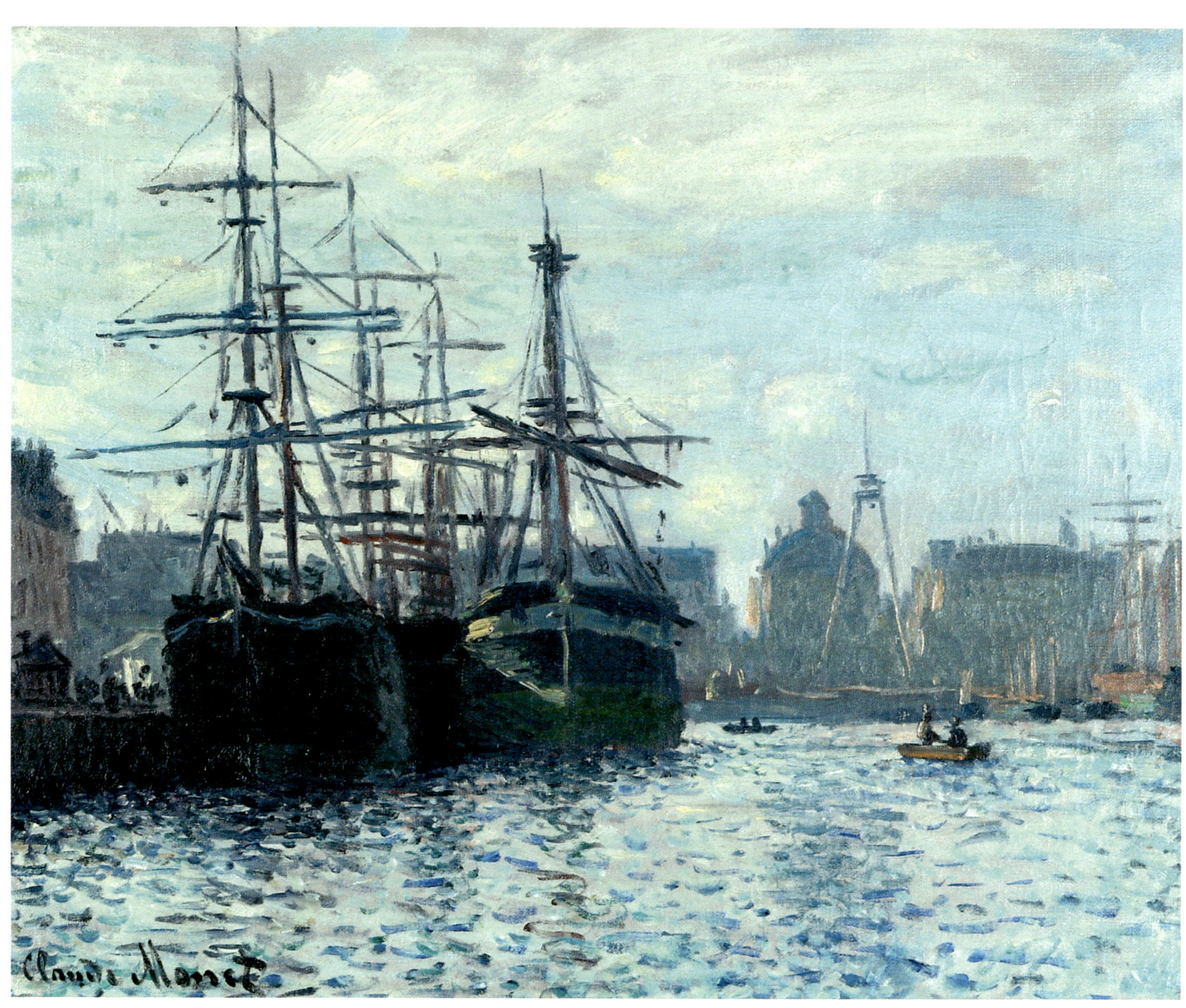

12. Claude Monet

The Bassin du Commerce in the Port of Le Havre, 1874
Oil on canvas, 38 × 46 cm (15 × 18 ¼ in.)
Signed lower left, W294
Collection of the Musée d'Art moderne et d'Art contemporain, Liège
Gift of Eugène Dumont, 1900, 399/151

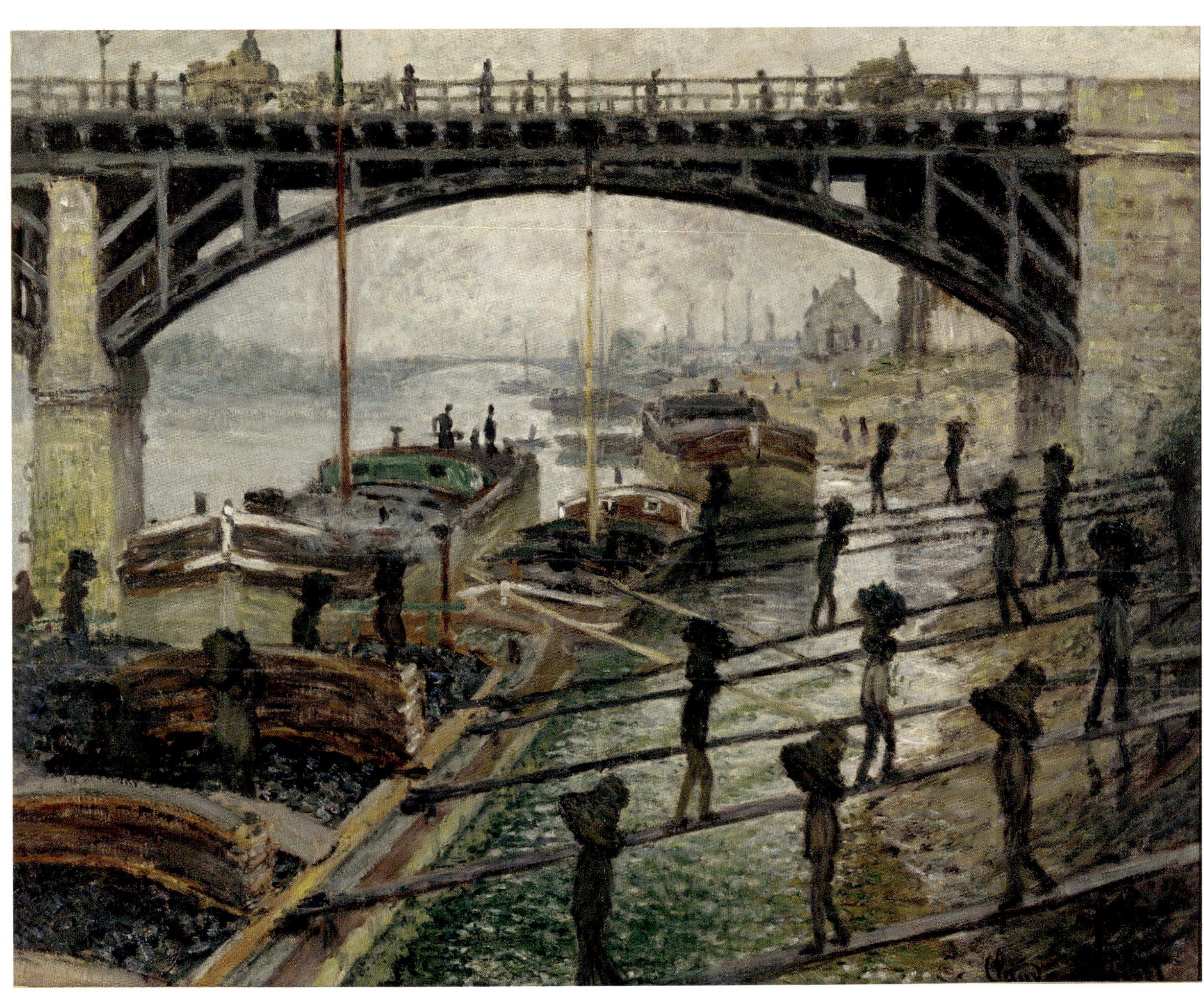

13. Claude Monet

The Coal-Dockers also known as *The Coalmen*, c. 1875
Oil on canvas, 55 × 66 cm (21 ½ × 26 in.)
Signed lower right, W364
Musée d'Orsay, Paris, RF 1993-21

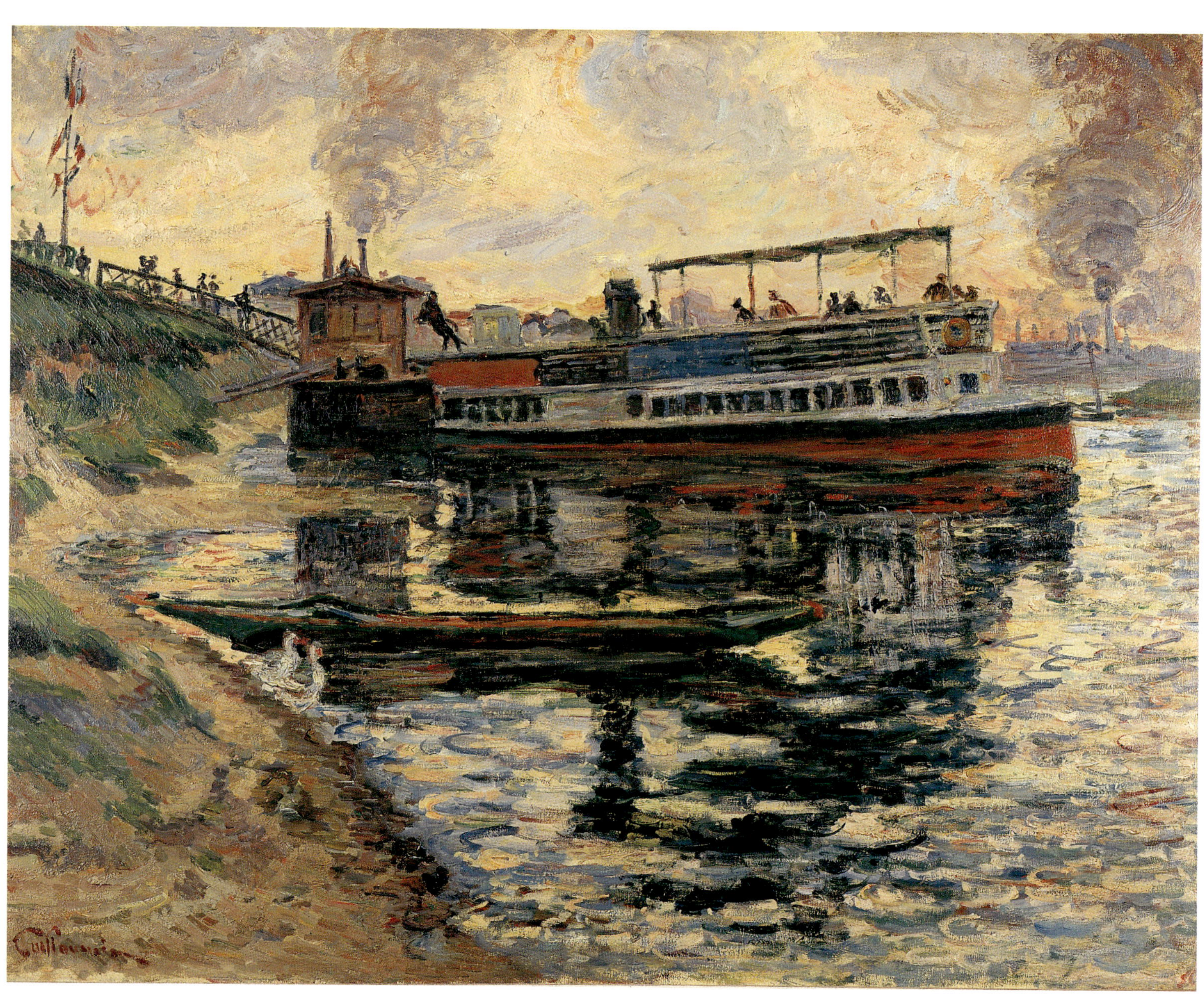

14. Armand Guillaumin

Riverboat (Charenton), c. 1875
Oil on canvas, 65 × 81 cm (25 ½ × 32 in.)
Signed lower left
Private collection
Courtesy of the Galerie Bernheim-Jeune, Paris

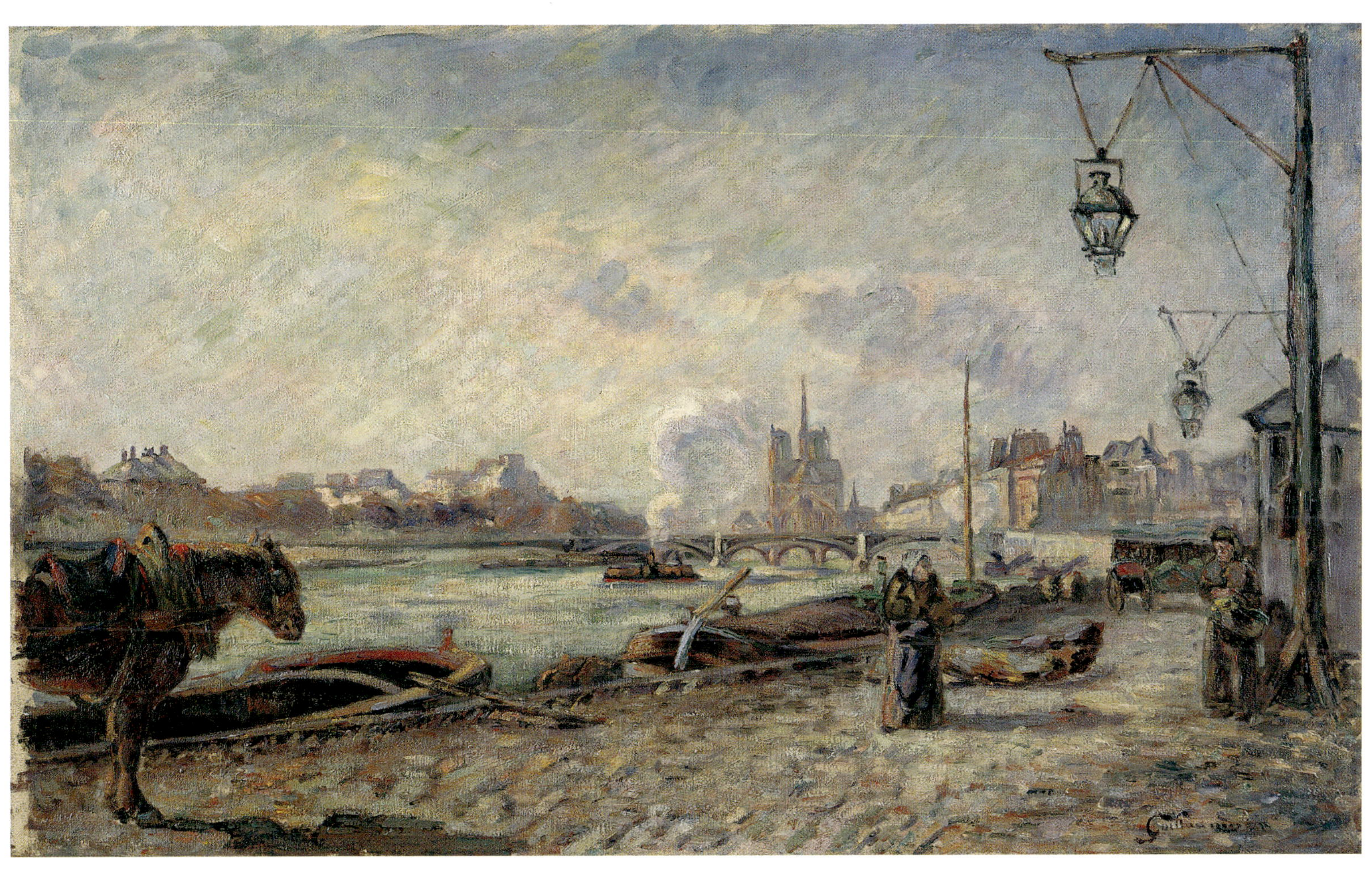

15. Armand Guillaumin

Quai de la Rapée, c. 1880
Oil on canvas, 50 × 79 cm (19 ¾ × 31 ¼ in.)
Signed lower right
Private collection

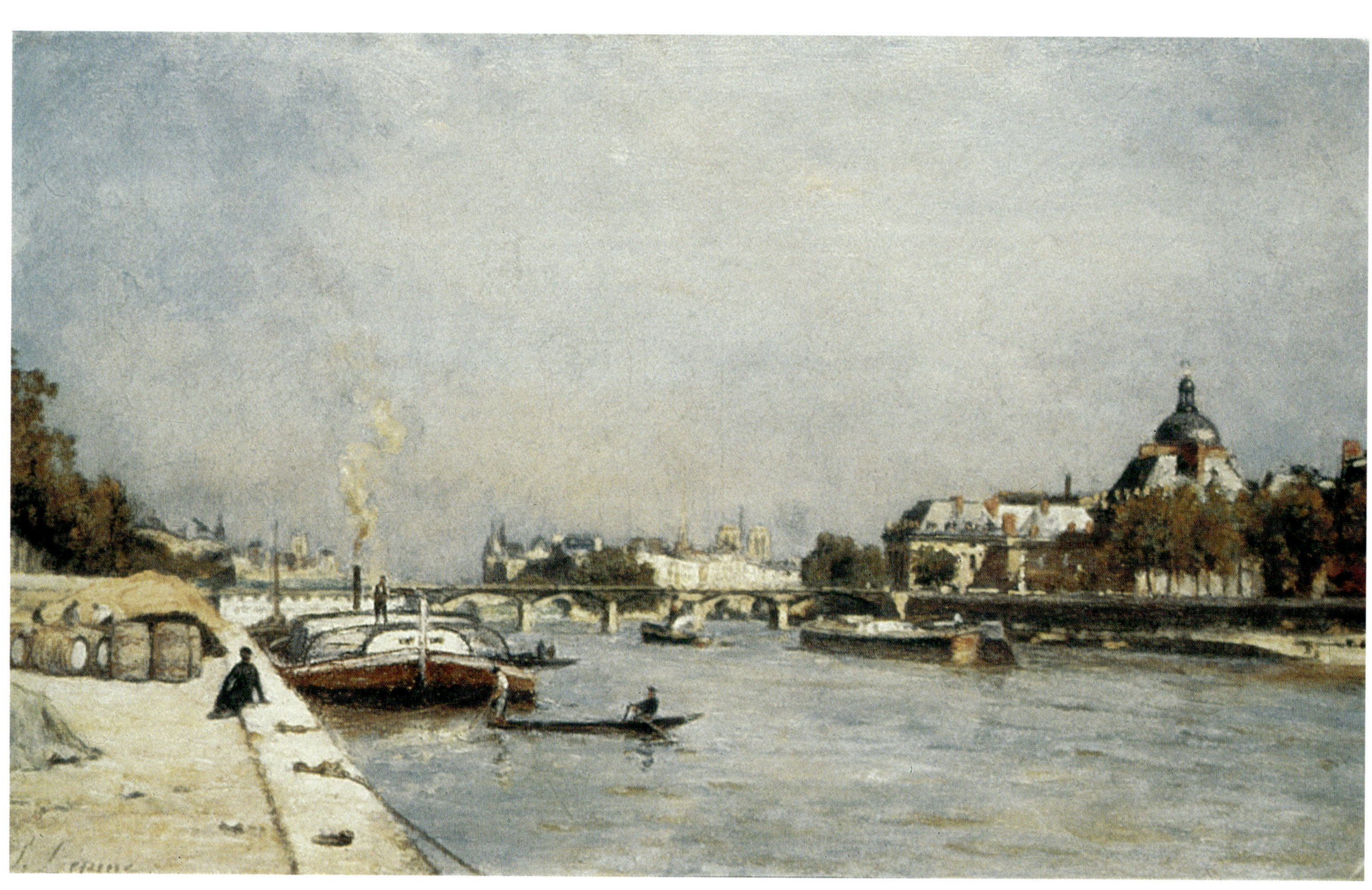

16. Stanislas Lépine

The Seine at Pont des Arts, c. 1878–83
Oil on canvas, 39 × 60 cm (15 ¼ × 23 ¾ in.)
Signed lower left, S 21
Fondation Bemberg, Toulouse, 2067

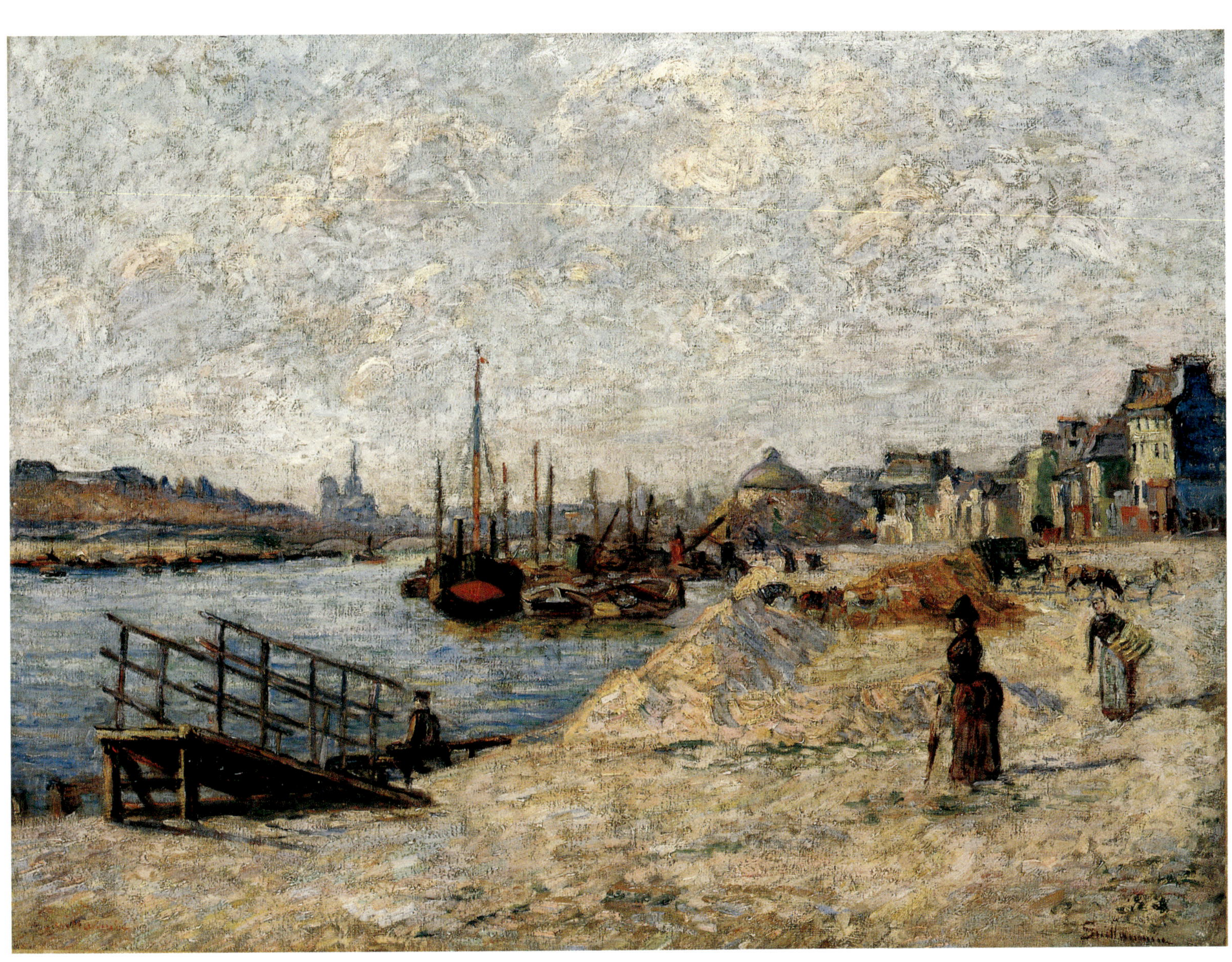

17. Armand Guillaumin

Quai de Bercy, c. 1881
Oil on canvas, 55 × 71 cm (21 ½ × 28 in.)
Signed lower right, SF 93
Association des Amis du Petit Palais, Geneva

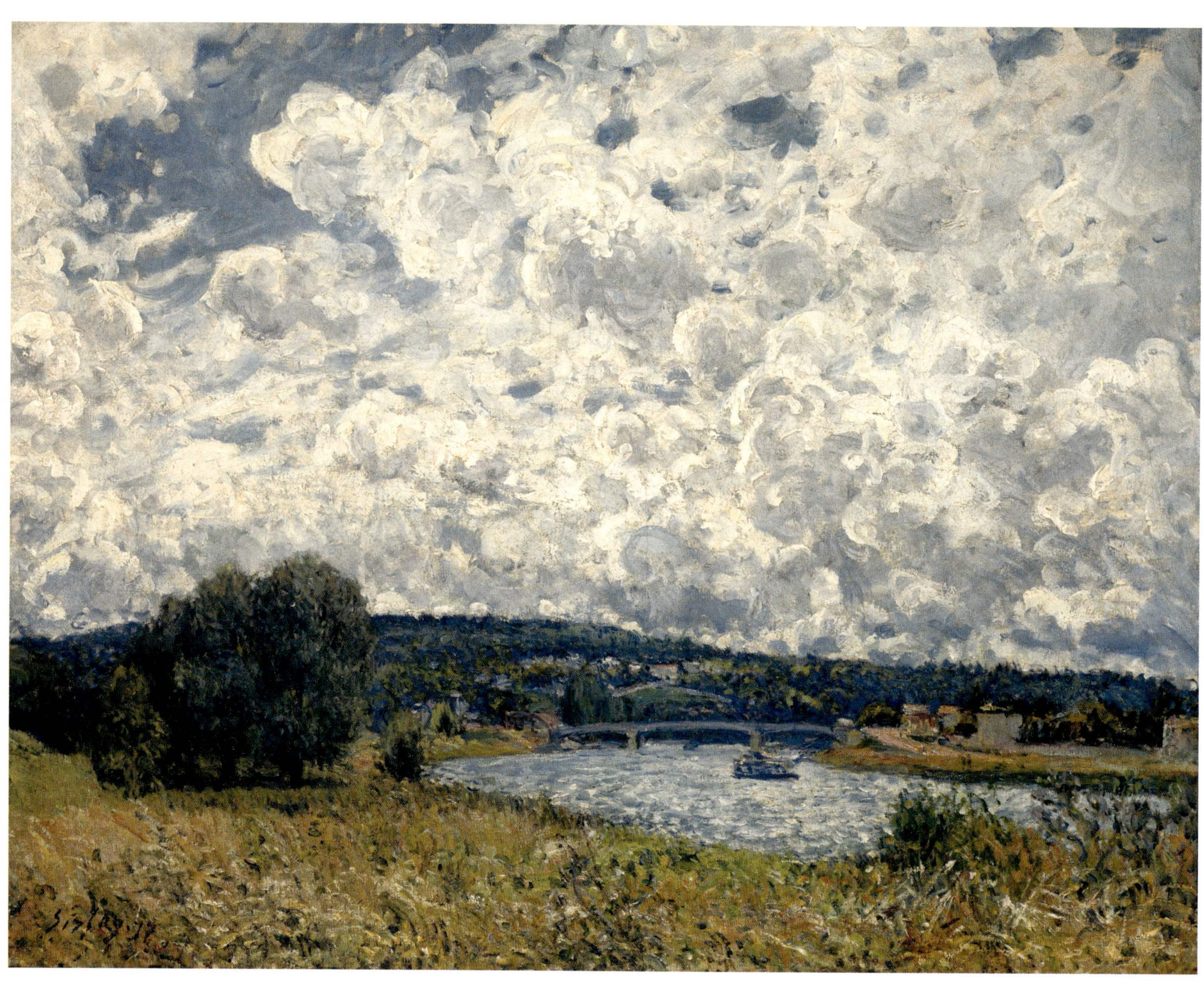

18. Alfred Sisley

The Seine at Suresnes, 1877
Oil on canvas, 60.5 × 73.5 cm (23 ¾ × 29 in.)
Signed and dated lower left, FD 267
Musée d'Orsay, Paris
Bequest of Gustave Caillebotte, 1894, RF 2786

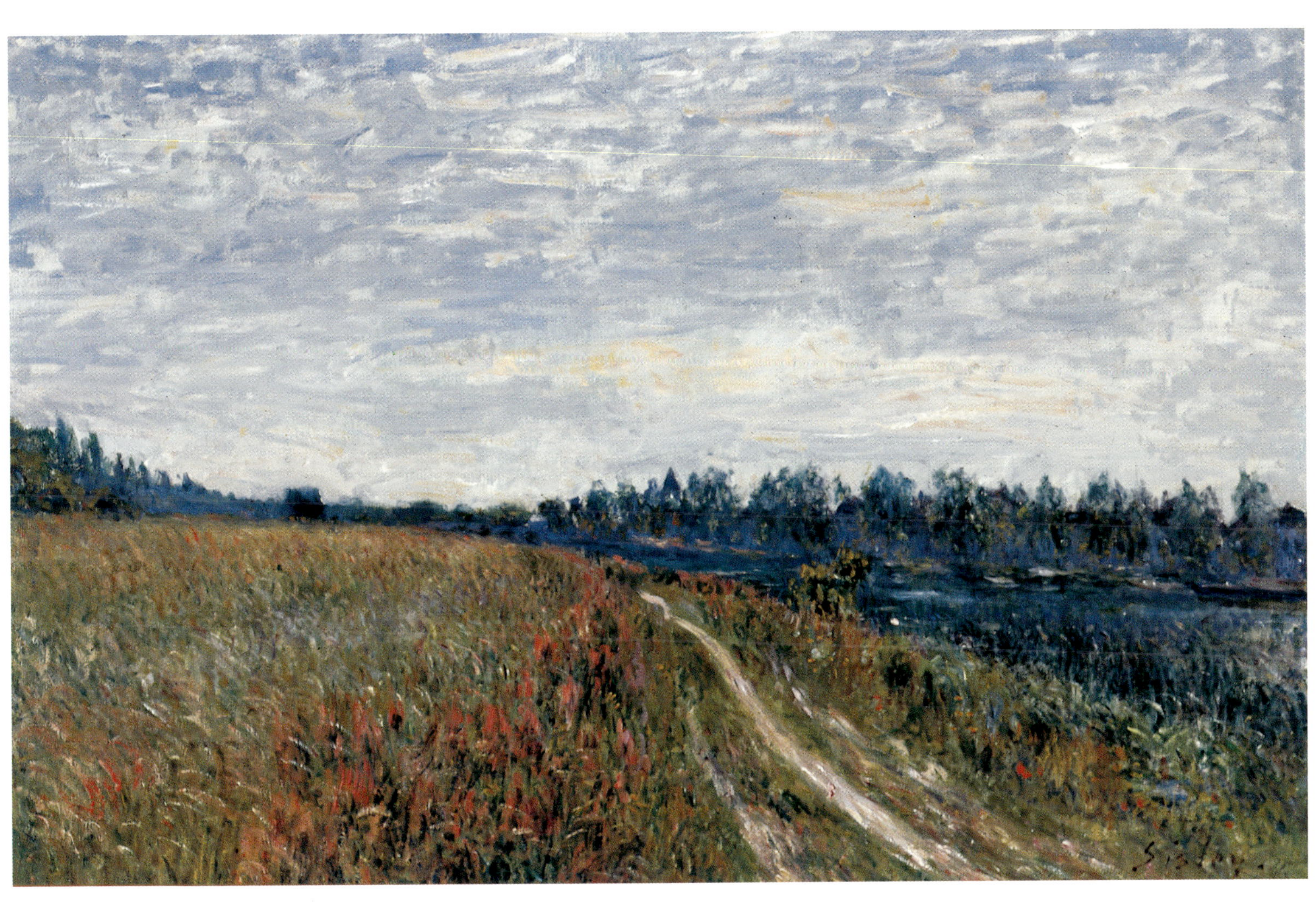

19. Alfred Sisley

The Prairie, 1880
Oil on canvas, 50 × 73 cm (19 ¾ × 28 ¾ in.)
Signed lower right, FD 377
Private collection

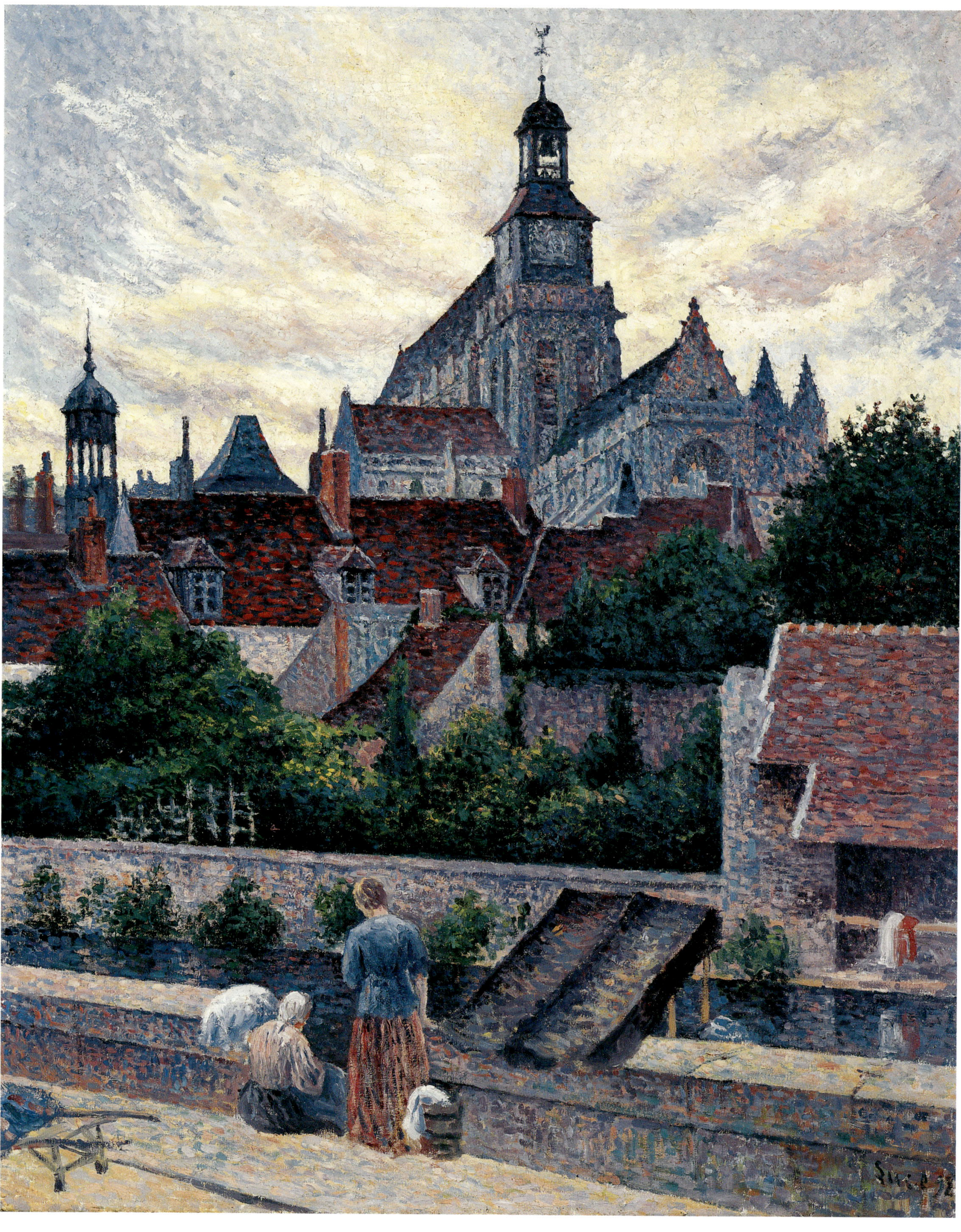

20. Maximilien Luce

Gisors Cathedral from the Fossé aux Tanneurs, 1898
Oil on canvas, 92 × 73 cm (36 ¼ × 28 ¾ in.)
Signed and dated lower right, JBL et DB 514
Private collection

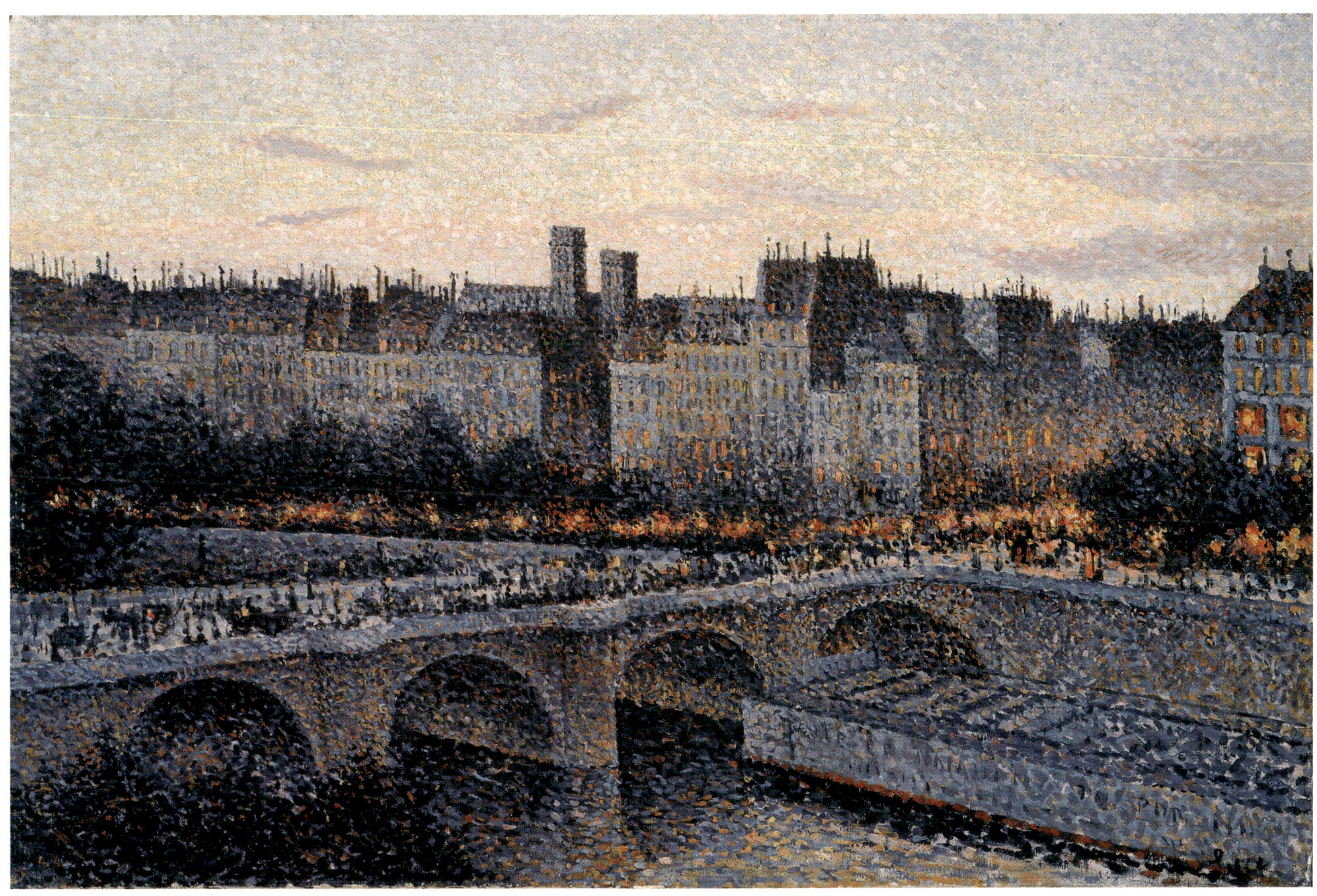

21. Maximilien Luce

Quai de l'École, Paris, Evening, 1889
Oil on canvas, 50.9 × 70 cm (20 × 27 ½ in.)
Signed lower right, JBL et DB 242
Private collection

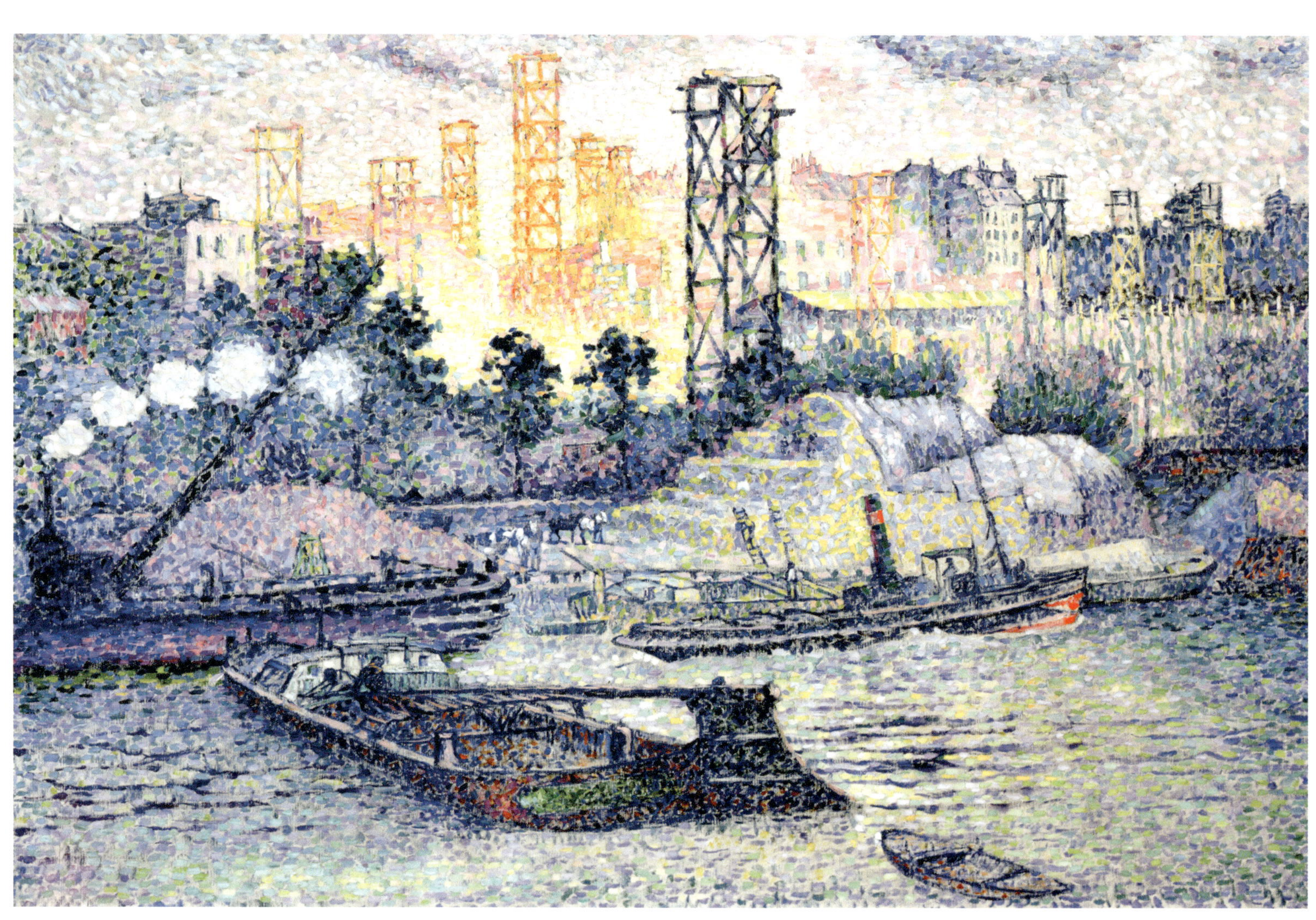

22. Henri-Edmond Cross

Quai de Passy, c. 1899
Oil on canvas, 65.5 × 92.1 cm (25 ¾ × 36 ¼ in.)
IC 76
Private collection

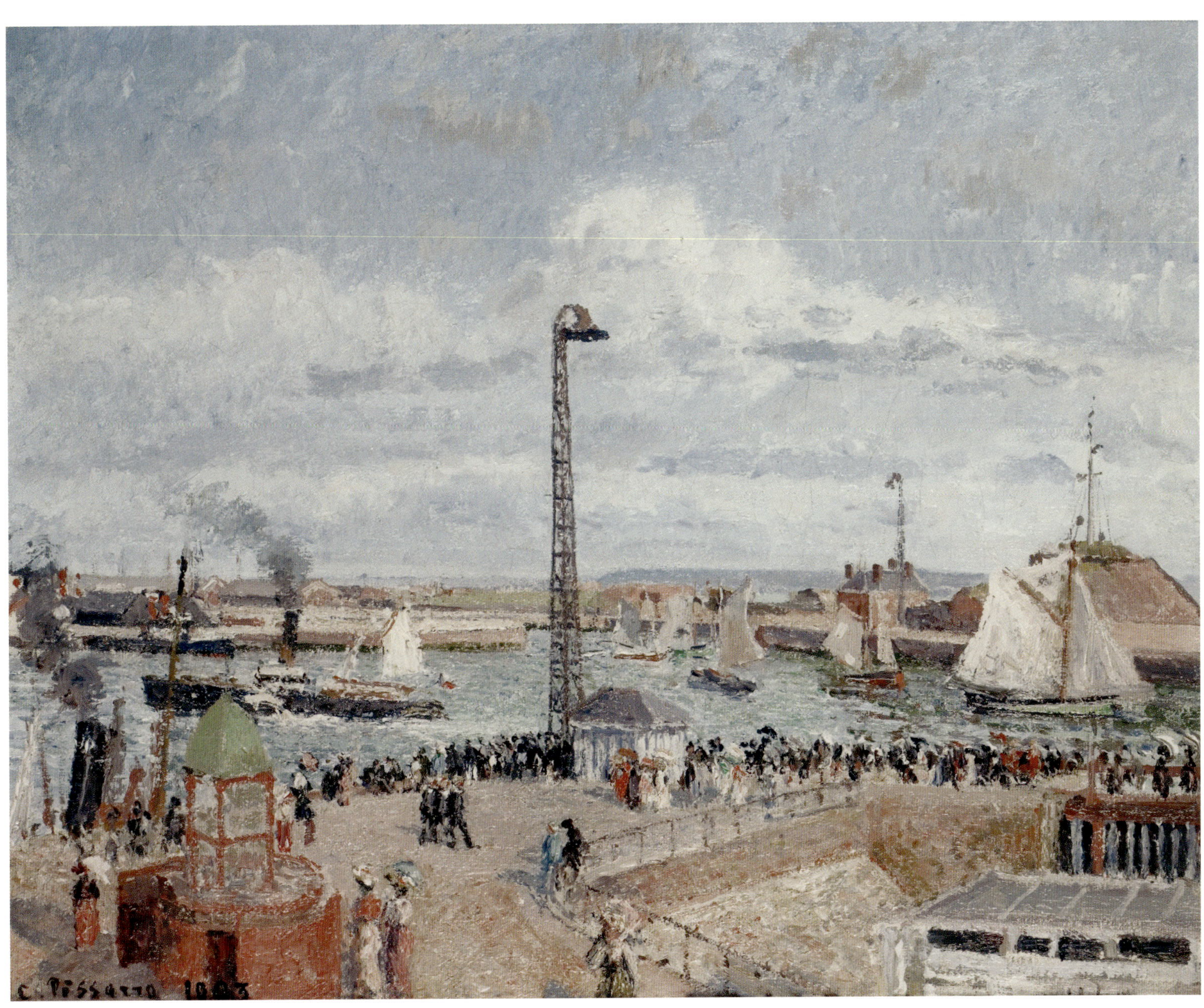

23. Camille Pissarro

The Pilots Jetty, Le Havre - High Tide, Afternoon Sun, 1903
Oil on canvas, 54.5 × 65.5 cm (21 ½ × 25 ¾ in.)
Signed and dated lower left, P et D-RS 1513
Musée Malraux, Ville du Havre, A 494

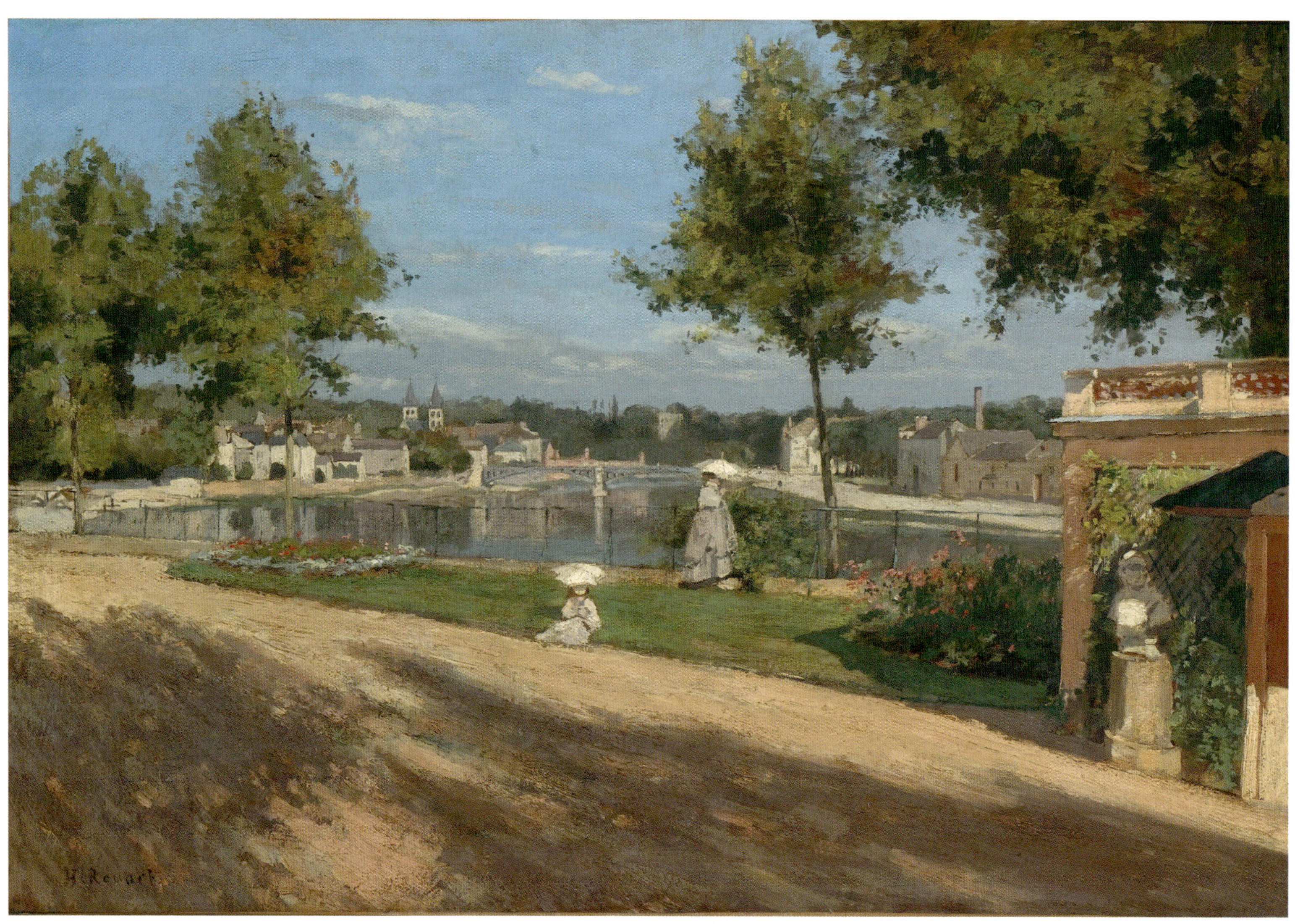

24. Henri Rouart

Terrace along the banks of the Seine at Melun, c. 1880
Oil on canvas, 46.5 × 65.5 cm (18 ¼ × 25 ¾ in.)
Signed lower left
Musée d'Orsay, Paris, RF 3832

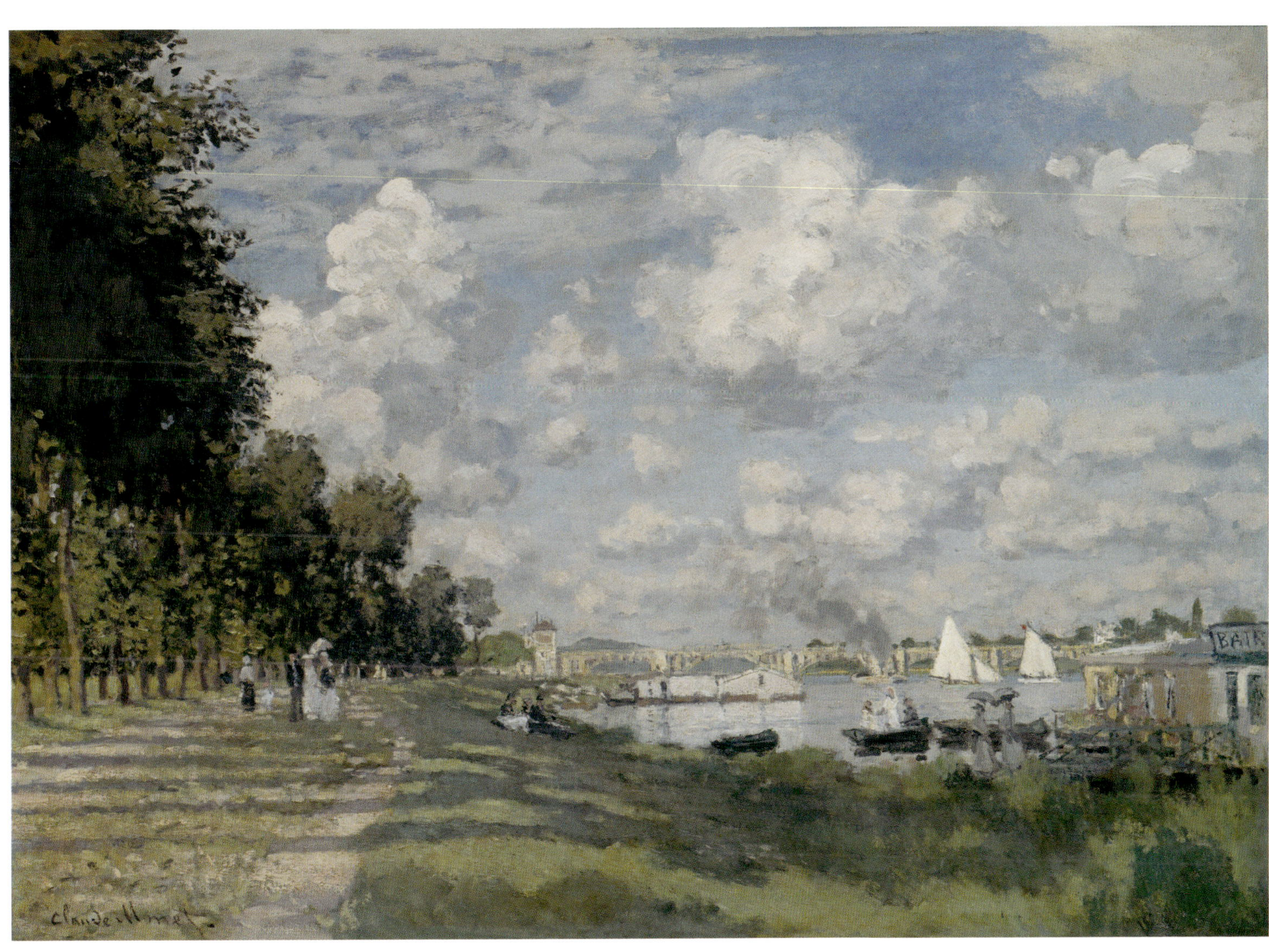

25. Claude Monet

The Port at Argenteuil, c. 1872
Oil on canvas, 60 × 80.5 cm (23 ¾ × 31 ¾ in.)
Signed lower left, W225
Musée d'Orsay, Paris
Bequest of Count Isaac Camondo, 1911, RF 2010

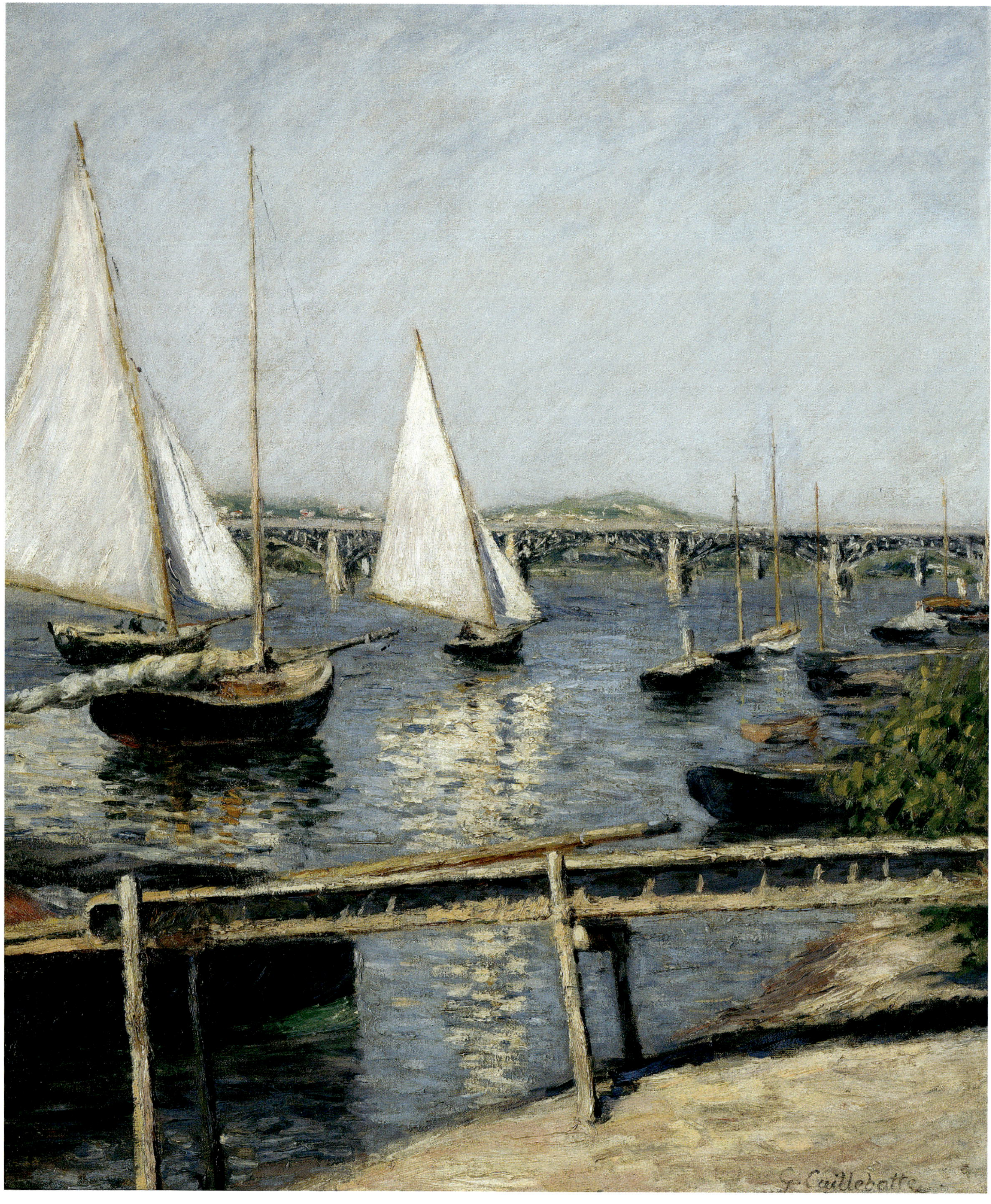
G. Caillebotte

26. Gustave Caillebotte

Sailing Boats at Argenteuil, c. 1888
Oil on canvas, 65 × 55 cm (25 ½ × 21 ¾ in.)
Signed lower right, MB 214
Musée d'Orsay, Paris, RF 1954-31

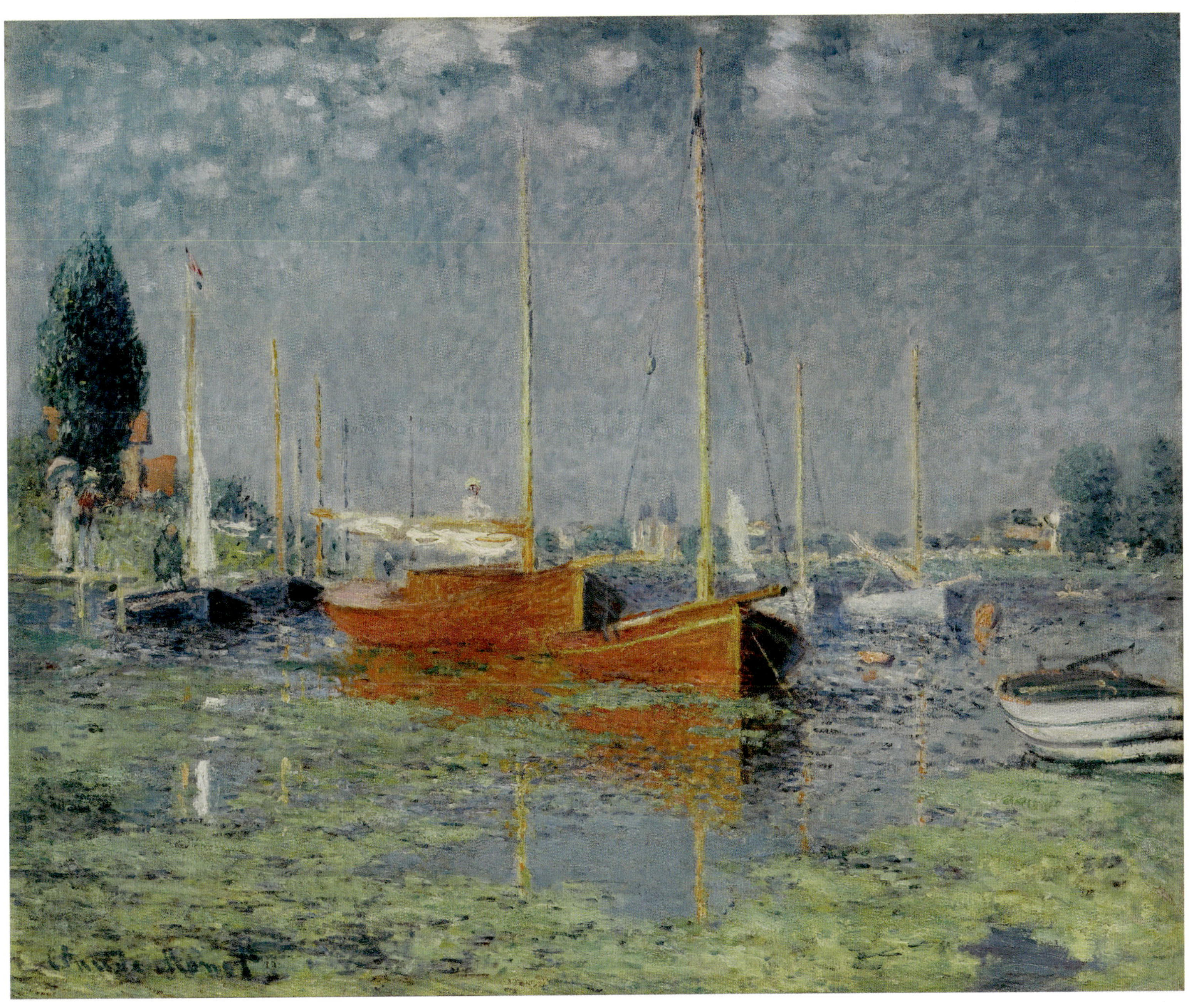

27. Claude Monet

Red Boats, Argenteuil, 1875
Oil on canvas, 56 × 67 cm (22 × 26 ½ in.)
Signed lower left, W370
Musée de l'Orangerie, Paris
Jean Walter and Paul Guillaume Collection, RF 1963-106

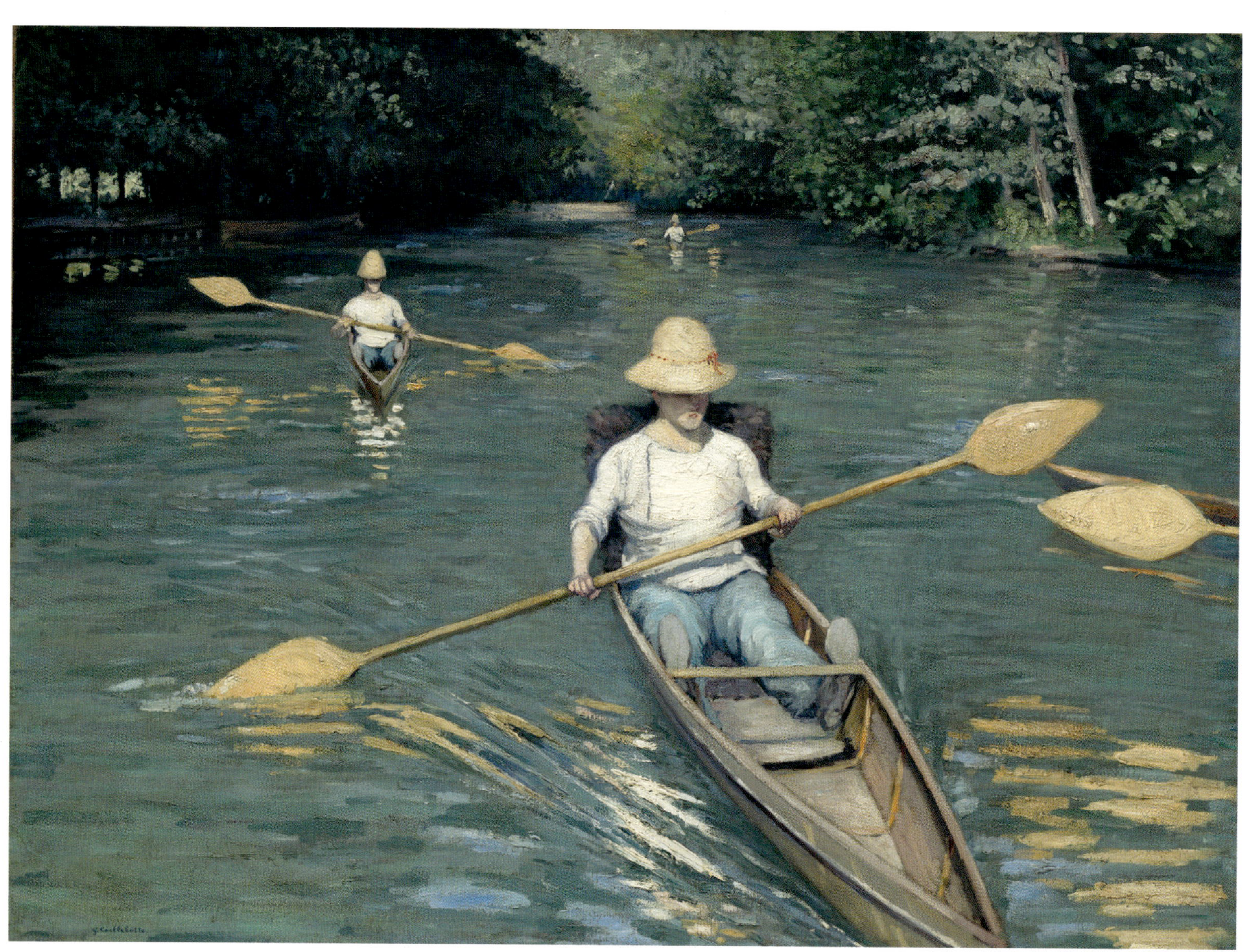

28. Gustave Caillebotte

Skiffs, 1877
Oil on canvas, 88.9 × 116.2 cm (35 × 45 ¾ in.)
Signed upper right, MB 87
National Gallery of Art, Washington
Mr. and Mrs. Paul Mellon Collection, 1985.64.6

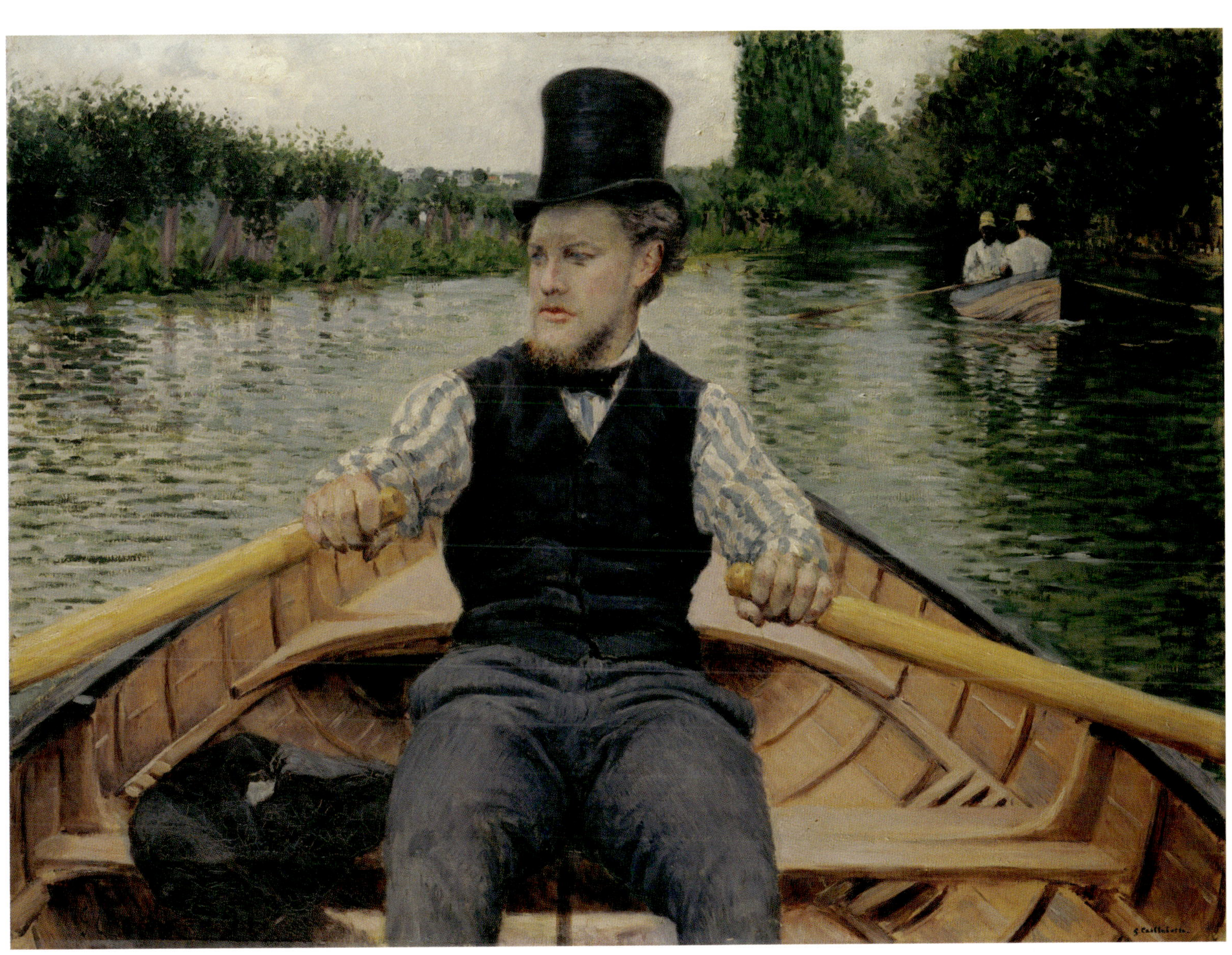

29. Gustave Caillebotte

Boating Party known as *Oarsman in a Top Hat*, 1878
Oil on canvas, 90 × 117 cm (35 ¾ × 46 in.)
Signed lower left, MB 122
Private collection

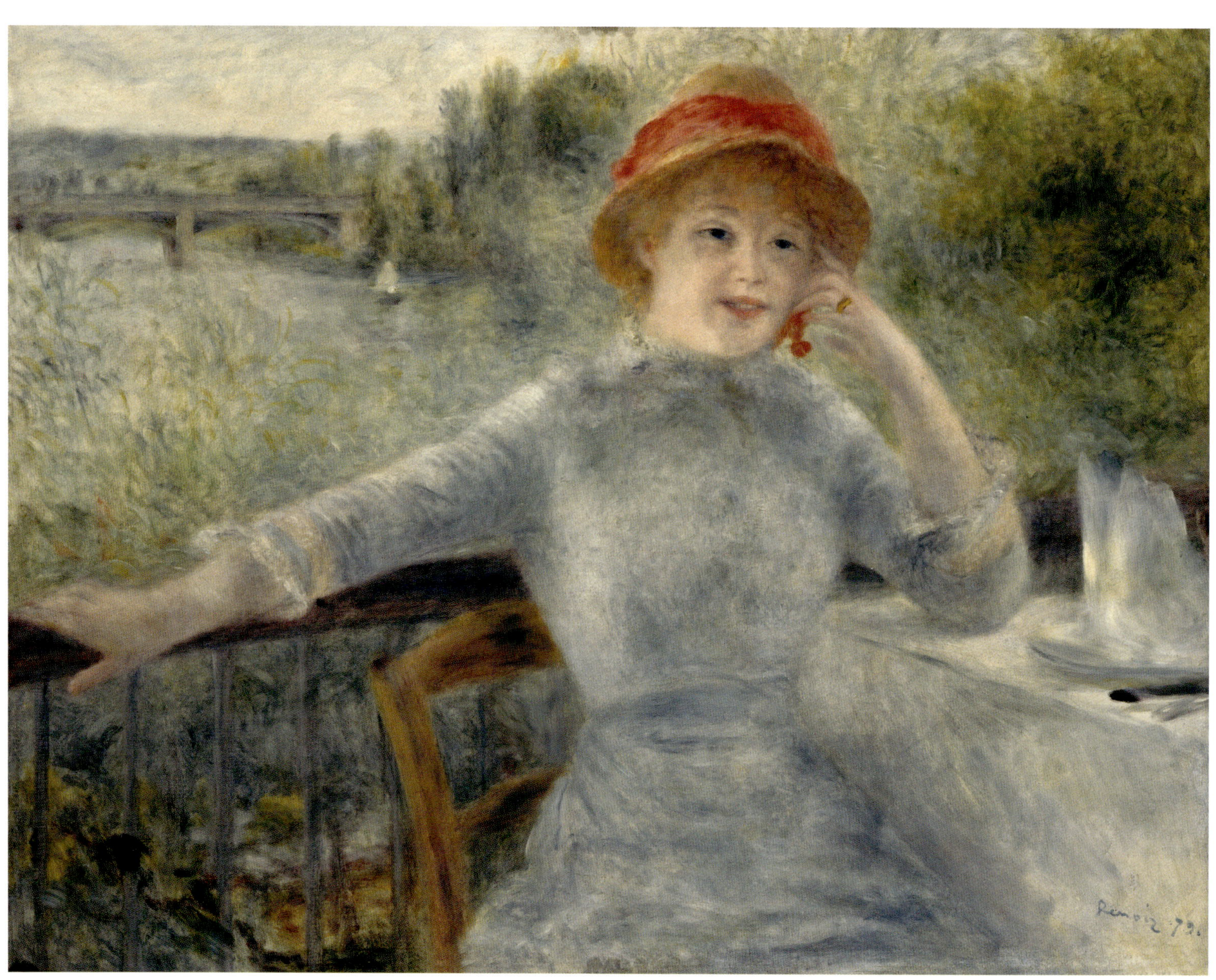

30. Auguste Renoir

Alphonsine Fournaise also known as *À la Grenouillère,* 1879
Oil on canvas, 73.5 × 93 cm (29 × 36 ¾ in.)
Signed and dated lower right, D 321
Musée d'Orsay, Paris. Gift of D. David-Weill, 1937, RF 1937-9

31. Auguste Renoir

Oarsmen at Chatou, 1879
Oil on canvas, 81.2 × 100.2 cm (32 × 39 ½ in.)
Signed and dated lower right, D 217
National Gallery of Art, Washington. Gift of Sam A. Lewisohn, 1951.5.2

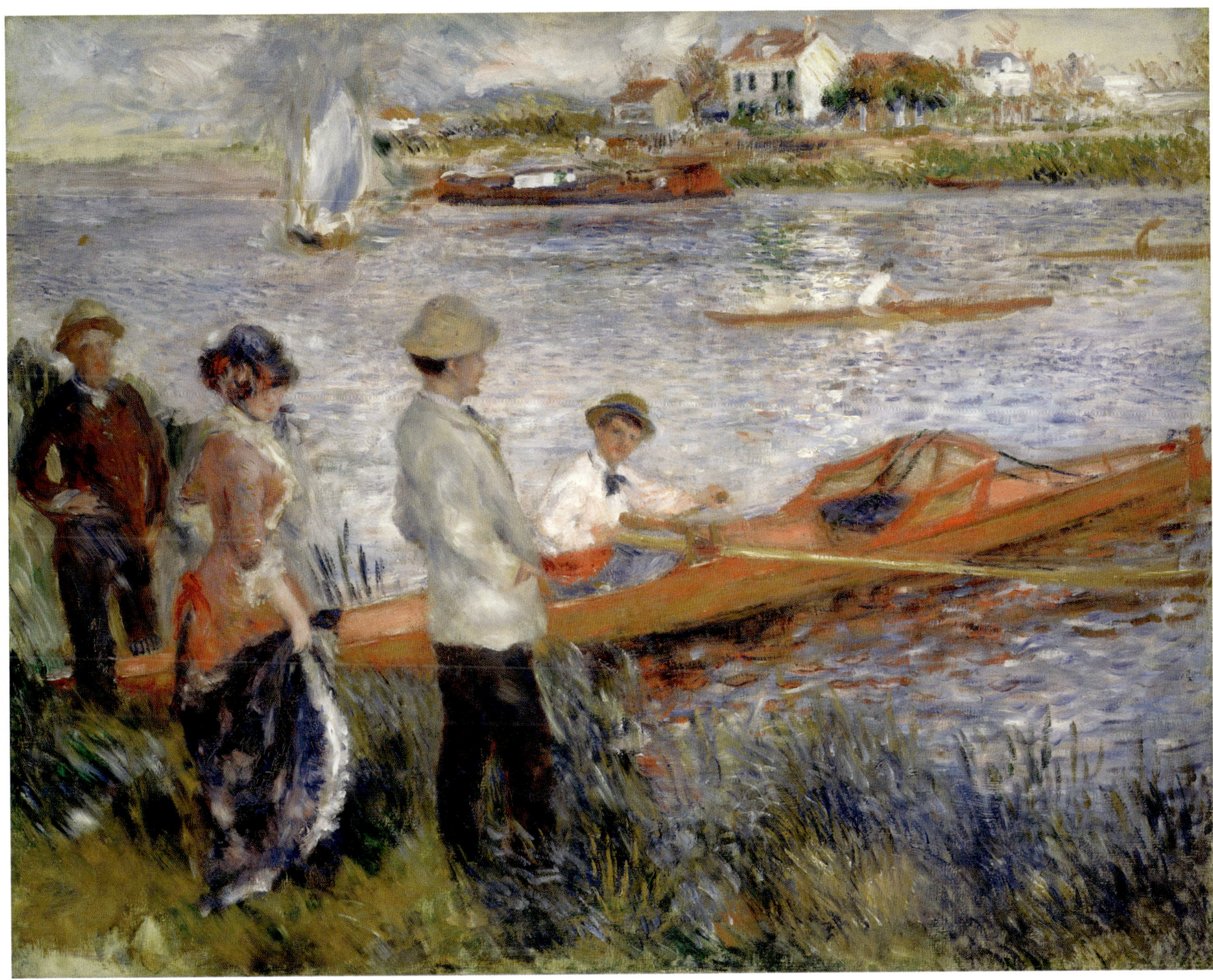

32. Georges Seurat (page 102)

The Seine at Courbevoie (By the Water), 1885
Oil on canvas, 81.5 × 65 cm (32 × 25 ½ in.)
Signed lower right, DH 134
Private collection

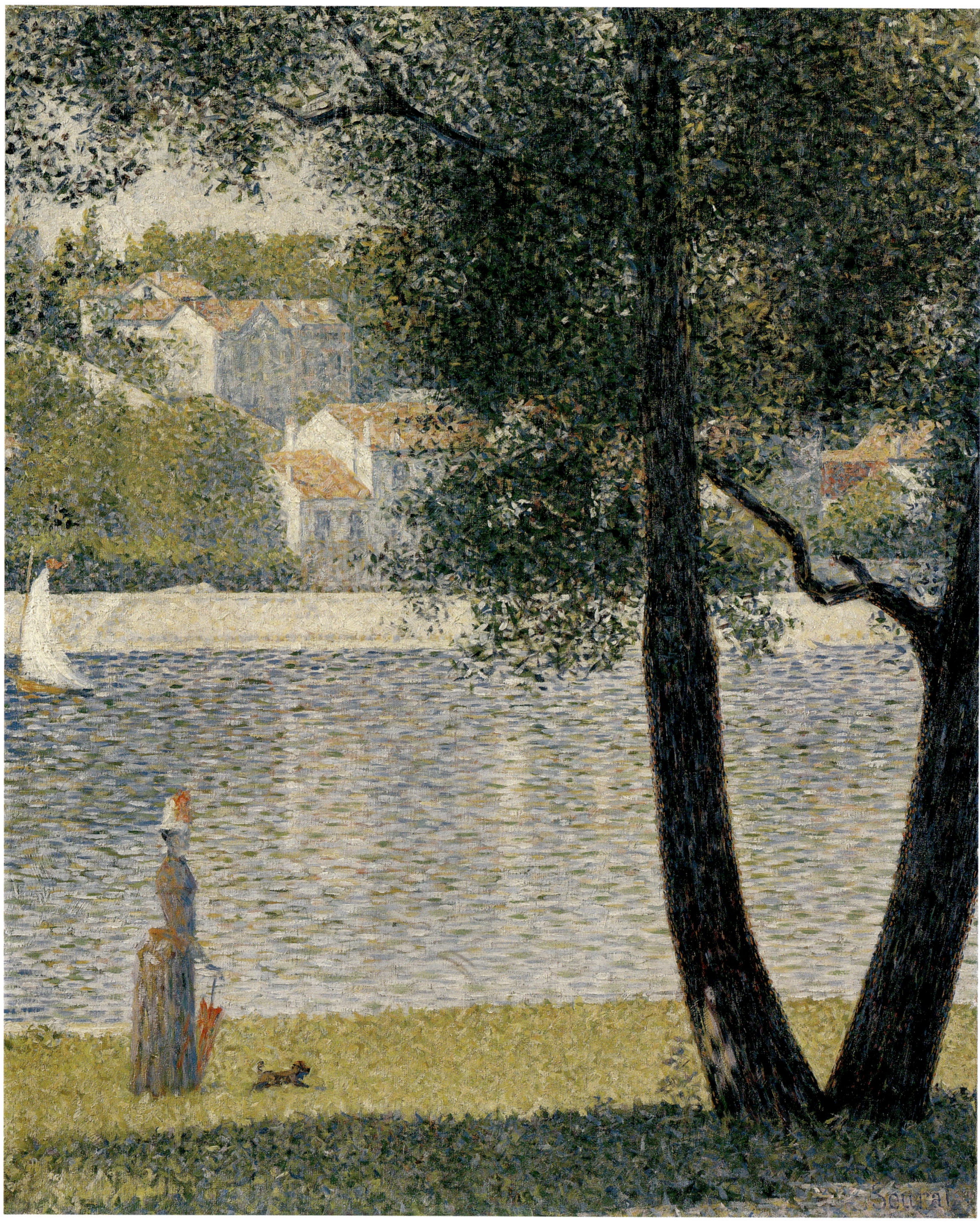
Seurat

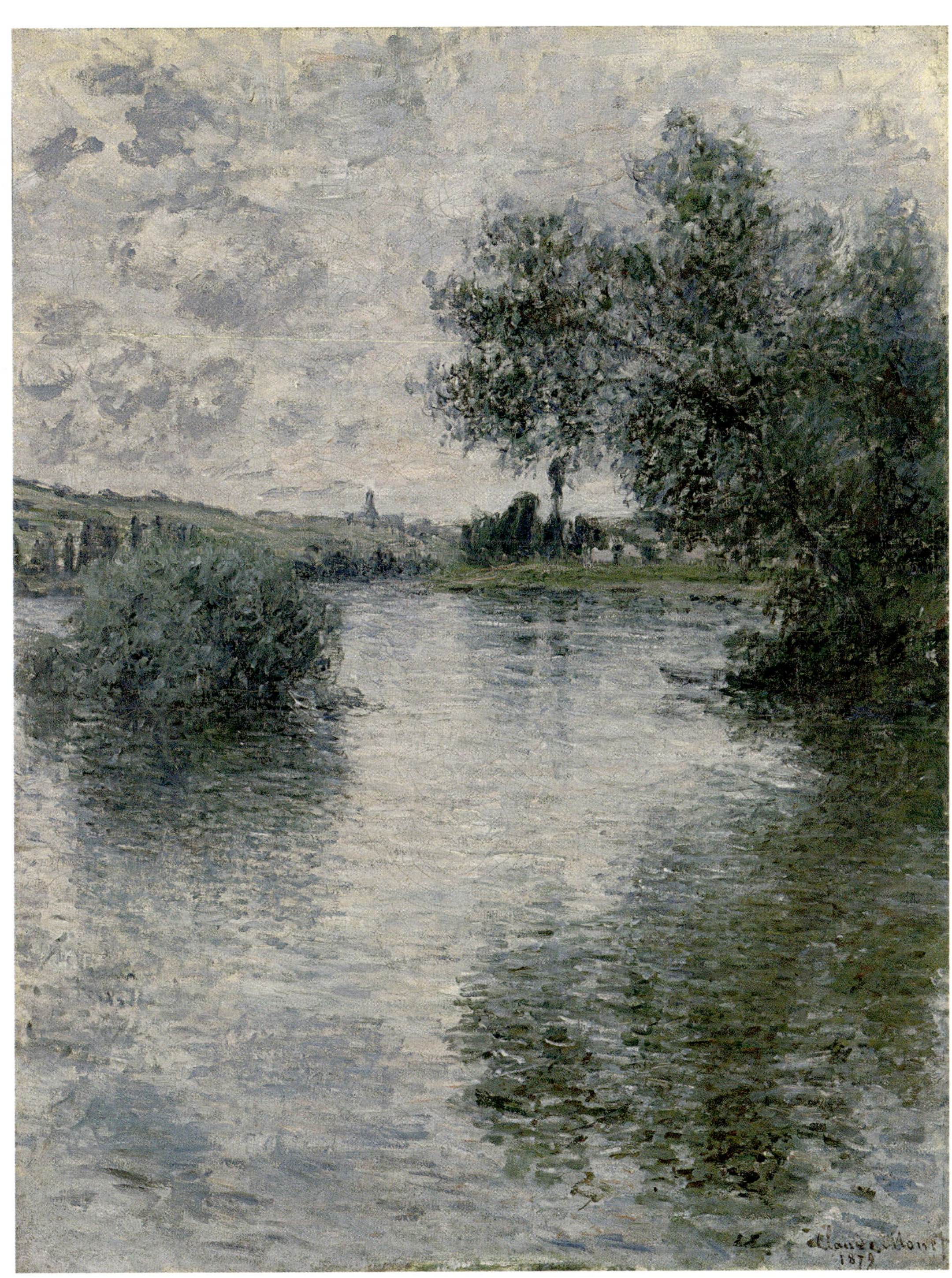

33. Claude Monet

The Seine at Vétheuil, 1879
Oil on canvas, 80 × 60 cm (31 ½ × 23 ¾ in.)
Signed and dated lower left, W537
Musée d'Orsay, Paris, on long term loan at the musée des Beaux-Arts de Rouen, MNR 205

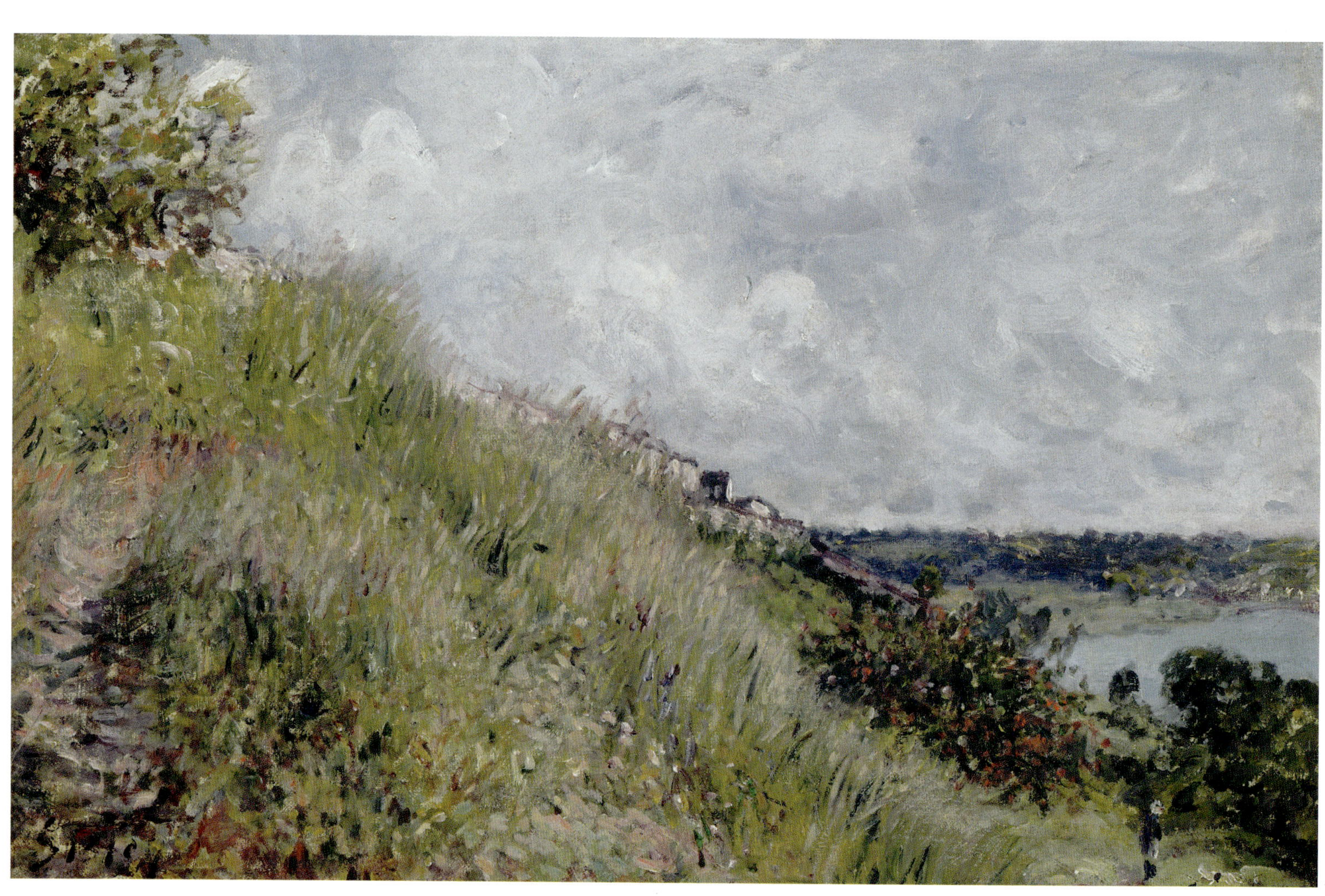

34. Alfred Sisley

The Seine from the Hills of By, 1881
Oil on canvas, 37 × 55 cm (14 ½ × 21 ¾ in.)
Signed lower right, FD 443
Musée d'Orsay, Paris, work recovered after the Second World War and entrusted to the musées nationaux, MNR 210 bis

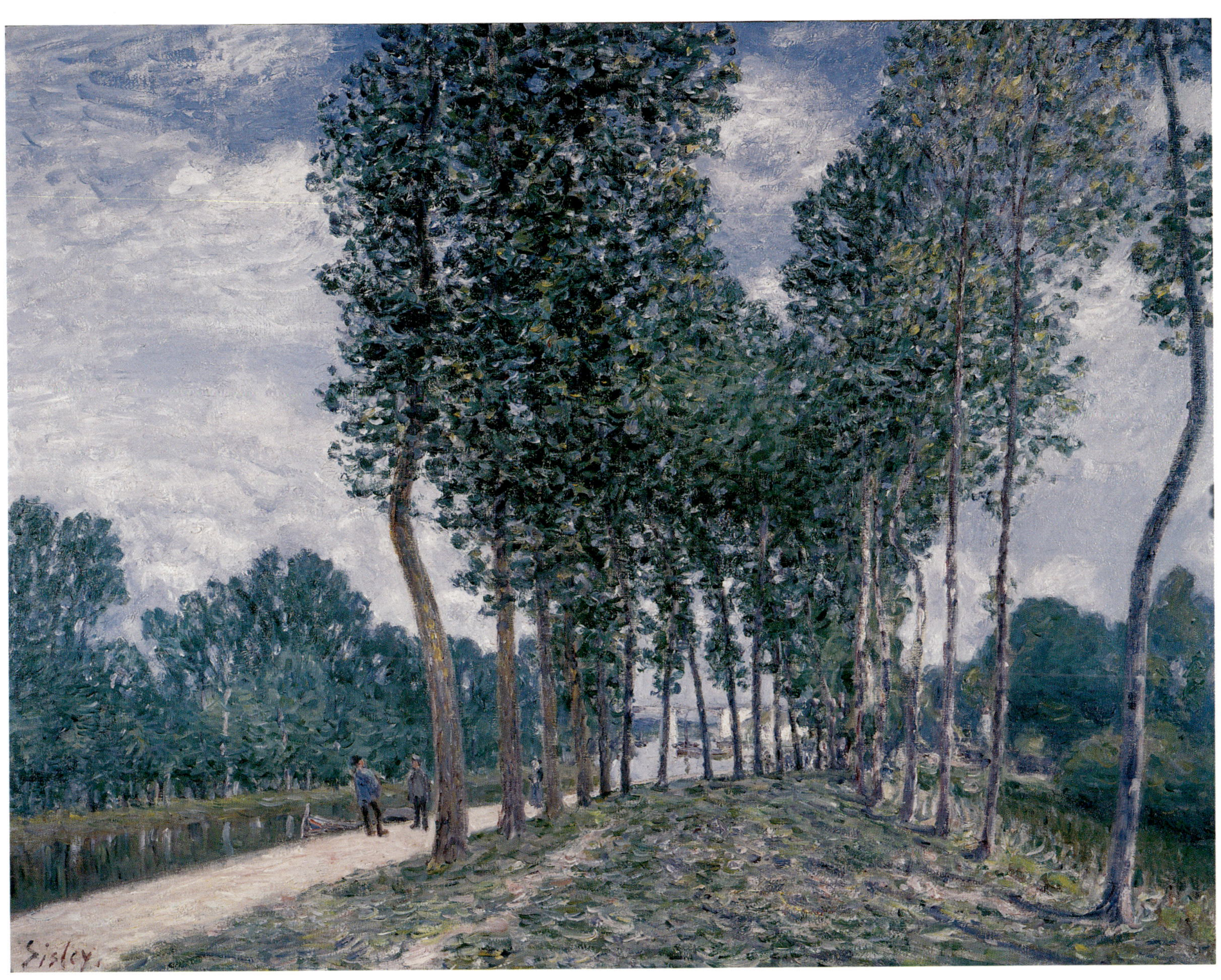

35. Alfred Sisley

Borders of the Loing at Moret, 1892
Oil on canvas, 73 × 92 cm (28 ¾ × 36 ¼ in.)
Signed lower left, FD 795
Collection Triton Foundation, The Netherlands

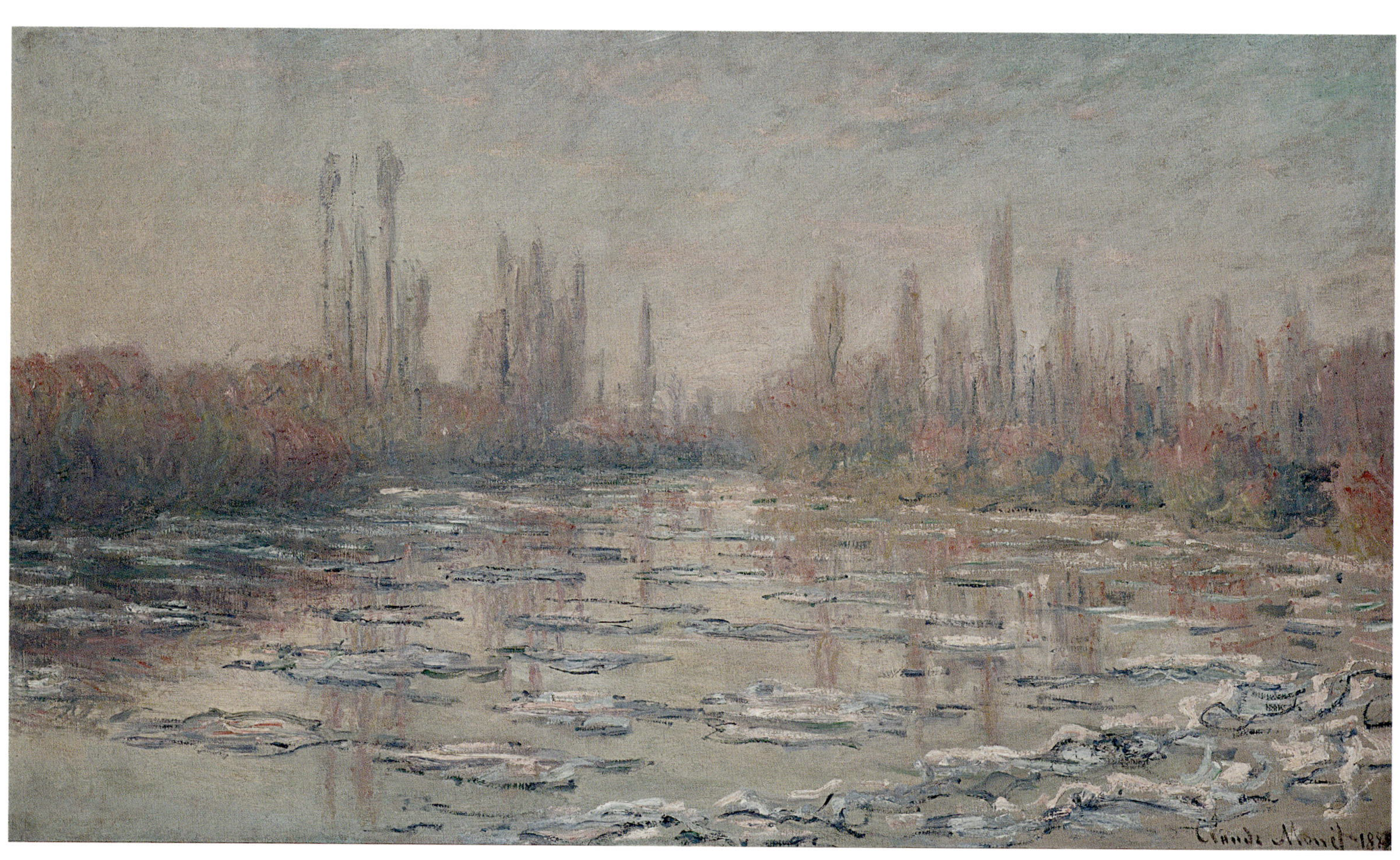

36. Claude Monet

Floating Ice also known as *Floes on the Seine*, 1880
Oil on canvas, 60 × 100 cm (23 ¾ × 39 ½ in.)
Signed and dated lower right, W567
Musée d'Orsay, Paris
Donation of Baroness Eva Gebhard-Gourgaud, 1965, RF 1965-10

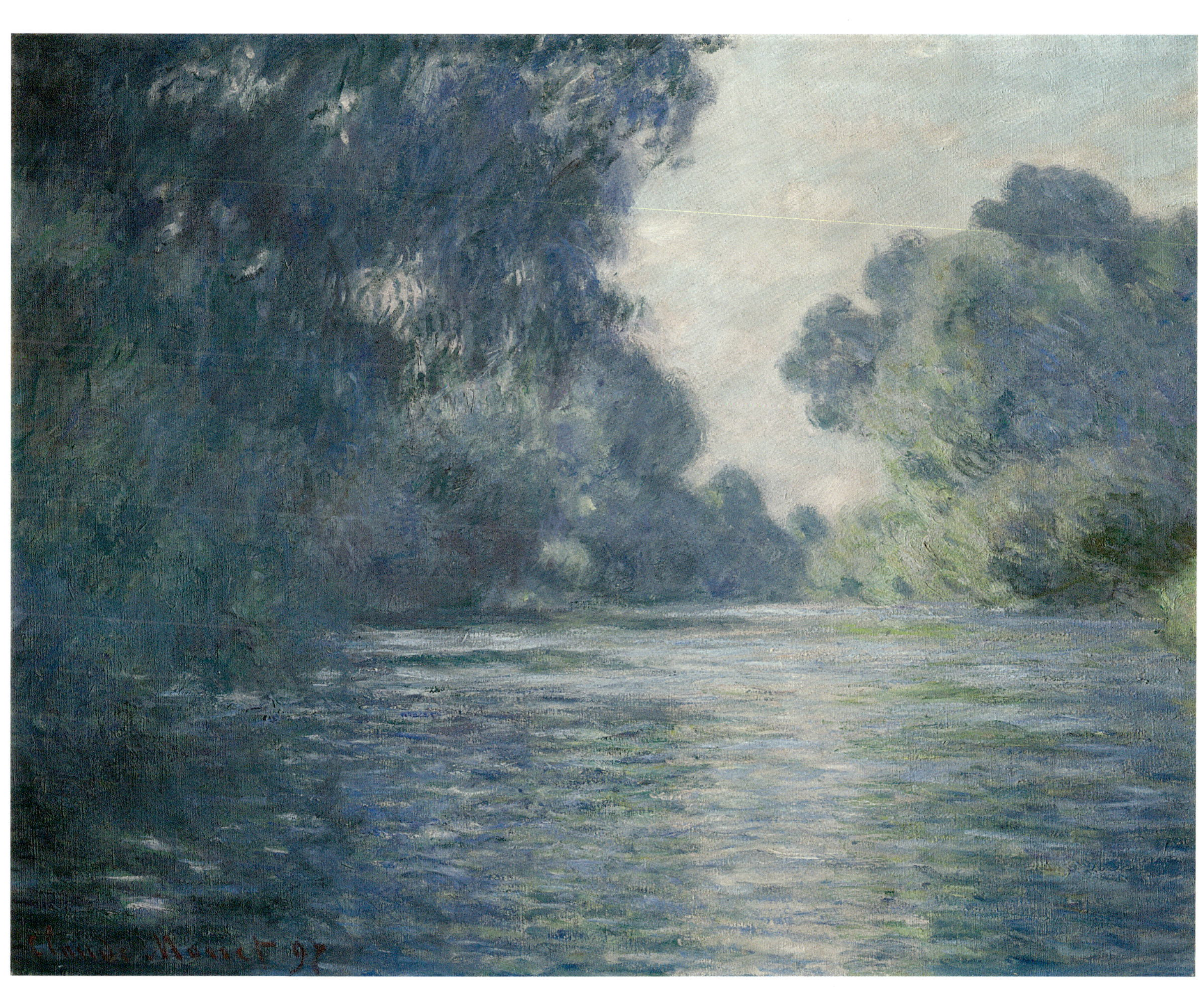

37. Claude Monet

Arm of the Seine near Giverny, 1897
Oil on canvas, 75 × 92.5 cm (29 ½ × 36 ½ in.)
Signed and dated lower left, W1487
Musée d'Orsay, Paris
Bequest of Count Isaac Camondo, 1911, RF 2003

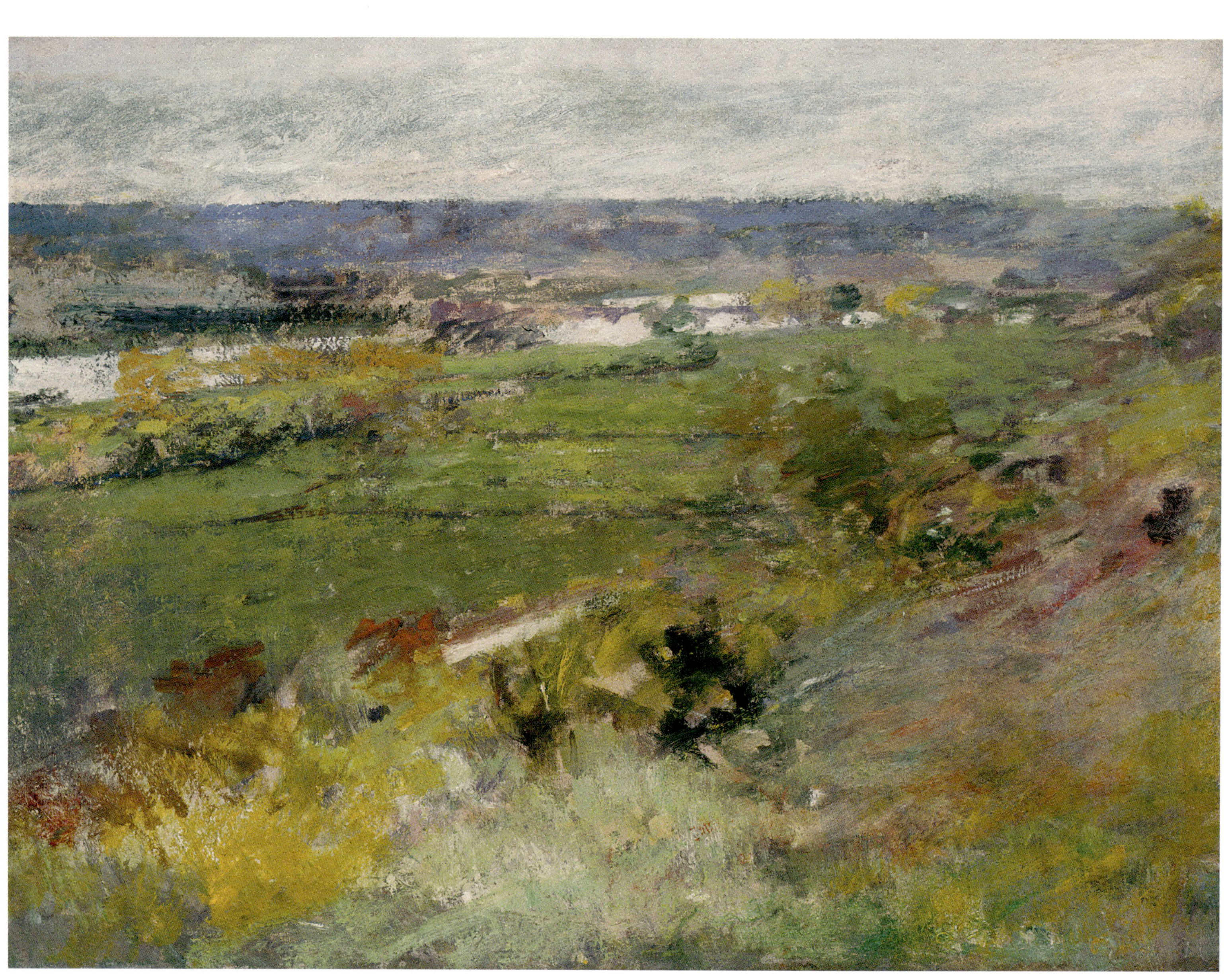

38. Theodore Robinson

Étude pour "Vallée de la Seine vue des hauteurs de Giverny", 1892
Oil on canvas, 58.1 × 73.3 cm (23 × 29 in.)
Terra Foundation for American Art, Chicago
Daniel J. Terra Collection, 1992.9

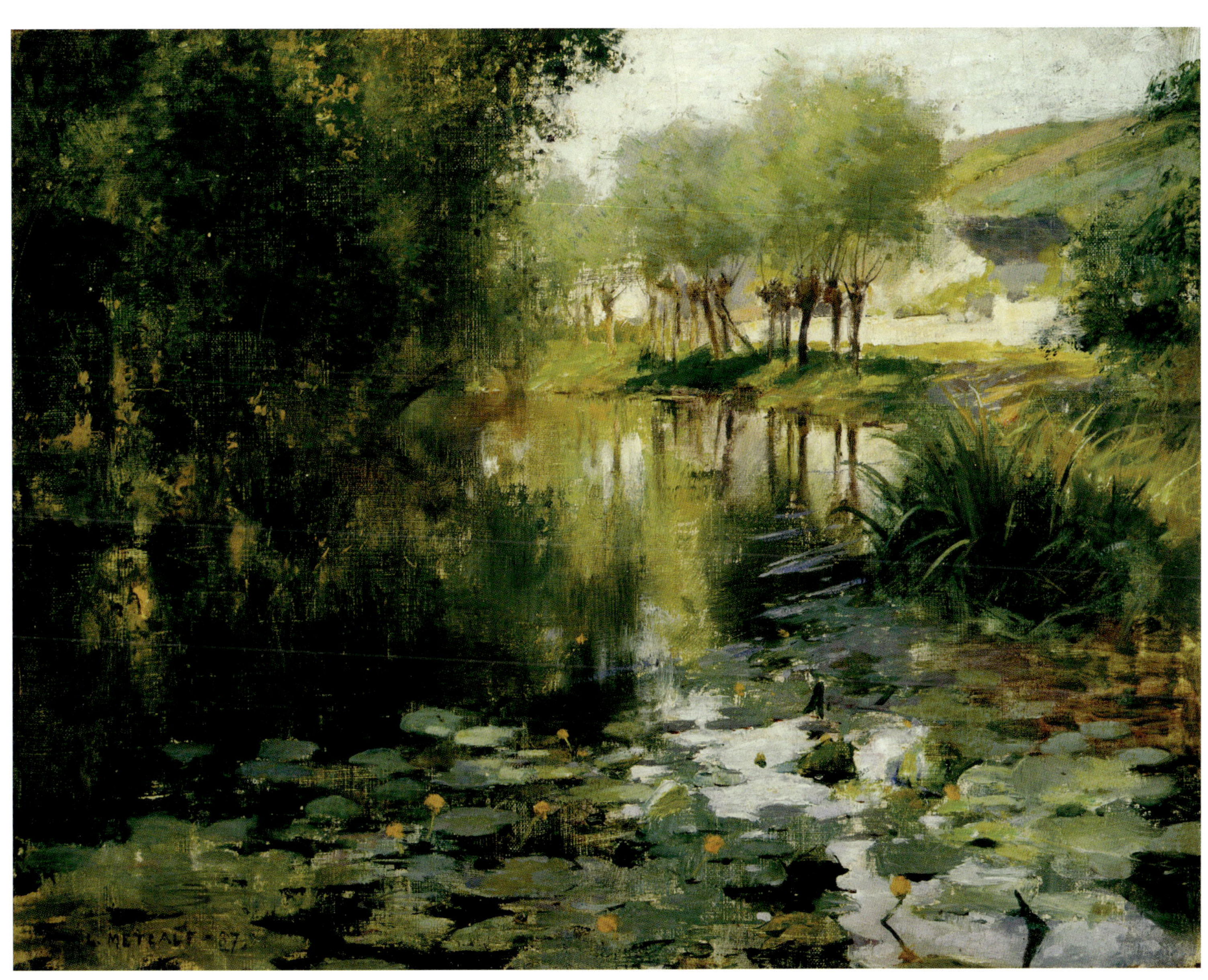

39. Willard Leroy Metcalf

The Lily Pond, 1887
Oil on canvas, 30.8 × 38.3 cm (12 ¼ × 15 in.)
Signed lower left
Terra Foundation for American Art, Chicago
Daniel J. Terra Collection, 1993.5

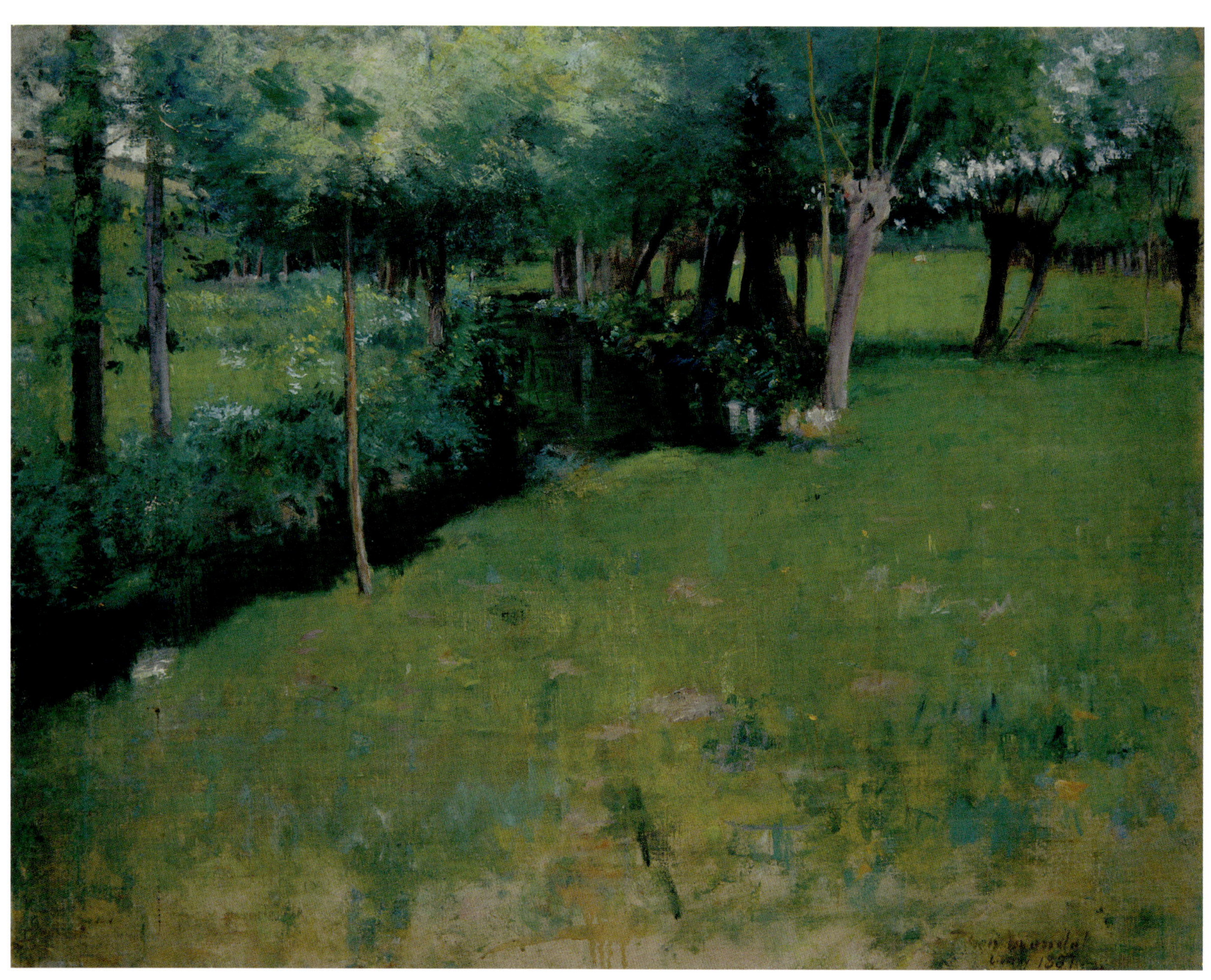

40. Theodore Wendel

Brook, Giverny, 1887
Oil on canvas, 72.4 × 90.5 cm (28 ½ × 35 ½ in.)
Signed lower right
Terra Foundation for American Art, Chicago
Daniel J. Terra Collection, 1987.13

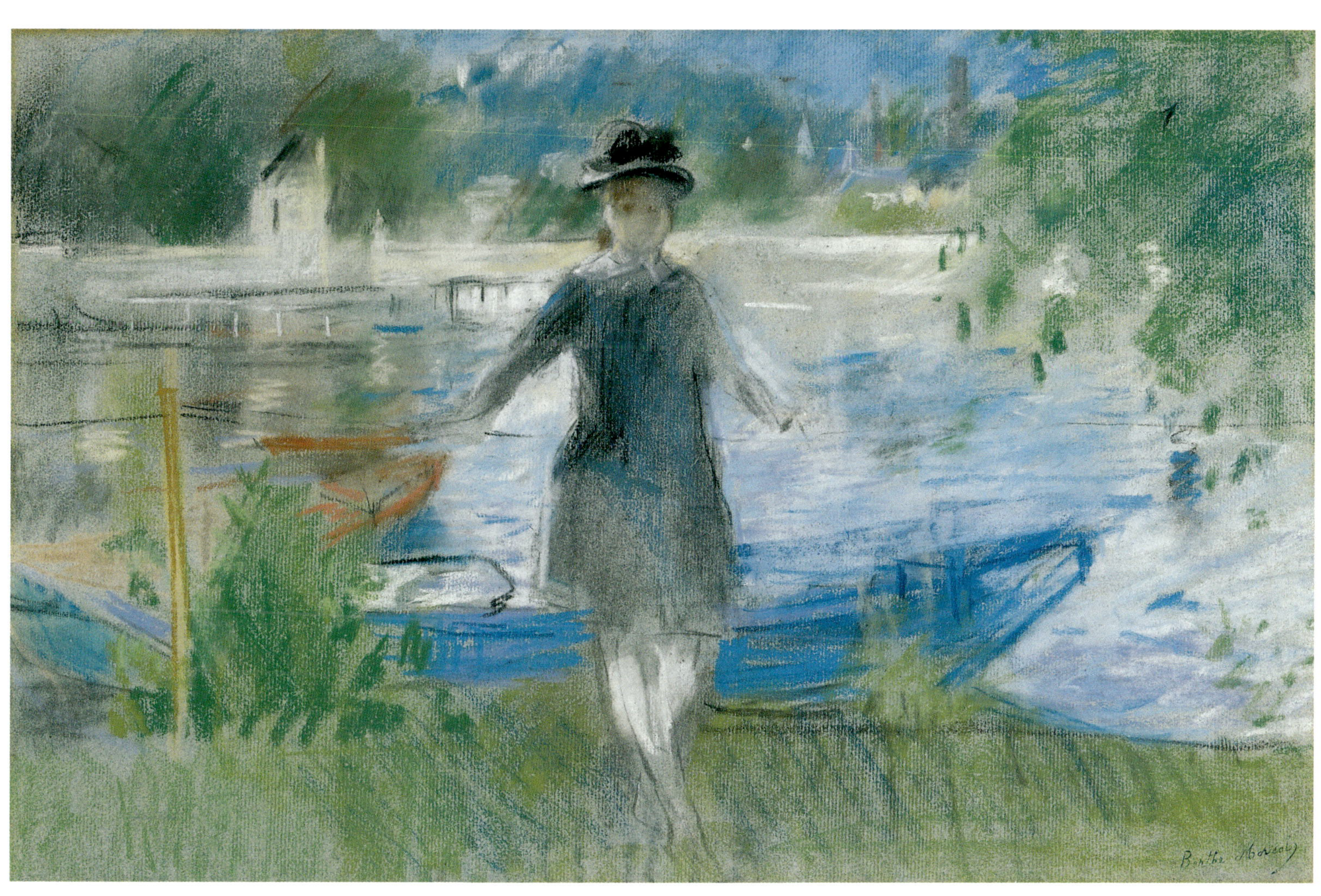

41. Berthe Morisot

Banks along the Seine at Épinay, 1881
Pastel, 29 × 44 cm (11 ½ × 17 ¼ in.)
Stamp of signature lower right, BW 454
Private collection

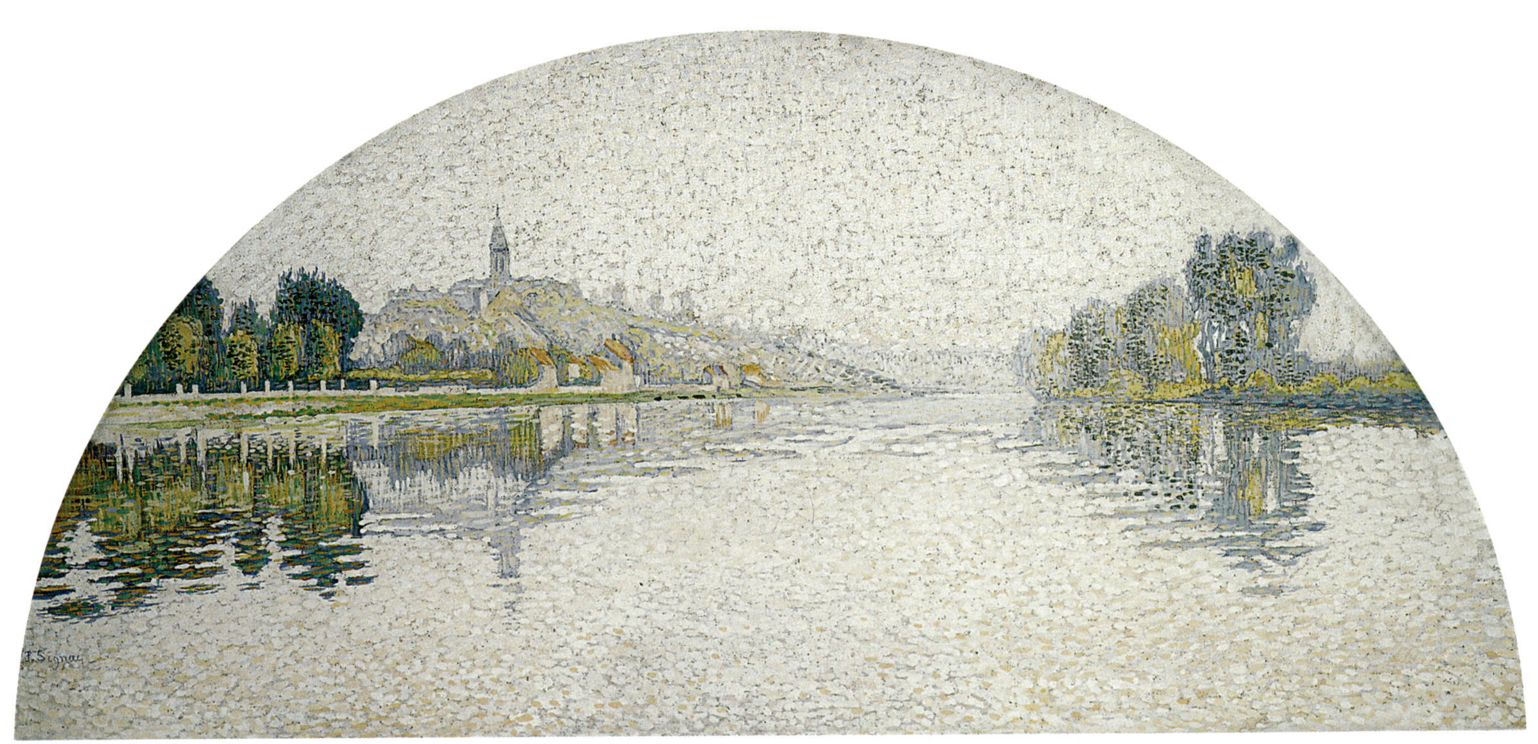

42. Paul Signac

Herblay, Fog, Opus 208, c. 1889–90
Oil on silk, 31.7 × 68.5 cm (12 ½ × 27 in.)
Signed lower left, FC 209
Musée Camille Pissarro, Pontoise, P.1983.2

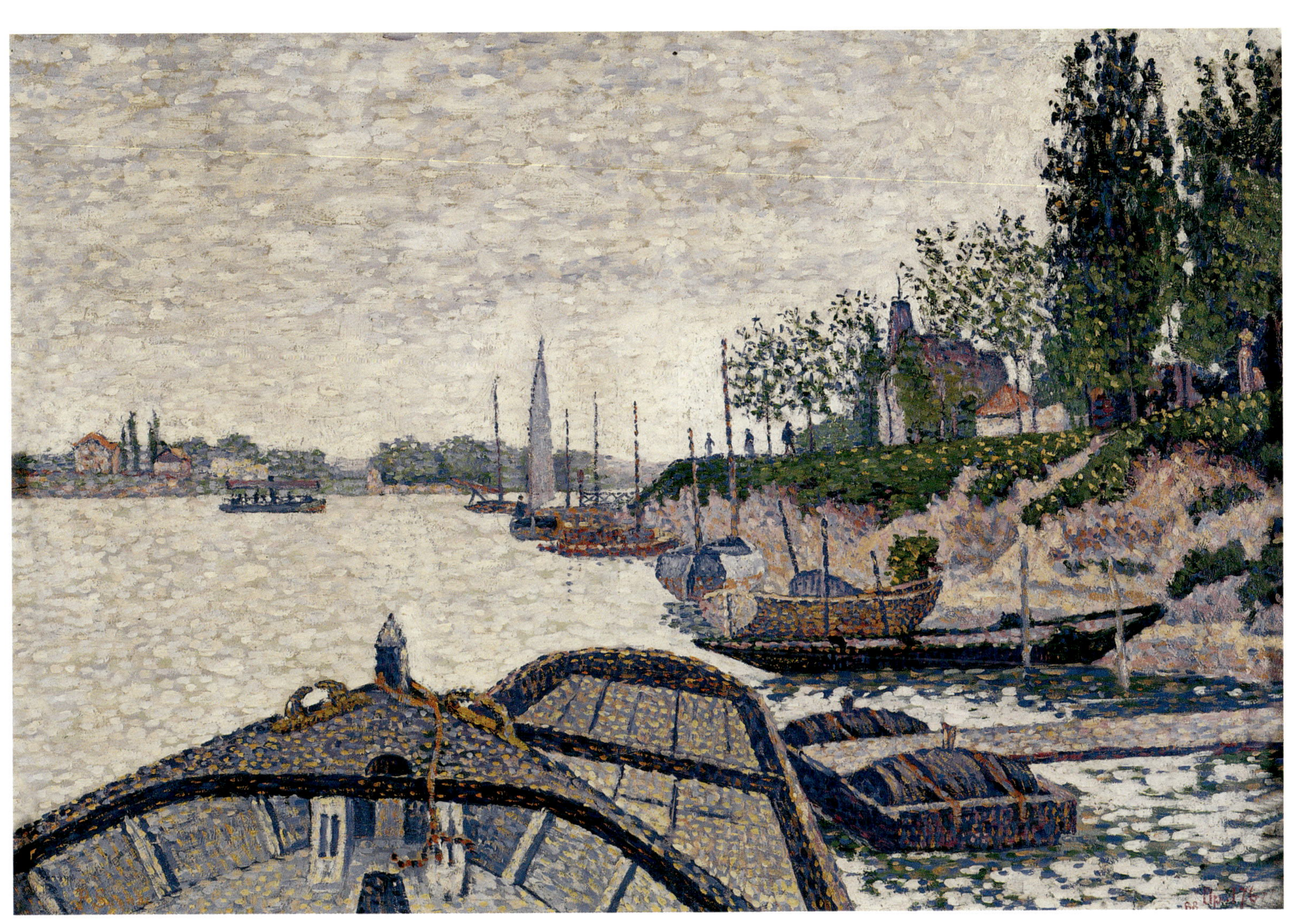

43. Paul Signac

Bow of the Tub, Opus 176, 1888
Oil on canvas, 45 × 65 cm (17 ¾ × 25 ½ in.)
Signed lower left, FC 162
Private collection

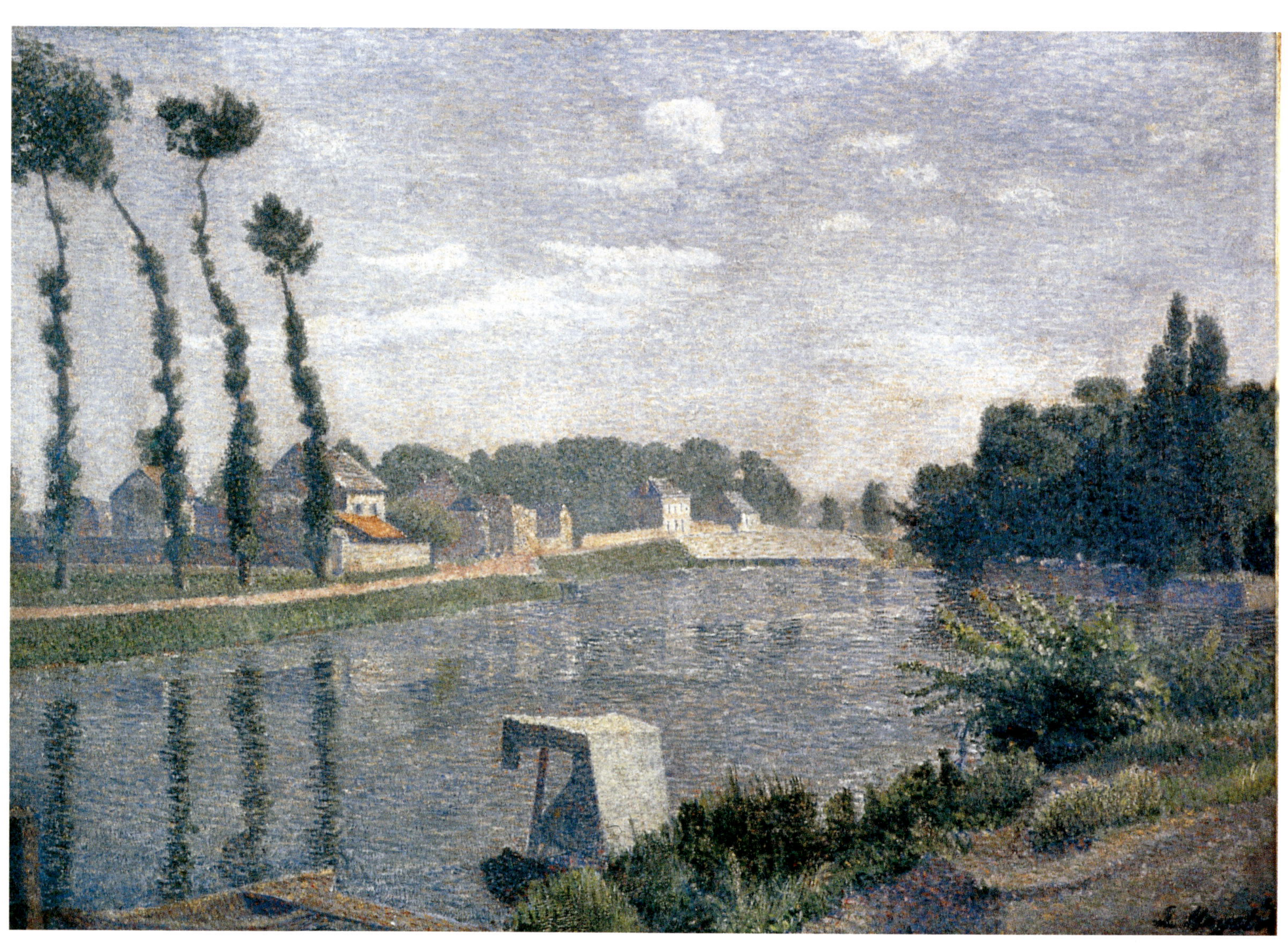

44. Louis Hayet

Bank along the Oise at Pontoise, c. 1888
Oil on canvas, 52 × 75 cm (20 ½ × 29 ½ in.)
Signed and dated lower right
Conseil général du Val d'Oise, Cergy-Pontoise, 11 146

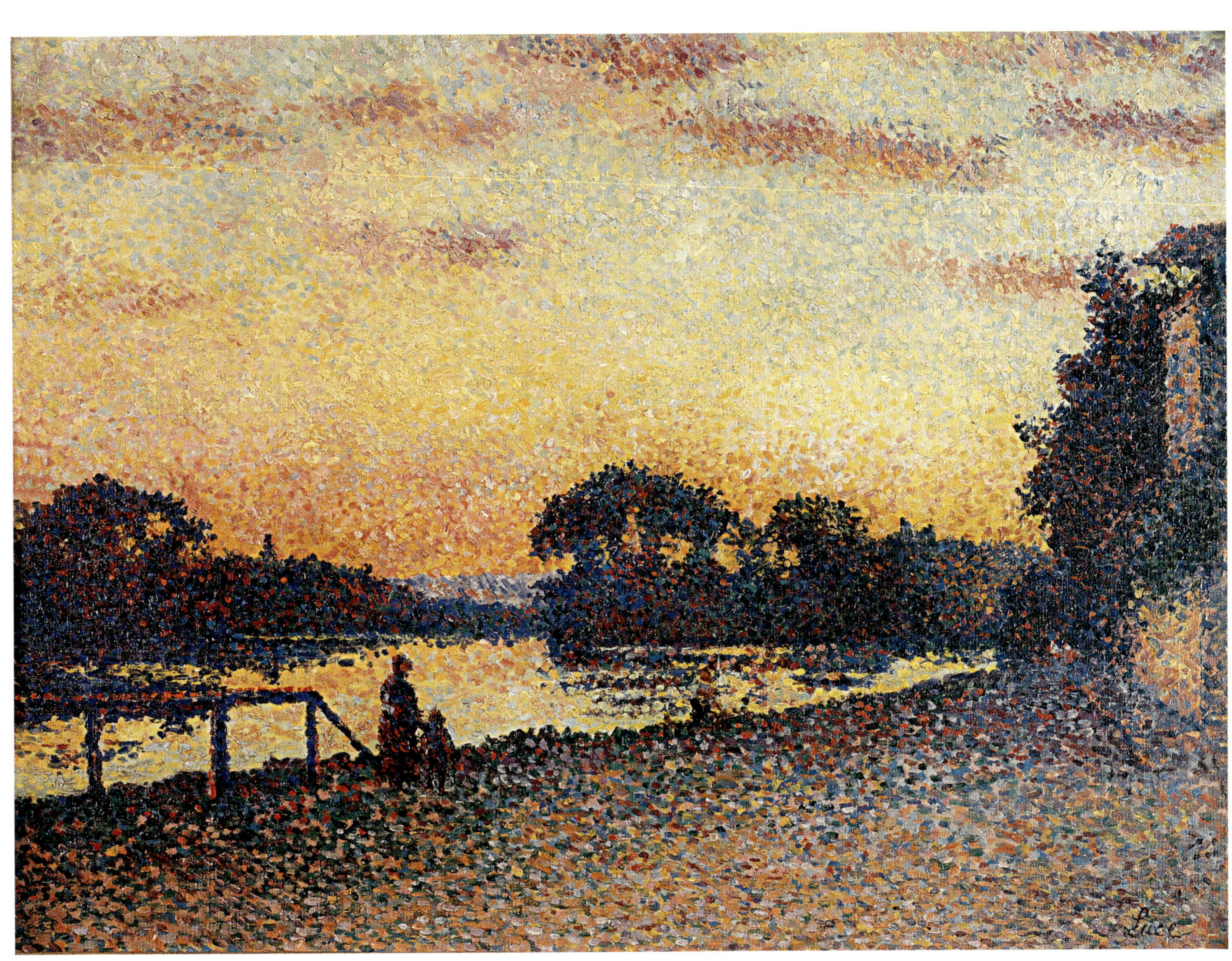

45. Maximilien Luce

Banks along the Seine at Herblay, Sunset, c. 1889
Oil on canvas, 50 × 65 cm (19 ¾ × 25 ½ in.)
Signed lower right, JBL et DB 58
Private collection

46. Maurice Denis

The Farandole, 1895
Oil on canvas,
49 × 211 cm (19 ½ × 83 ¼ in.)
Signed vertical monogram
and dated lower right
Private collection

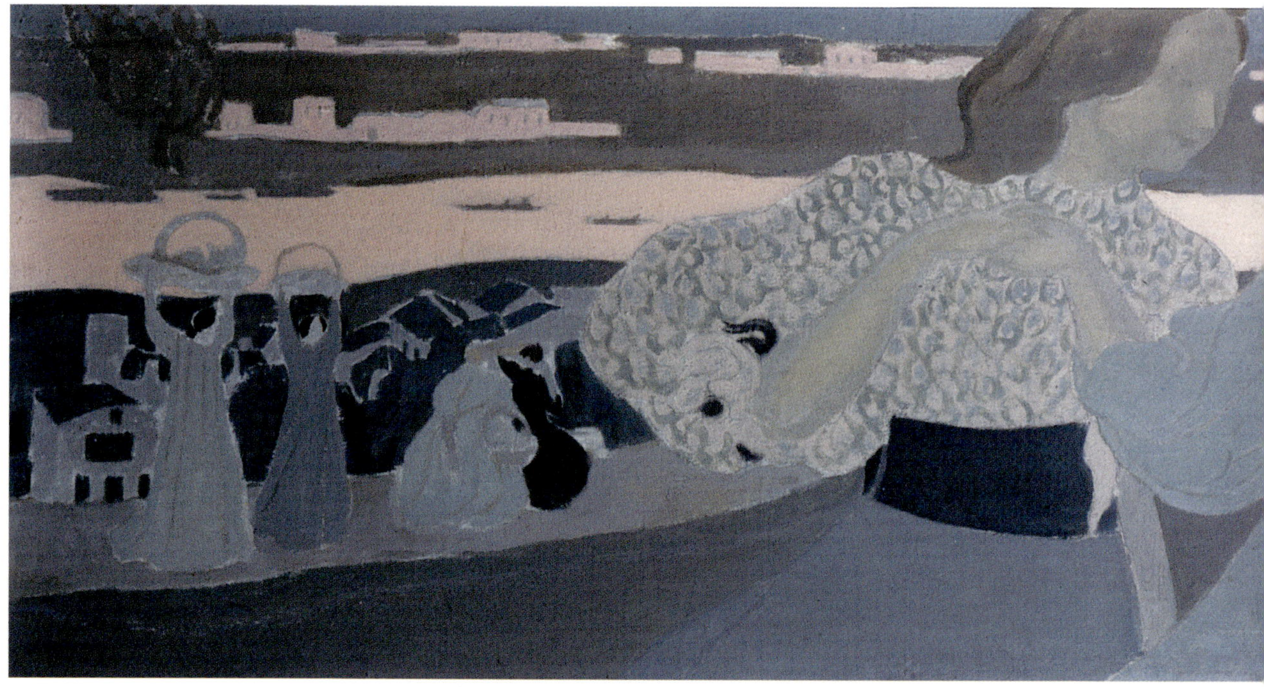

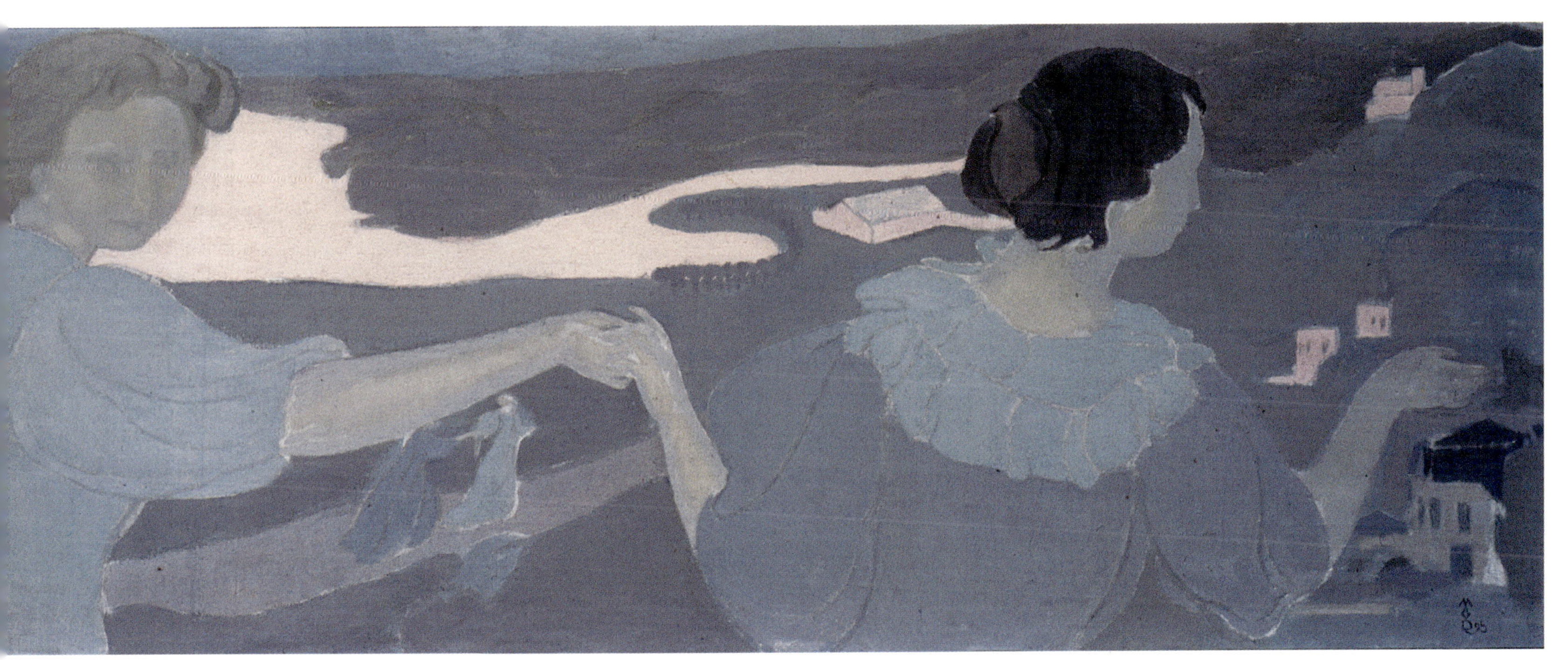

47. Pierre Bonnard (page 118)

Balcony at Vernonnet
also know as *Bloomy Apple Tree*, c. 1920
Oil on canvas, 100 × 78 cm (39 ½ × 30 ¾ in.)
Signed lower right, D 1000
Musée des beaux-arts, Brest

48. Pierre Bonnard (page 119)

Sunbeam
(Terrace of "La Roulotte" at Vernonnet), 1916
Oil on canvas, 53 × 41 cm (21 × 16 ¼ in.)
Signed lower right, D 862
Private collection

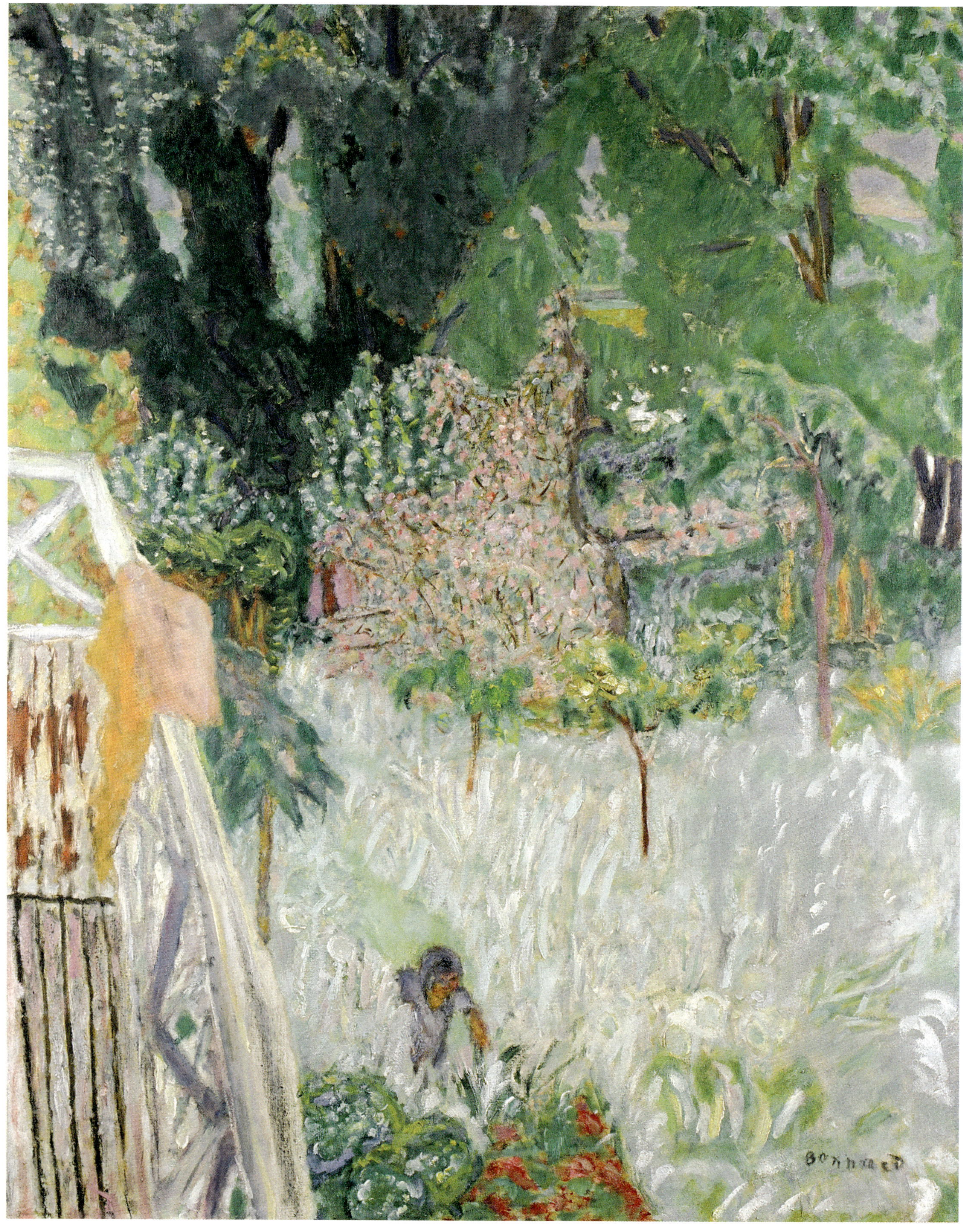
Bonnard

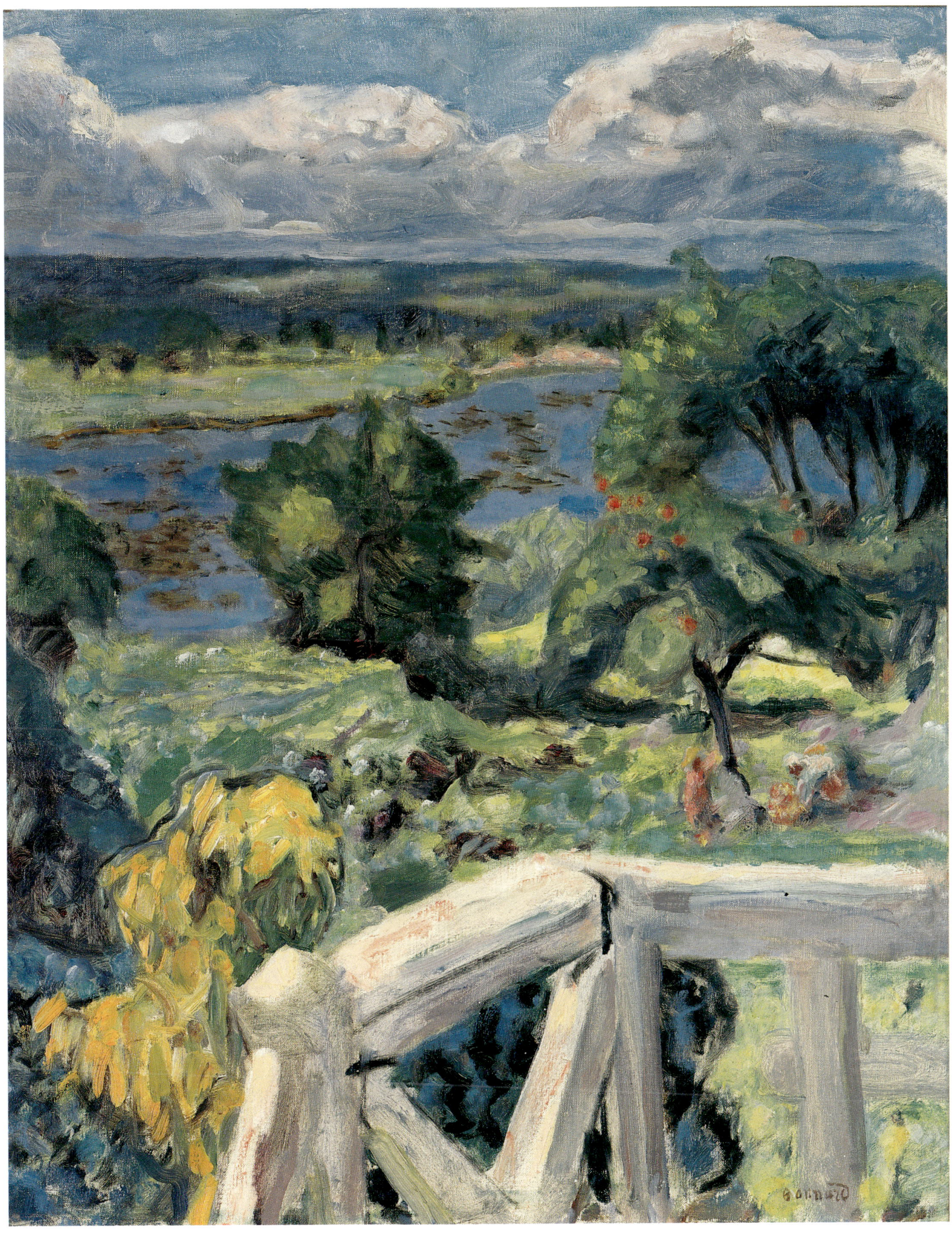

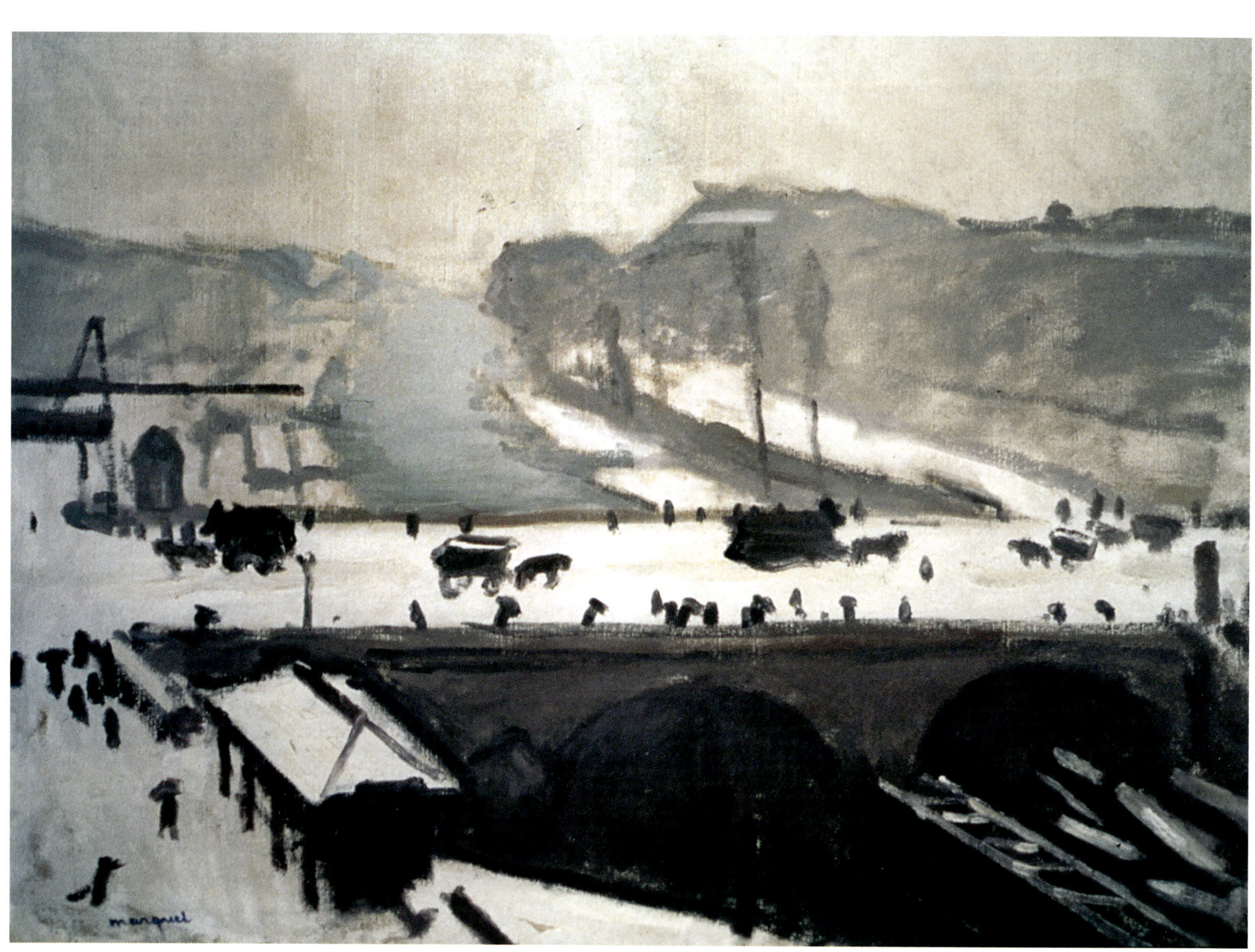

49. Albert Marquet

Pont Saint-Michel, Mist and Snow, c. 1908
Oil on canvas, 65 × 81 cm (25 ½ × 32 in.)
Signed lower left
Private collection
Courtesy of the Galerie de la Présidence, Paris

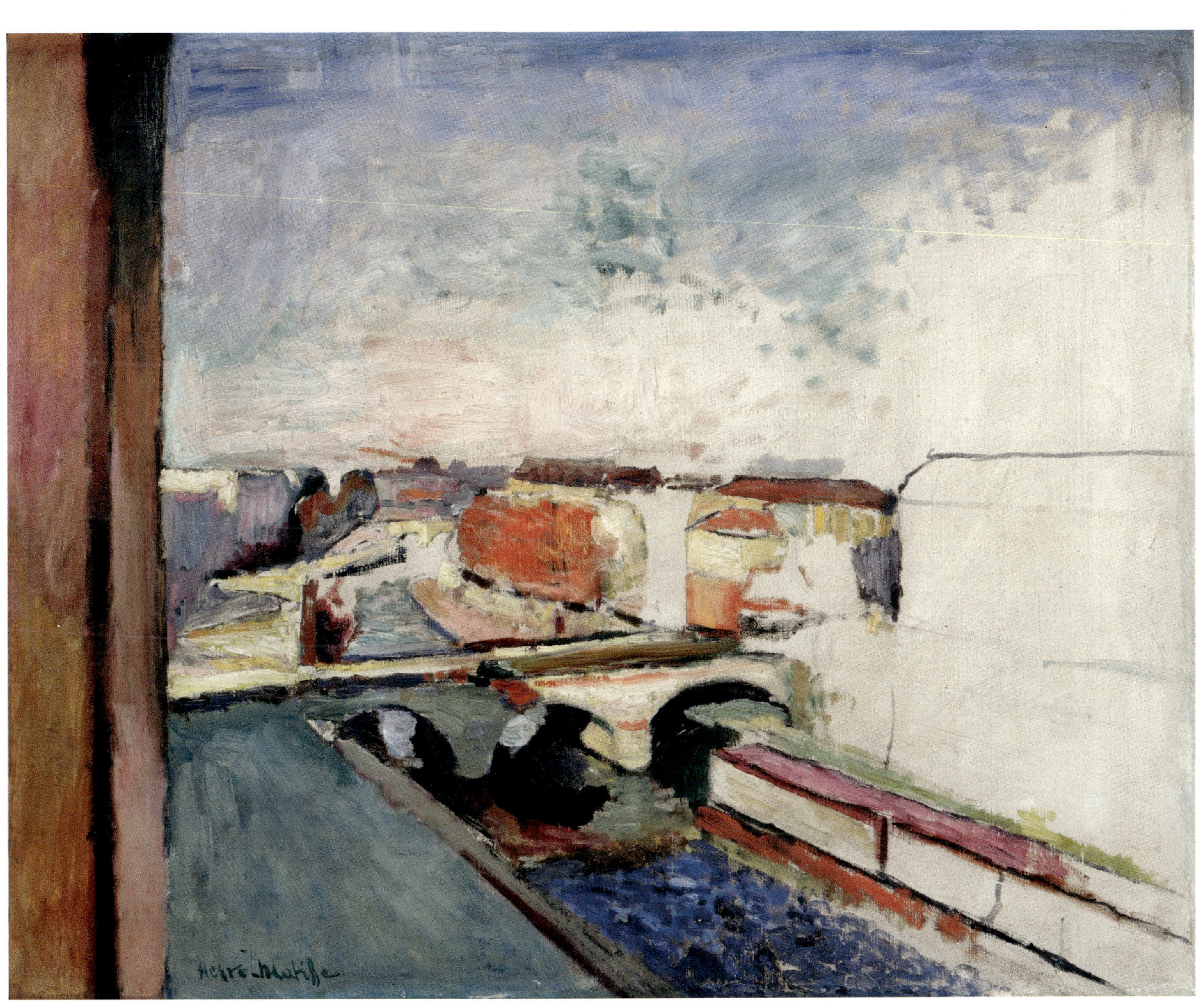

50. Henri Matisse

Pont Saint-Michel, c. 1900
Oil on canvas, 58 × 71 cm (22 ¾ × 28 in.)
Signed lower left
Centre Pompidou, musée national d'art moderne / Centre de création industrielle, Paris, dation 2001, AM 2001-213

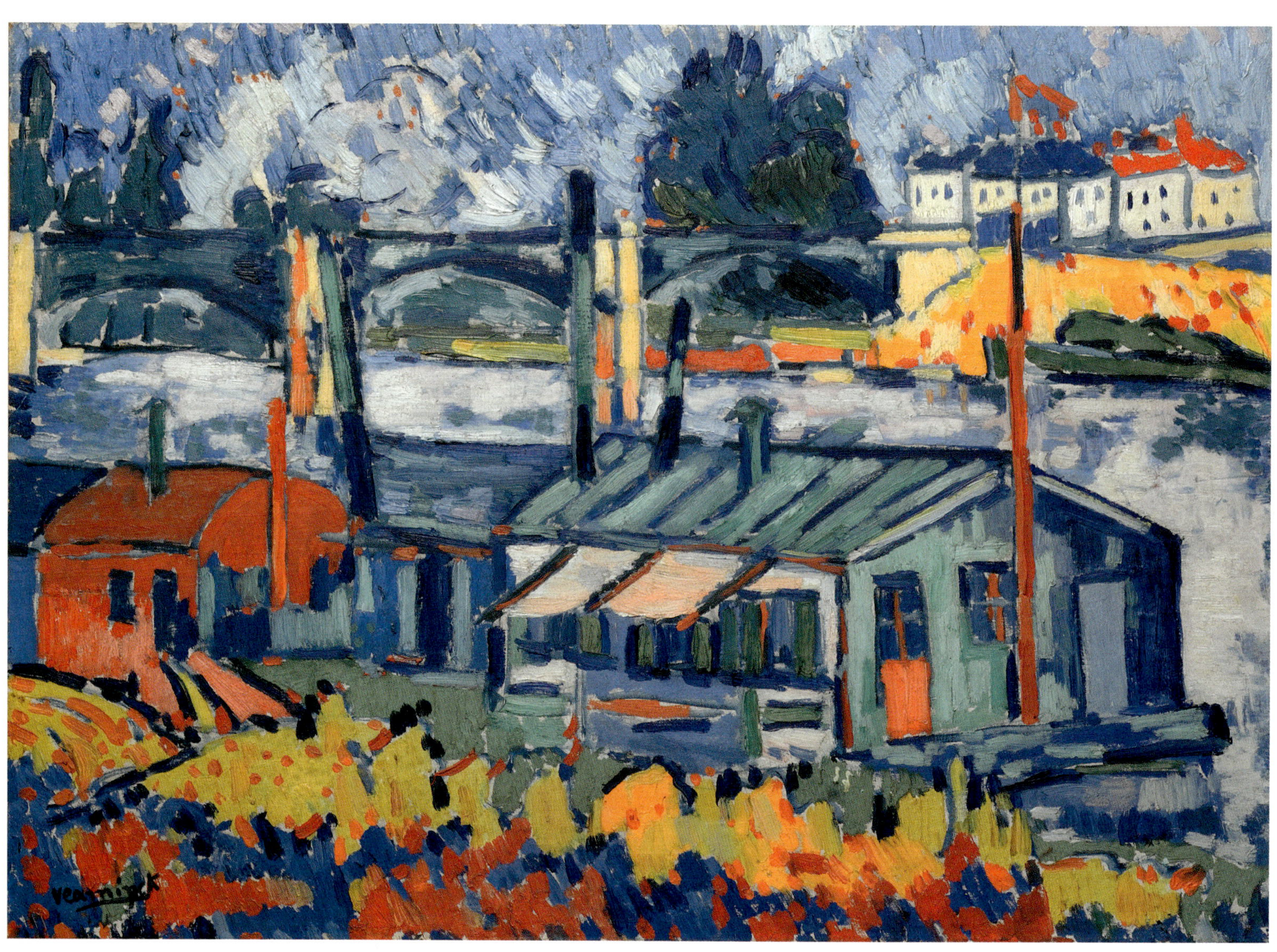

51. Maurice de Vlaminck

Pont de Chatou, 1906
Oil on canvas, 54 × 73 cm (21 ¼ × 28 ¾ in.)
Signed lower left
Centre Pompidou, musée national d'art moderne / Centre de création industrielle, Paris
Bequest of Georges Grammont 1959, AM 3846, on long term loan at L'Annonciade, musée de Saint-Tropez

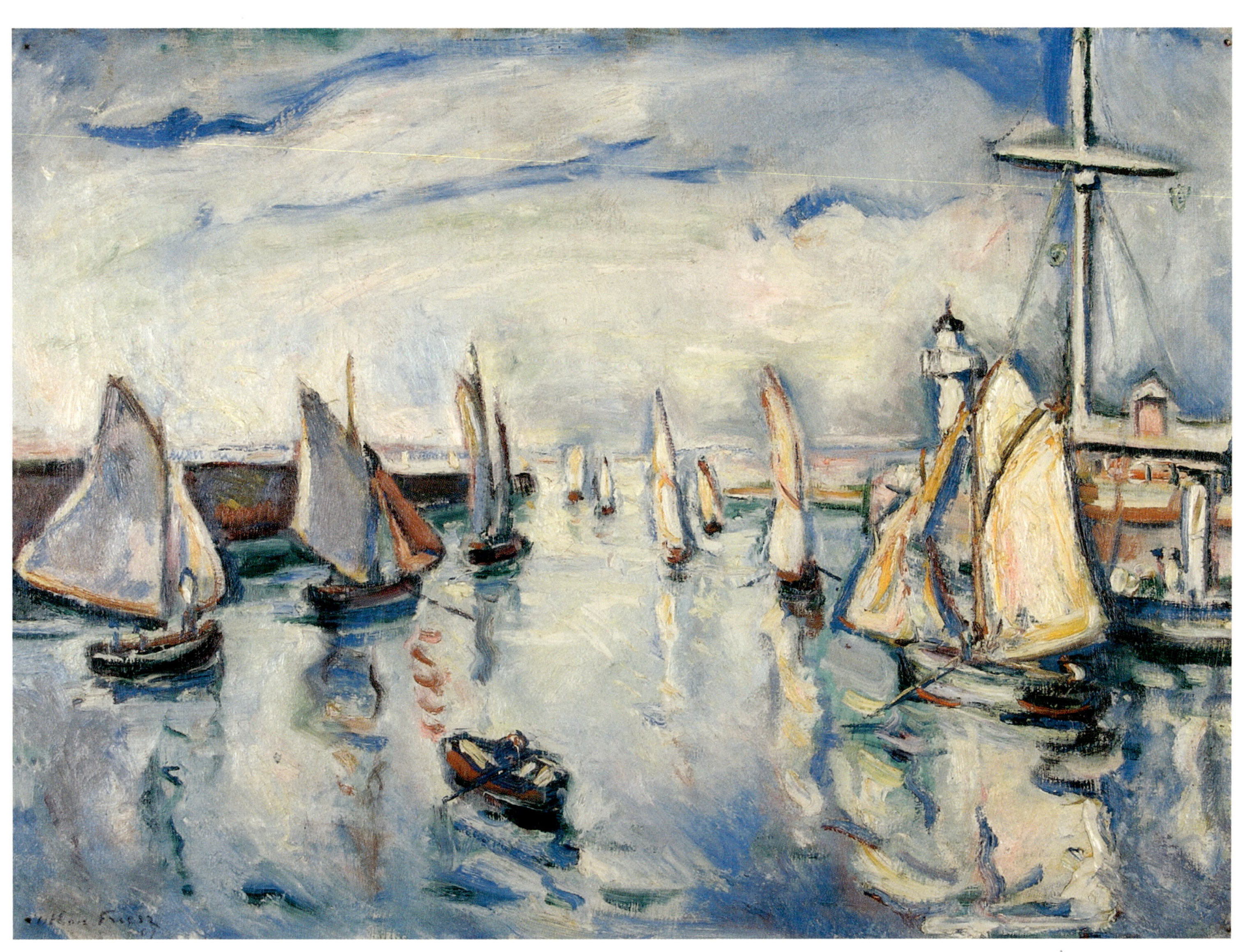

52. Othon Friesz

Sailing Boats Leaving the Port of Honfleur, 1907
Oil on canvas, 46 × 60 cm (18 × 23 ¾ in.)
Signed and dated lower left
Private collection
Courtesy of Galerie de Berthet-Aittouarès, Paris

appendix

marked a turning point. He initially retained a palette influenced by Duveneck in its predominance of earthy colors but quickly adopted the bright palette of the Impressionists. He returned to the United States in 1889 and settled in Boston, where he exhibited regularly, applying the Impressionist approach to the landscapes of Massachusetts, especially in places with an Old World charm like Gloucester and Ipswich. Despite Wendel's pioneering role in the discovery of Impressionism by American artists, his work remains comparatively unknown because of the losses incurred during a fire at his studio in 1897 or 1898.

H.F.

Selected Bibliography

La Rivière de Seine et ses peintres. Exh. cat., Sceaux, Orangerie du Châteaux de Sceaux. Sceaux: musée de l'Île de France, 1991.

ADHÉMAR, Hélène, DISTEL, Anne, GACHE, Sylvie. *Hommage à Claude Monet : 1840-1926*. Exh. cat., Paris, Galeries nationales du Grand Palais. Paris: Éditions de la Réunion des musées nationaux, 1980.

AGAMEMNON, Jean, GALLOYER, Anne, LESPINASSE, François. *Inspirations de bords de Seine : Maximilien Luce et les peintres de son époque*. Exh. cat., Mantes-la-Jolie, musée de l'Hôtel-Dieu. Paris: Somogy, 2004.

ALEXANDRE, Arsène, GEFFROY, Gustave. *Catalogue des tableaux, études, pastels par Alfred Sisley et de tableaux, aquarelles, pastels et dessins offerts à ses enfants*. Auction catalogue. Paris: Galerie Georges Petit, 1st May 1899.

ALPHANT, Adolphe. *Les Promenades de Paris*. 2 Vols. Paris: Veuve A. Morel, 1863.

Association des conservateurs de Haute-Normandie. *Scènes de la Seine*. Exh. cat., Bernay, Caudebec-en-Caux, Elbeuf, Louviers, Rouen, musée des Beaux-Arts. Rouen: ASHN, 1986.

AUFFRET, François. *Johan Barthold Jongkind (1819-1891), héritier, contemporain et précurseur. Biographie illustrée*. Paris: Éditions Maisonneuve et Larose.

BAILEY, Colin B., Anne. *Renoir's Portraits: Impressions of an Age*. Exh. cat., Ottawa, Musée des beaux-arts du Canada, The Art Institute of Chicago, Forth Worth, Kimbell Art Museum. New Haven: Yale University Press, 1997.

BAILEY, Colin B., RIOPELLE, Christopher. *Renoir Landscapes 1865–1883*. Exh. cat., London, The National Gallery, Ottawa, Musée des beaux-arts du Canada, Philadelphia, Philadelphia Museum of Art. London: National Gallery Company, 2007.

BAILLY-HERZBERG, Janine. *Correspondance de Camille Pissarro, 1865-1885*. Vol 1. Paris: PUF, 1980.

BAILLY-HERZBERG, Janine. *Correspondance de Camille Pissarro, 1865-1885*. Vol. 2. Paris: Éditions du Valhermeil, 1986.

BAILLY-HERZBERG, Janine. *Correspondance de Camille Pissarro, 1891-1894*. Vol. 3. Paris: Éditions du Valhermeil, 1988.

BAILLY-HERZBERG, Janine. *Correspondance de Camille Pissarro, 1895-1898*. Vol. 4. Paris: Éditions du Valhermeil, 1989.

BAKHUYS, Diederick, GOUJARD, Lucie, HAUDIQUET, Annette, JOUBERT, Caroline. *Voyages pittoresques, Normandie 1820-2009*. Exh. cat., Rouen, musée des Beaux-Arts, Le Havre, musée Malraux, Caen, musée des Beaux-Arts. Milan: Silvana Editoriale, 2009.

BATAILLE, M.-L., WILDENSTEIN, Guy, *Berthe Morisot. Catalogue des peintures, pastels et aquarelles*. Paris: Les Beaux-Arts, 1961.

BAUDELAIRE, Charles. *Œuvres complètes*. Paris: Éditions Gallimard, Bibliothèque de La Pléïade, 1987.

BAZETOUX, Denise, BOUIN-LUCE, Jean. *Maximilien Luce : catalogue de l'œuvre peint*. Vols. 1 and 2. La Celle Saint-Cloud: Éditions JBL, 1986.

BAZETOUX, Denise. *Maximilien Luce : catalogue de l'œuvre peint*. Vol. 3. Paris: Avril Graphiques éditions, 2005.

BEAUDOUIN, François, BOURCELOT, Henri, CHERRIER, Claude, CORNÈDE, Martine, et al. *Seine et Marne*. Paris: Bonneton, 1989.

BEAUDOUIN, François. *Paris / Seine*. Paris: Éditions de La Martinière, 1993.

BERHAUT, Marie, new edition revised and increased with the support of PIETRI, Sophie. *Gustave Caillebotte : catalogue raisonné des peintures et pastels*. Paris: Wildenstein Institute, 1994.

BERSON, Ruth. *The New Painting. Impressionism 1874-1886*. 2 Vols. San Francisco: Fine Arts Museum of San Francisco, 1996.

BHATTACHARYA-STETTLER, Therese, DUCREY, Marina, KOELLA, Rudolf, FREHNER, Matthias. *Félix Vallotton: les couchers de soleil*. Martigny: Fondation Pierre Gianadda, 2005.

BRETELL, Richard R., LACLOTTE, Michel, GACHE-PATIN, Sylvie. *A Day in the Country: Impressionism and the French Landscape*. Exh. cat., Los Angeles County Museum of Art, The Art Institute of Chicago Paris, Galeries nationales du Grand Palais. Los Angeles: Los Angeles County Museum of Art, 1984.

CACHIN, Françoise. *Félix Fénéon. Au-delà de l'impressionnisme*. Texts by Félix Fénéon reunited and presented by Françoise Cachin. Paris: Hermann, 1966.

CACHIN, Françoise, MOFFETT, Charles S. *Manet, 1832–83*. Exh. cat., Paris, Galeries nationales du Grand Palais, New York, The Metropolitan Museum of Art. New York: The Metropolitan Museum of Art, 1983.

CACHIN, Françoise. "Le Paysage du peintre", in NORA, Pierre (ed.). *Les Lieux de mémoire*. Vol. 11, La Nation. Paris: Éditions Gallimard, 1986.

CACHIN, Françoise, WELSH-OVCHAROV, Bogomila. *Van Gogh à Paris*. Exh, cat., Paris, musée d'Orsay. Paris: Éditions de la Réunion des musées nationaux, 1988.

CACHIN, Françoise, in collaboration with FERRETTI BOCQUILLON, Marina. *Signac : Catalogue raisonné de l'œuvre peint*. Paris: Éditions Gallimard, 2000.

CHAPUS, Eugène. *De Paris au Havre*. Paris: L. Hachette, 1855.

CHARDEAU, Jean. *Les Dessins de Caillebotte*. Paris: Hermé, 1989.

CLAIRET, Alain, MONTALANT, Delphine, ROUART, Yves, in collaboration with HOPKINS, Waring and THOMAS, Alain. *Berthe Morisot, 1841-1895 : catalogue raisonné de l'œuvre peint*. Montolivet: CÉRA-nrs Éditions, 1997.

CLARETIE, Jules. *Voyages d'un parisien*. Paris: A. Faure, 1865.

CLARKE, Michael, THOMSON, Richard. *Monet. The Seine and The Sea*. Edimburgh: National Galleries of Scotland, 2003.

CLÉMENT, Auguste. *Le Village et l'ancien prieuré de Saint-Mammès*. Dammarie-les-Lys: Éditions Amatteis, 1985 [1900].

COMPIN , Isabelle. *H.E. Cross*. Paris: Quatre Chemins – Editart, 1964.

CORBIN, Alain. *L'Avènement des loisirs, 1850-1960*. Paris: Flammarion, 2009 [Paris: Aubier, 1995].

COWE, Anne L. *Community and Nation: The Representation of the Village in French Landscape Painting 1870-1890*. Thesis, Edinburgh, 2005.

DAUBERVILLE, Jean et Henry, *Bonnard. Catalogue raisonné de l'œuvre peint,* 1888-1905. Paris: Éditions J. et H. Bernheim-Jeune, 1966.

DAUBERVILLE, Jean et Henry, *Bonnard. Catalogue raisonné de l'œuvre peint,* 1906-1919. Paris: Éditions J. et H. Bernheim-Jeune, 1968.

DAUBERVILLE, Jean et Henry, *Bonnard. Catalogue raisonné de l'œuvre peint,* 1920-1939. Paris: Éditions J. et H. Bernheim-Jeune, 1973.

DAUBERVILLE, Jean et Henry, *Bonnard. Catalogue raisonné de l'œuvre peint,* 1940-1947. Paris: Éditions J. et H. Bernheim-Jeune, 1974.

DAUBERVILLE, Guy-Patrice and Michel, in collaboration with FREMONTIER-MURPHY, Camille. *Renoir : catalogue raisonné des tableaux, pastels, dessins et aquarelles, 1858-1881*. Vol. 1. Paris: Bernheim-jeune, 2007.

DAUBERVILLE, Guy-Patrice and Michel. *Renoir : catalogue raisonné des tableaux, pastels, dessins et aquarelles, 1882-1894*. Vol. 2. Paris: Éditions Bernheim-jeune, 2009.

DAULTE, François. *Sisley*. Paris: Braun et Cie, 1954.

DAULTE, François. *Alfred Sisley. Catalogue raisonné de l'œuvre peint*. Paris: Éditions Durand-Ruel, 1959.

DISTEL, Anne, HOUSE, John, WALSH Jr., John. *Renoir*. Exh. cat., London, Hayward Gallery, Paris, Galeries nationales du Grand Palais, Boston, Museum of Fine Arts. Boston: Harry N. Abrams Inc, 1985.

DISTEL, Anne, DRUICK, Douglas W., GROOM, Gloria, RAPETTI, Rodolphe. *Gustave Caillebotte Urban Impressionist*. Exh. cat., Paris, Galerie nationales du Grand Palais, The Art Institute of Chicago. Chicago: The Art Institute of Chicago, 1995.

DISTEL, Anne, LEIGHTON, John, STEIN, Susan Alyson, FERRETTI BOCQUILLON, Marina. *Signac ,1863–1935*. Exh. cat., Paris, Galeries nationales du Grand Palais, Amsterdam, Van Gogh Museum, New York, The Metropolitan Museum of Art. New York / New Haven / London: The Metropolitan Museum of Art in association with Yale University Press, 2001.

DUCREY, Marina, JOURDAN, Patrice. *Félix Vallotton : le paysage composé, Norman-*

die et Bretagne. Morlaix: musée des Jacobins, 1998.

DUCREY, Marina. *Félix Vallotton, 1865-1925, Honfleur et la Normandie*. Exh. cat., Honfleur, musée Eugène Boudin. Arcueil: Anthèse, 1999.

DUCREY, Marina, in collaboration with POLETTI, Katia. *Félix Vallotton, 1865-1925 : l'œuvre peint*. Exh. cat., Lausanne, Institut suisse pour l'étude de l'art, Zurich / Lausanne, Fondation Félix Vallotton. Milan: 5 Continents Éditions, 2005.

DUCREY, Marina. *Félix Vallotton. His Life, His Technique, His Paintings*. Lausanne: Edita, 1989.

DULAURE, Jacques-Antoine. *Histoire physique, civile et morale des environs de Paris, depuis les premiers temps historiques jusqu'à nos jours*. Paris: Furne, 1838.

DULON, Guy, DUVIVIER, Christophe. *Louis Hayet, 1864-1940 : peintre et théoricien du néo-impressionnisme*. Exh. cat., musée de Pontoise, Ville de Pontoise, Conseil Général du Val d'Oise, 1991.

FAURE, Alain (ed.). *Les premiers banlieusards : aux origines des banlieues de Paris : 1860-1940*. Paris: Créaphis, 1991.

FÉNÉON, Félix. *Les Impressionnistes en 1886*. Paris: publications de *La Vogue*, 1886.

FERRETTI BOCQUILLON, Marina. *Signac Watercolors*. Paris: Vilo International, 2001.

FERRETTI BOCQUILLON, Marina. *Paul Signac*. Martigny: Fondation Pierre Gianadda, 2003.

FOWLE, Frances, et al. *Monet and French Landscape: Vétheuil and Normandy*. Edinburgh: National Galleries of Scotland, 2006.

GAUDICHON, Bruno, BUTCHER, David, HAUDIQUET, Annette, MATAMOROS, Joséphine. *Othon Friesz. Le Fauve Baroque, 1879-1949*. Paris: Éditions Gallimard, 2007.

GEORGEL, Chantal. *La Forêt de Fontainebleau : un atelier grandeur nature*. Exh. cat., Paris, musée d'Orsay. Paris: Éditions de la Réunion des musées nationaux, 2007.

GIRAULT de SAINT-FARGEAU, Pierre. *Guide pittoresque du voyageur en France*. Vol. 6. Paris: Firmin-Didot Frères, 1838.

GLOUVET, Jules de. *Le marinier : au bord de la Loire*. Coudray-Macouard: Cheminements, [1881], 2002.

GONCOURT, Edmond and Jules de. *Manette Salomon*. Paris: A. Lacroix et Verboeckhoven, 1867.

GUISAN, Gilbert, JAKUBEC, Doris. *Félix Vallotton. Documents pour une biographie et pour l'histoire d'une œuvre, Journal 1914-1921*. Lausanne / Paris: La Bibliothèque des Arts, 1973.

HAUKE, César M. De. *Seurat et son œuvre* Paris: Gründ, 1961.

HERBERT, Robert. *Impressionism: Art, Leisure and Parisian Society*. New Haven & London: Yale University Press, 1988.

HERBERT, Robert L., CACHIN, Françoise, DISTEL, Anne, TINTEROW, Gary. *Georges Seurat, 1859–1891*. Exh. cat., Paris, Galeries nationales du Grand Palais, and New York, The Metropolitan Museum of Art. New York: The Metropolitan Museum of Art, 1991.

JEAN-AUBRY, Georges. *Eugène Boudin, d'après des documents inédits. L'Homme et l'œuvre*. Paris: Bernheim-Jeune, 1922.

JOUAN, Lucienne. *Asnières-sur-Seine au cours des siècles*. Asnières: L. Unal, 1976.

JOANNE, Adolphe. *Les Environs de Paris illustrés*. Paris: L. Hachette, 1868.

JOANNE, Adolphe. *La Normandie*. Collection of guides Joanne, guides Diamant. Paris: L. Hachette, 1867.

KARR, Alphone. *Le canotage en France*. Paris: J. Taride, 1858.

KLEIN, Jacques-Sylvain. *La Normandie, berceau de l'impressionnisme 1820-1900*. Rennes: Éditions *Ouest-France*, 1999.

KORNFELD, Eberhard W., WICK, Peter Arms. *Catalogue raisonné de l'œuvre gravé et lithographié de Paul Signac*. Bern: Kornfeld et Klipstein, 1974.

KÜSS, René, BEAUDOIN, François, BERGERET-GOURBIN, Anne-Marie. *La Seine sous ses ponts : de Paris à Honfleur*. Exh. cat., Honfleur, musée Eugène Boudin. Arcueil: Anthèse, 1995.

LA BÉDOLLIÈRE, Émile de. *Histoire des environs du nouveau Paris*. Paris: G. Barba, 1861.

LACLOTTE, Michel, et al. *L'Impressionnisme et le paysage français*. Exh. cat., Los Angeles County Museum of Art, The Art Institute of Chicago, Paris, Galeries nationales du Grand Palais. Paris: Éditions de la Réunion des musées nationaux, 1985.

LA FAILLE, Jacob Baart de. *Vincent Van Gogh*. Paris: Hypérion, 1939.

LEIGHTON, John, THOMSON, Richard. *Seurat and the Bathers*. Exh. cat., London, The National Gallery. London: National Gallery Publications Limited, 1997.

LEMOINE, Serge, FERRETTI BOCQUILLON, Marina, *Le néo-impressionnisme : de Seurat à Paul Klee*. Exh. cat., Paris, musée d'Orsay. Paris: Éditions de la Réunion des musées nationaux, 2005.

LESPINASSE, François. *La Seine vue par les peintres*. Lausanne: Edita, 1993.

LIOT, David, PANTAZZI, Michel, POMARÈDE, Vincent. *De Corot à l'art moderne, souvenirs et variations*. Exh. cat., Reims, musée des Beaux-Arts. Paris: Hazan, 2009.

LLOYD, Christopher, STERN SHAPIRO, Barbara, DISTEL, Anne, CACHIN, Françoise, et al. *Pissarro*. Exh. cat., London, Hayward Gallery, Paris, Galeries nationales du Grand Palais, Boston, Museum of Fine Arts. London: Arts Council of Great Britain, 1981.

LLOYD, Christopher. "An Unknown Sketchbook by Gustave Caillebotte." *Master Drawings*, Vol. XXVI, 1988, p. 107–18.

LOBSTEIN, Dominique. *Au temps de l'impressionnisme : 1863-1886*. Paris: Éditions Gallimard / Éditions de la Réunion des musées nationaux, 1994.

LOYRETTE, Henri, TINTEROW, Gary. *Origins of Impressionism*. Exh. cat., Paris, Galeries nationales du Grand Palais, New York, The Metropolitan Museum of Art. New York: The Metropolitan Museum of Art, 1994.

MANCERON, Vanessa. *Saint-Mammès, terre de mariniers, approche ethnologique d'une population et d'un territoire*. Dammarie-lès-Lys : Musée départemental des Pays de Seine et Marne, 1994.

MAUPASSANT, Guy de. *Contes et nouvelles 1*. Paris: Éditions Gallimard, Bibliothèque de La Pléiade, 1974.

MAUPASSANT, Guy de. *Contes et nouvelles 2*. Paris: Éditions Gallimard, Bibliothèque de La Pléiade, 1979.

MAUPASSANT, Guy de. *Chroniques 2*. [1883]. Paris: Union générale d'éditions, 1980.

MICHELET, Jules. *Histoire de France*. Paris: Flammarion, 1870.

MONNERET, Sophie. *L'Impressionnisme et son époque : dictionnaire international*. 2 Vols. Paris: Robert Laffont, 1987.

MONNIER, Geneviève, SERVOT, Martine, TOUSSAINT, Hélène, LACLOTTE, Michel. *Hommage à Corot : peintures et dessins des collections françaises*. Exh. cat., Paris, musée de l'Orangerie. Paris: Éditions de la Réunion des musées nationaux, 1975.

MORIN, Louis. *Les dimanches parisiens. Notes d'un décadent*. Paris: L. Conquet, 1898.

NOEL, Benoît, HOURNON, Jean. *La Seine au temps des canotiers*. Garches: AROM, 1997.

NORD, Philip G. *Impressionists and politics: art and democracy in the nineteenth century*. London / New York: Routledge 2000.

PACH, Walter. "Une visite à Claude Monet : Giverny, novembre 1907." *Scriber's Magazine*, Vol. XLIII, n° 6, New York, june 1908, translated from english by Patrice Cotensin. Paris: L'Échoppe, 2009.

PATIN, Sylvie. *L'Impressionnisme*. Lausanne / Paris : La Bibliothèque des Arts, 2002.

PATRY, Sylvie, WILHELM, Hugues and PATIN, Sylvie. *Berthe Morisot, 1841-1895*. Exh. cat., Lille, Palais des beaux-arts, Martigny, Fondation Pierre Gianadda. Paris: Éditions de la Réunion des musées nationaux, 2002.

PATRY, Sylvie, GAËTAN, Isabelle. *Renoir in the 20th century*. Exh. cat., Paris, Galerie nationales du Grand Palais, Los Angeles, Los Angeles County Museum of Art, Philadelphia, Philadelphia Museum of Art. Ostfildern: Hatje Cantz Publishers, 2009.

PICKVANCE, Ronald. *Van Gogh*. Martigny: Fondation Pierre Gianadda, 2000.
PISSARRO, Camille. *Lettres à son fils Lucien*. Published by John Rewald. Paris: Albin-Michel, 1950.

PISSARRO, Joachim. *Camille Pissarro*. Paris: Hermé, 1995.

PISSARRO, Joachim, DURAND-RUEL SNOLLAERTS, Claire. *Pissarro. Critical Catalogue of Paintings*, 3 Vols. Milan: Skira, Paris: Wildenstein Institute Publications, 2005.

POMARÈDE, Vincent, LEROY, Christiane, AYME, Jean-Louis, et al. *Reflets de la Seine impressionniste*. Exh. cat., Rueil-Malmaison, Atelier Grognard. Saint-Ouen-l'Aumône: Éditions du Valhermeil, 2008.

PUGET, François. "Signac, le marin." *Chasse-marée*, n° 220, January 2010, p. 30–41.

RATHBONE, Eliza E., ROTHKOPF, Katherine, BRETTELL, Richard R., MOFFET, Charles S. *Impressionists on the Seine. A celebration of Renoir's Luncheon of the Boating Party*. Exh. cat., Washington, The Phillips Collection. Washington D.C.: Counterpoint, 1996.

REGNAULT, Jean-Michel. *Veneux-les-Sablons : histoire de mon village*. Le Mée-sur-Seine: Amattéis, 1991.

REWALD, John. "Extraits du Journal inédit de Paul Signac I, 1894-1895." *Gazette des Beaux-Arts,* 36, July-Septembre 1949, 97–128, english translations 166–74.

REWALD, John. "Extraits du Journal inédit de Paul Signac II, 1897-1898." *Gazette des Beaux-Arts*, Vol. 39, April 1952, p. 265–84, english translations p. 298–304.

REWALD, John. "Extraits du Journal inédit de Paul Signac III, 1898-1899." *Gazette des Beaux-Arts*, Vol. 42, July-August 1953, p. 27–57, english translations p. 72–80.

REWALD, John. *Histoire de l'Impressionnisme* [1955]. Paris: Albin Michel, 1986.

REWALD, John. *Post-Impressionism from Van Gogh to Gauguin*. New York: Museum of Modern Art, 1956, reviewed in 1962.

RITCHIE, Leitch. *Wanderings by the Seine, from Rouen to the Source*. London, Longman Rees, Orme Brown, Green and Longman, 1835.

ROBAUT, Alfred. *L'Œuvre de Corot, par Alfred Robaut, catalogue raisonné et illustré, précédé de l'histoire de Corot et de ses œuvres par Etienne Moreau-Nélaton*. 4 Vols. Paris: H. Floury, 1905.

ROUART, Denis, WILDENSTEIN, Daniel. *Édouard Manet : catalogue raisonné*. Paris / Lausanne: La Bibliothèque des Arts, 1975.

RUBIN, James H. *Impressionism and the Modern Landscape. Productivity, Technology, and Urbanization from Monet to Van Gogh*. London, Los Angeles: Berkeley, University of California Press, 2008.

SCHMIDT, Robert. *Eugène Boudin*, 1824-1898. 5 Vols. Paris: Robert Schmidt, 1973–93.

SCHMIDT, Robert and Manuel. *Stanislas Lépine, 1835-1892. Catalogue raisonné de l'œuvre peint*. Paris: Éditions galerie Schmidt, 1992.

SCHULMAN (Michel), *Théodore Rousseau 1812-1867. Catalogue raisonné de l'œuvre peint*, Paris, Les Éditions de l'Amateur, 1999.

SERRET, Georges, FABIANI (Dominique), *Armand Guillaumin 1841-1927. Catalogue raisonné de l'œuvre peint*, Paris, Éditions Mayer, 1971.

SHONE, Richard. *Sisley*. New York: Harry N. Abrams, 1992.

SIGNAC, Paul. *D'Eugène Delacroix au néo-impressionnisme*. Paris: Éditions de la *Revue blanche*, 1899.

SMITH, Cecil O. Jr. "The Longest Run: Public Engineers and Planning in France." *American Historical Review*, Vol. 95, n° 3, June 1990, p. 657–92.

SPATE, Virginia. *The Colour of Time*. London: Thames & Hudson, [1992], 2001.

STEIN, Adolphe, BRAME, Sylvie, LORENCEAU, François, SINIZERGUES, Janine, *Jongkind. Catalogue critique de l'œuvre. Peintures I*, Brame & Lorenceau Éditions, Paris, 2003.

STEVENS, Mary Anne, DUMAS, Ann, LLOYD, Christopher, PATIN, Sylvie. *Alfred Sisley*. Exh. cat., London, Royal Academy of Arts, Paris, musée d'Orsay, Baltimore, The Walters Art Gallery, New Haven, Yale University Press. London : Royal Academy of Arts, 1992.

STEVENS, Mary Anne, DUMAS, Ann, POMARÈDE, Vincent, et al. *Alfred Sisley*. Exh. cat., Lyon, musée des Beaux-Arts, Paris: Éditions de la Réunion des musées nationaux, 2002.

TAVERNIER, Adolphe. *L'Atelier de Sisley*. Paris: Galerie Bernheim Jeune et Cie, Paris, Bernheim Jeune, 1907 [préface].

TERRASSE, Antoine. *Bonnard.* Paris: Éditions Gallimard, 1988.

THIÉBAULT-SISSON, François. "Claude Monet : les années d'épreuves." *Le Temps*, n° 14414, 26 November 1900, p. 3.

THOMSON, Richard. *Camille Pissarro: Impressionism, Landscape and Rural Labour.* Exh. cat., Birmingham, City Museum and Art Gallery, Glasgow, The Burrell Collection, 1990. London: Herbert press, 1990.

THOROLD, Anne. *The Letters of Lucien to Camille Pissarro, 1883-1903.* Cambridge: Cambridge University Press, Department of Western Art, Ashmolean Museum Oxford, 1993.

TUCKER, Paul Hayes. *Claude Monet. Life and Art.* New Haven / London: Yale University Press, 1995.

TUCKER, Paul Hayes. *Monet at Argenteuil.* New Haven / London: Yale University Press, 1982.

VALENCIENNES, Pierre Henri de. *Éléments de perspective pratique à l'usage des artistes, suivis de Réflexions et Conseils à un élève sur la Peinture et particulièrement le genre du Paysage.* Paris: An VIII, 1800.

VALLÈS-BLED, Maithé. *Vlaminck catalogue critique des peintures et céramiques de la période fauve.* Paris: Wildenstein Institute Publication, 2008.

VAN DEPUTTE, Jocelyne. *Ponts de Paris.* Monaco: Sauret. Paris: Paris Musées, 1994

WARRELL, Ian. *Turner on the Seine*, London: Tate Gallery Publishing, 1999.

WILDENSTEIN, Daniel. *Claude Monet, biographie et catalogue raisonné.* 5 Vols. Lausanne / Paris: La Bibliothèque des Arts, 1974–91.

WILLI-COSANDIER, Juliane, WUHRMANN, Sylvie. *Caillebotte : au cœur de l'Impressionnisme.* Exh. cat., Lausanne, Fondation de l'Hermitage. Lausanne / Paris: La Bibliothèque des Arts, 2005.

WILSON-BAREAU, Juliet. *Manet, Monet, and the Gare Saint-Lazare.* Exh. cat., Paris, musée d'Orsay, Washington, National Gallery of Art. New Haven / Washington: Yale University Press copublished with the National Gallery of Art, Washington, 1998.

ZOLA, Émile. *L'Œuvre* [1886]. Paris: Éditions Gallimard, 1983.

Photograph Credits

Every effort has been made to trace individual copyright holders. Our sincere apologies to those whose names we may have omitted to mention.

Amsterdam
Van Gogh Museum: p. 47 (fig. 5)

Birmingham
Birmingham Museums & Art Gallery: p. 20 (fig. 4)

Boston
Museum of Fine Arts: p. 28 (detail), p. 32 (fig. 3), 37 (fig. 6), 39 (fig. 8)

Brest
Musée des beaux-arts: p. 118 (cat. 47)

Brussels
Musées royaux des Beaux-Arts de Belgique / Photo Speltdoorn & Fils, Brussels: p. 71 (cat. 1)

Cergy-Pontoise
Conseil général du Val d'Oise / Photo Jean-Yves Lacôte: p. 114 (cat. 44)

Chicago
Terra Foundation of American Art: p. 108 (cat. 38), 109 (cat. 39), 110 (cat. 40)
The Art Institute: p. 24 (fig. 8), 54 (detail), 58 (fig. 3)

Columbus
Columbus Museum of Art: p. 37 (fig. 5)

Dammarie-les-Lys
Éditions Amatteis: p. 31 (fig. 2)

Évreux
Musée d'Art, Histoire et Archéologie / Photo J.-P. Godais: p. 80 (cat. 10)
Archives départementales de l'Eure: p. 59 (fig. 4)

Geneva
Association des Amis du Petit Palais: p. 87 (cat. 17)

Lausanne
Fondation Félix Vallotton: p. 61 (fig. 6), 63 (fig. 7)

Le Havre
Musée Malraux / Photo Florian Kleinefenn: p. 93 (cat. 23)

Liège
Collection du Musée d'Art moderne et d'Art contemporain: p. 82 (cat. 12)

London
The National Gallery: p. 46 (fig. 4), 59 (fig. 5), 79 (cat. 9)

Munich
Bayrische Staatsgemäldesammlungen, Neue Pinakothek / Photo BPK, Berlin, Dist RMN / Image BStGS: p. 23 (fig. 7)

New York
Metropolitan Museum of Art, Dist RMN / Image of the MMA: p. 23 (fig. 6)
Museum of Modern Art / Photo Scala, Florence: p. 42 (detail), 48 (fig. 6)

Oxford
University of Oxford-Ashmolean Museum: p. 49 (fig. 8)

Paris
Bibliothèque nationale de France: p. 45 (fig. 3), 57 (fig. 1, 2)
Centre Pompidou, musée national d'art moderne / Centre de création industrielle, Dist. RMN / Photo Georges Meguerditchian: p. 121 (cat. 50) / Photo Philippe Migeat: p. 122 (cat. 51)
Galerie Bernheim-Jeune: p. 84 (cat. 14)
Galerie Berthet-Aittouarès / Photo Bertrand Michau: p. 123 (cat. 52)
Galerie Hopkins-Custot: p. 111 (cat. 41)
Galerie de la Présidence: p. 120 (cat. 49)
RMN / Agence Bulloz: p. 16 (fig. 2)
RMN / Photo Jean-Gilles Berizzi: p. 34 (fig. 4)
RMN (musée de l'Orangerie) / Photo Franck Raux: p. 97 (cat. 27)
RMN (Musée d'Orsay) / Photo Hervé Lewandowski: p. 38 (cat. 7), 73 (cat. 3), 78 (cat. 8), 88 (cat. 18), 94 (cat. 24), 95 (cat. 25), 96 (cat. 26), 100 (cat. 30), 104 (cat. 34), 106 (cat. 36), 107 (cat. 37) / Photo Jean-Gilles Berizzi: p. 81 (cat. 11), 83 (cat. 13) / Photo Thierry Le Mage: p. 75 (cat. 5) / Rights reserved: p. 19 (fig. 3)
RMN / Photo Daniel Arnaudet: p. 99 (cat. 29)
RMN / Photo Gérard Blot: p. 103 (cat. 33)

Pontoise
Musée Camille Pissarro: p. 76 (cat. 6), 112 (cat. 42)

Reims
Musée des Beaux-Arts / Photo C. Devleeschauwer: p. 74 (cat. 4)

Rotterdam
Museum Boijmans Van Beuningen: p. 30 (fig. 1)

The Hague
Galerie Ivo Bouwman / Photo Ed Brandon-Art View: p. 72 (cat. 2)

The Netherlands
Collection Triton Foundation: p. 105 (cat. 35)

Tournai
Musée des Beaux-Arts Collection: p. 15 (fig. 1)

Toulouse
Fondation Bemberg: p. 86 (cat. 16)

Washington
National Gallery of Art: p. 98 (cat. 28), 101 (cat. 31)
The Phillips Collection: p. 22 (fig. 5)

Zurich
The Foundation E. G. Bührle Collection: p. 48 (fig. 7)

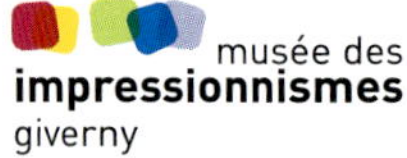

Edition
Vanessa Lecomte assisted by Céline Mittelette

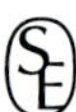

Silvana Editoriale

Produced by
Arti Grafiche Amilcare Pizzi Spa

Direction
Dario Cimorelli

Art Director
Giacomo Merli

Copy Editor
Viviana Vai

Layout
Annamaria Ardizzi

Translations
Paul Metcalfe and Mark Eaton for Scriptum, Rome

Production Coordinator
Michela Bramati

Editorial Assistant
Valentina Miolo

Iconographic office
Deborah D'Ippolito,
Alessandra Olivari

Press office
Lidia Masolini,
press@silvanaeditoriale.it

Silvana Editoriale

via Margherita De Vizzi, 86
20092 Cinisello Balsamo, Milan
tél. +39 02 61 83 63 37
fax +39 02 61 72 464
www.silvanaeditoriale.it

Reproductions, printing and binding
by Arti Grafiche Amilcare Pizzi Spa
Cinisello Balsamo, Milan

Printed
March 2010